TEACHING
with Visual
Frameworks

CORWIN
PRESS

The Corwin Press logo—a raven striding across an open book—represents the happy union of courage and learning. We are a professional-level publisher of books and journals for K–12 educators, and we are committed to creating and providing resources that embody these qualities. Corwin's motto is "Success for All Learners."

TEACHING
with Visual
Frameworks

**Focused Learning and Achievement Through
Instructional Graphics Co-Created by Students and Teachers**

Christine Allen Ewy

Foreword by Robert J. Marzano   Illustrations by Katrina Ewy

CORWIN PRESS, INC.
A Sage Publications Company
Thousand Oaks, California

Illustrations and Multimedia Design by Katrina A. Ewy, artprana@yahoo.com

For information:

Corwin Press, Inc.
A Sage Publications Company
2455 Teller Road
Thousand Oaks, California 91320
www.corwinpress.com

Sage Publications Ltd.
6 Bonhill Street
London EC2A 4PU
United Kingdom

Sage Publications India Pvt. Ltd.
M-32 Market
Greater Kailash I
New Delhi 110 048 India

Printed in the United States of America

Library of Congress Cataloging-in-Publication Data

Ewy, Christine Allen.
Teaching with visual frameworks: Focused learning and
achievement through instructional graphics co-created by students and teachers /
Christine Allen Ewy; foreword by Robert J. Marzano; illustrations by Katrina A. Ewy.
      p. cm.
Includes bibliographical references (p.   ) and index.
ISBN 0-7619-4664-0 — ISBN 0-7619-4665-9 (pbk.)
1. Visual education. 2. Teaching-aids and devices. 3. Graphic arts. I. Title.
LB1043.5 .E99 2003
371.33'5—dc21   2002009750

This book is printed on acid-free paper.

02   03   04   05   06   10   9   8   7   6   5   4   3   2   1

Acquisitions Editor: Faye Zucker
Corwin Editorial Assistant: Julia Parnell
Production Editor: Diana E. Axelsen
Copy Editor: Stacey Shimizu
Typesetter: Christina Hill
Illustrator: Katrina Ewy
Cover Designer: Michael Dubowe
Production Artist: Michelle Lee

Contents

Foreword

One of the biggest breakthroughs in our understanding of how the human mind operates and, therefore, how human beings learn is our growing awareness of the importance of imagery. Psychologist Allan Paivio (1971, 1991) is probably best known for his explanation of this dynamic within his dual coding theory or DCT. Briefly, within DCT Paivio explains that anything we have in permanent memory is stored in two ways—hence the title "dual coding."

One way of storing information is as abstract characteristics that manifest as semantic or linguistic elements. Paivio refers to these representations as *logogens*. To illustrate, a student who knows the concept of an atom has stored logogens about it. The student knows the abstract characteristics of atoms—they are the smallest component of an element having the characteristics of the element, they contain a nucleus made up of neutrons and protons, they contain electrons bound to the nucleus by an electrical attraction, the number of protons determines the identity of the element, and so on.

The second way knowledge is stored in permanent memory is as images. These are referred to as *imagens*. There are a number of very interesting aspects of imagens that have strong implications for classroom instruction. First, imagens are not merely mental pictures. Rather, they are composed of mental images, smells, tastes, sounds, and kinesthetic sensations. For example, along with the abstract characteristics of an atom, a student would have a mental picture of the neutrons, protons, electrons, and their interactions. These images might include sound, smell, taste, and kinesthetic sensations.

Second, images are absolutely necessary for understanding. Without imagery or imagens, we really don't know something in depth even if we can recite its abstract characteristics. Many teachers have experienced students who can provide succinct definitions or descriptions of concepts such as the atom but who do not truly understand them. It is our rich images about concepts that allow us to understand them and manipulate them.

Unfortunately, when we examine current classroom practice we see that the vast majority of instructional activities are geared toward the linguistic aspects of learning—in Paivio's terminology, geared toward the development of logogens. We talk to students, we read to them, we have them read, and so on. Yet if we do nothing explicitly to enhance the generation of images, we leave this process up to the student. In fact, one might say we leave the better part of learning up to students.

Fortunately, there are creative teachers who systematically employ instructional activities that enhance the development of images relative to the content being taught. Even more fortunately, there are educators who develop imagery-based instructional systems that can be used by a wide range of teachers across a wide range of subject areas. Christine Ewy is one of those educators. The system and techniques described in this book mark the beginning of what may be nothing short of a revolution in classroom pedagogy. The reader will find this book not only highly practical but also quite provocative in its implications.

—Robert J. Marzano
Senior Scholar, Mid-Continent Research for Education and Learning
Adjunct Professor, Cardinal Stritch University

REFERENCES

Paivio, A. (1971). *Imagery and verbal processes*. New York: Holt, Rinehart & Winston.

Paivio, A. (1991). Dual coding theory: Retrospect and current status. *Canadian Journal of Psychology*, 45, 255-287.

Acknowledgments

Helpful people defy categories, but the groupings below assist me in expressing an expansive "thank you" to

- Predecessors whose work contributed to my conception of this work

- Students, parents, teachers, and other educators mentioned by name and included anonymously in this book, as well as others over the years who have had faith enough to try the ideas I brought to them and to influence their improvement. Particular thanks to those willing to share their work and thoughts publicly in this book

- Friends and family who encouraged and supported me through excitement and struggle—the lifelines that kept me going, especially Barb Easley, Elisa Kuriyagawa, Sandra Williams, and my husband—Bob Ewy—for his abundant personal and professional support

- People who contributed, in direct and indirect ways, with a style and generosity that nourished me: Donna Berg, Matt Fuller, Jo Ann Kratz, Agnes Lagerquist, Julie Looye, Bob Marzano, Mike Mlynski, Carol Ann Rush, Faye Zucker, and especially my daughter—Katrina Ewy—who gave me even more reasons to love her through her enthusiasm, professionalism, talent, and personal support. Katrina transformed my clip art, sketches, and photos with her original art and multimedia skills. She also proved to me, as did her father, that professional relationships could thrive alongside very close personal ones

- Teachers who read drafts of this manuscript as it was written, and whose timely responses improved it. I list them separately so you may also see some of the perspectives that informed the work:

  - Ginger Benning, Sixth Grade, General Education
  - Paula Bullis, Third Grade, General Education

– Dr. Mary Crambes, High School, ESL

– Araceli Johnson, First Grade, Bilingual

– Elizabeth Kurubus, Second Grade, Bilingual

– Darlene Solano, First Grade, General Education

The publisher also gratefully acknowledges the contributions of the following reviewers:

Sandra Enger
Assistant Professor/Coordinator of Science Education
The University of Alabama in Huntsville
Institute for Science Education
Huntsville, AL

Barbara Flanagan, Ph.D.
Co-Director, Training and Technical Assistance Center (T/TAC)
College of Human Resources and Education
Virginia Tech
Blacksburg, VA

Dr. Xiufeng Liu
Associate Professor
Faculty of Education
University of Prince Edward Island
Charlottetown, Prince Edward Island
Canada

About the Author

Christine Ewy has a business called Results Through Alignment, dedicated to helping students, teachers, and administrators achieve their goals through the areas of curriculum, instruction, and assessment. She applies expertise from 30 years in education as a classroom teacher of preschool through adults, an instructional resource teacher, a curriculum and inservice specialist, a building- and district-level administrative intern, an adjunct professor, a consultant, and an author.

In addition to assisting practical understanding of national and state goals and standards, Christine has led standards-based curriculum development with engaged learning, integrated technology, UVF design, and strong assessment components. She has taught methods and assessment courses at the graduate level, coordinated the development of statewide standardized and alternative assessment projects, written assessment articles for professional journals—including one coauthored with students—and written test items for statewide assessments.

Language acquisition, literacy development, and bilingual education are also strands of Christine's staff development, consulting, and products. She coauthored *Literacy Development Strategies for Teachers and Students,* is one of the featured speakers in a video on the use of a state writing rubric in the classroom, participates in state writing validation, has done freelance writing in materials for English language learners, and is coauthor of a textbook series with international leaders in the field of second-language acquisition.

Christine's passion for bringing students' voices into their own learning process runs through all areas of work, including two innovations she created: *Teaching the Teacher Within and Learning From the Inside.* This passion has also guided Christine's work with inquiry- and problem-based learning, and her role as an Essential School's coach.

Christine's contact information is

Results Through Alignment
852 Fairway Drive
Palatine, Illinois
60067-3416
Phone: 847-776-9613
E-mail: info@resultsthroughalignment.com

Results Through Alignment

Unit Visual Framework 1

Making Ongoing Sense of a Unit of Study

At dinner one night, a colleague asked me what I was writing. Trying to be brief, I said it was a book about a specific kind of graphic organizer. As the words left my mouth and I saw her response, I knew that with brevity I had sacrificed clarity. In borrowing a term whose literal meaning works in my mind, I had used a term that has other associations for each person who uses it.

As a result, my colleague was thinking about visuals, but not quite the kind that fill this book. I had not communicated the organizer's essential function of creating coherent and cohesive learning for a whole unit of study. Nor had I mentioned the fact that students and teacher co-create the evolving visual, and, in so doing, are actively engaged in making ongoing sense of the unit and its teaching and learning events. Therefore, my colleague had no way of knowing that this collaborative interaction and cumulative understanding are as important as the visuals themselves. Our brief dinner conversation was not the right context in which to communicate these details or to share my mental picture of the visual organizer's use (see Figure 1.1) and its broad applicability, which can only be seen through multiple examples.

In trying to give my colleague a quick sense of what I was doing, I omitted the visual organizer's name, *Unit Visual Framework.* The name fits for me, because each word describes its function. Unfortunately, however, it's hard to say quickly. That's why I actually refer to it as a UVF, just as I've learned to say IEP instead of "individual education plan" or KWL for "know, want to know, and learn." Back to why I chose this particular name:

> *Unit.* A UVF organizes a whole unit of study from its beginning to end. A unit is defined as a progression of learning experiences that work together to ensure deep learning of clear targets.

Figure 1.1. Teaching and Learning With Visual Frameworks: My Mental Picture

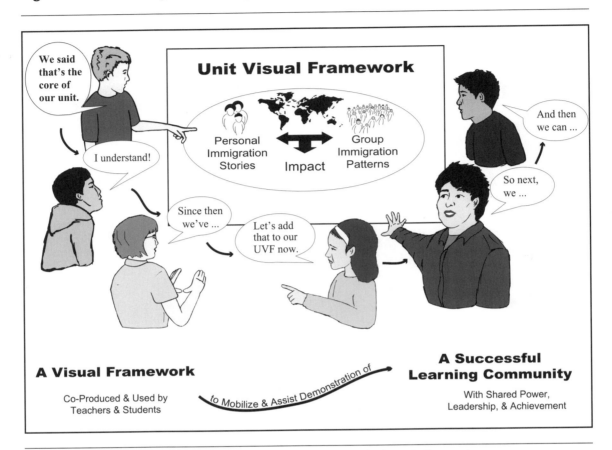

Visual. Students and teacher co-develop an ongoing class wall display (or other format where wall space is scarce) including a core visual with illustrations and text. They also make portable versions of the core visual for individual use.

Framework. The UVF provides and maintains a clear focus on instructional targets, so that students and teachers have ongoing awareness of what they are learning, relative to what they will be held accountable for, as they pursue multiple teaching and learning experiences.

Of course, one reason I was writing the book was to show what UVFs are. Another was to illustrate why principals and teachers in my workshops, teachers who've tried them in their classrooms, and I all think UVFs make a difference. Moreover, because people have requested additional information about them, I wrote the book so UVFs can be used more widely. The book begins with answers to very direct questions using the voices, classroom samples, and viewpoints of others as well as my own.

WHAT ARE UNIT VISUAL FRAMEWORKS?

> A UVF is an organic, class display that focuses, supports, and documents a unit of study from its beginning to end. Students and teachers collaboratively create and expand the display.
>
> The UVF begins as a **core visual**, with pictures and key text representing the essentials of what is studied and assessed, and it overtly establishes the focus. After co-developing it as a class, a copy of this portion of the UVF is made for, or by, each student to use as a **portable UVF**.
>
> The core visual grows into an **expanded display,** organized by the core visual to show learning paths and evolving, cumulative understanding of the unit.

As I watched my colleague's face at dinner that night, and listened to her tone and words, I could almost hear her thinking, "There are lots of graphic organizers already. Why would you design more?"

Had she known what I've now shared with you, she may have realized that I am not creating more graphic organizers, but instead am writing about a kind of central graphic representation that teachers and students co-create to help them get the results they want from the work they do. This kind of graphic display helps make their desired results—the "what's important" to teachers and students in a given unit of study—clear from the beginning through the end of the teaching-learning cycle, while honoring the spontaneity and freedom we treasure in the learning process.

The display begins with the co-development of a core visual that depicts the unit's overall focus. Prepared with knowledge of the students, curriculum, materials, and instructional targets, the teacher elicits student prior knowledge or responses to initial concrete experiences. During this process, the teacher helps establish a mental picture of the unit focus that students and teacher share. That mental picture is transferred using pictures and words onto chart paper or another format to form a tangible display, the beginning of a UVF. This display of the unit focus—and the class's understanding of that focus—is the core visual that will be expanded upon over the course of the unit, again by eliciting students' ideas, language, and experiences. If, in the unit's performance or product, a student can demonstrate understanding of the concepts anchored by the UVF, instructional targets should be achieved.

The core UVF may be a relatively simple one, such as the draft UVF for reading comprehension in Figure 1.2. On the other hand, it may be a more complex graphic, such as Figure 1.3, which is a draft core UVF that a teacher uses in planning the unit outlined in *Conflict and Resolution: Interpersonal and Political* (Ewy et al., 1998a). In all cases, the UVFs designed by teachers are drafts until

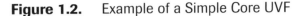
Figure 1.2.   Example of a Simple Core UVF

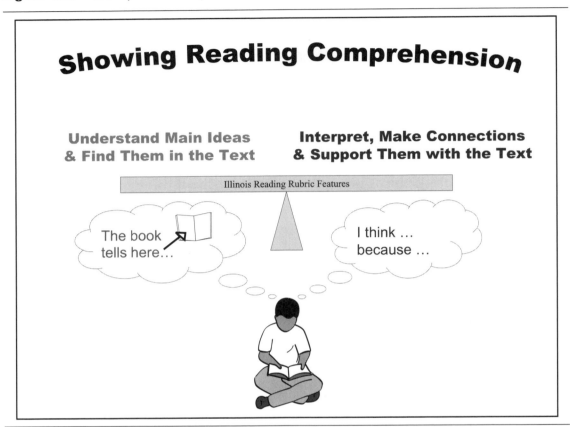

they are co-developed with the students who will use them, because UVFs must be shaped by student prior knowledge and reflect the concrete learning experiences that precede or help elicit the unit targets.

Figures 1.2 and 1.3 are only two of the many forms that a UVF can take. Additional examples from varied disciplines and grade levels fill this book. Please note that UVF examples in this book were chosen for their value in helping readers understand UVFs and their use in the classroom. If readers use them as drafts to adapt with their classes, it would be important for the content-area specialist to review them for content validity to ensure that accurate representation of concepts and principles occur when co-developing them with the class.

Because the UVF is a framework, it grows with the unit. Indeed, over time there may be multiple graphic organizers and/or visuals connected to the core UVF in such a way that they create a metagraphic of the unit's work, learning, and accountability. The result, like the one in Figure 1.4, may be confusing or overwhelming to an observer who hasn't been part of the unit's experiences, contributing along the way. However, an effective expanded UVF is organized and visually represented in ways that each participating student and the teacher can trace learning paths, and witness and express cumulative

Figure 1.3. Complex Core UVF

Unit Visual Framework				Illinois State Board of Education Content-Based Assessment Exemplars			
Conflict and Resolution		**Interpersonal**		**& Political**			
Social Sciences Scoring Rubric	**Model for Conflict Resolution**	**Drama Example**	**Personally Important Current Conflict** Task One	**American Revolution**			
				Task Two-A	Task Two-B	Task Two-C	Task Three
				Prewar through Boston Tea Party, 1773	Boston Tea Party to Close of First Continental Congress, 1774	First Continental Congress to Lexington & Concord 1775	Lexington & Concord to Yorktown & Treaty
Knowledge	**Get the FACTS** Actions & Reactions						
	Get the VIEWPOINTS						
	List What Each WANTS						
Reasoning	**Brainstorm POSSIBLE ACTIONS** All Types of Resolutions						
	Consider Best, Worst, Short-term & Long-term OUTCOMES of Each Action						
	Choose/Decide & ACT						
Communication	**Examine Short-term & Long-term Impacts & Use Criteria to EVALUATE Effectiveness**			Use primary and secondary sources to ensure accuracy of information.			Impacts on USA Impacts on Lives

From *Conflict and Resolution: Interpersonal and Political* (Ewy et al., 1998a). Reprinted with permission of the Illinois State Board of Education.

understanding. The UVF guides teaching and learning events by supporting the pursuit of student, teacher, and curricular goals. In fact, something dear to my heart is that these UVFs give students and teachers a concrete tool to manage the unit together with wide open eyes.

WHAT TEACHING/LEARNING SITUATIONS DO UVFs SERVE?

A UVF, like any tool, is useful for a particular purpose. The last sentence in the previous section said that the UVF is a tool to manage a unit together. There are two important parts to that statement: *unit* and *together*.

As the definition that opened this chapter indicated, UVFs serve complete units of study that allow time for a progression of experiences, which cumulatively lead to deep learning of clear targets. A UVF would be unnecessary for a brief mini-lesson or spontaneous short study. Similarly, certain types of academic work do and do not lend themselves to using a UVF, depending on

Figure 1.4. Expanded UVF of Unit's Work

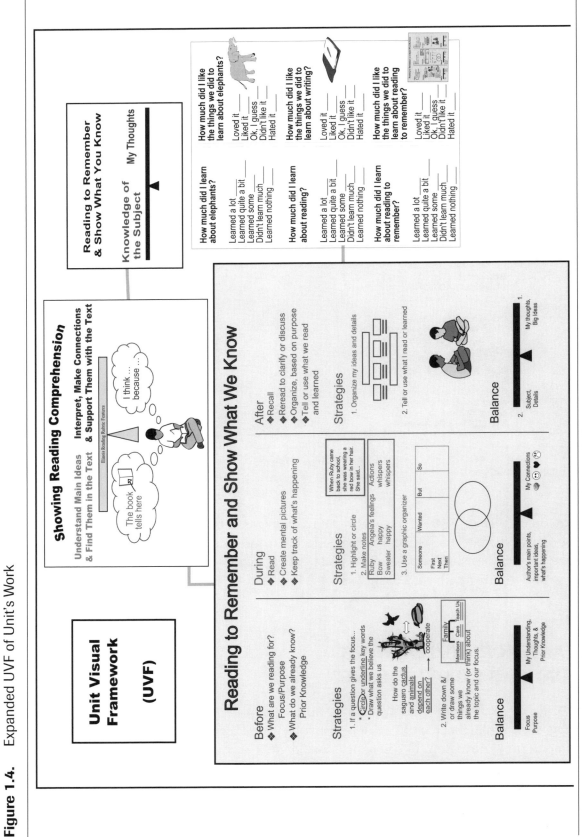

Figure 1.4. (Continued)

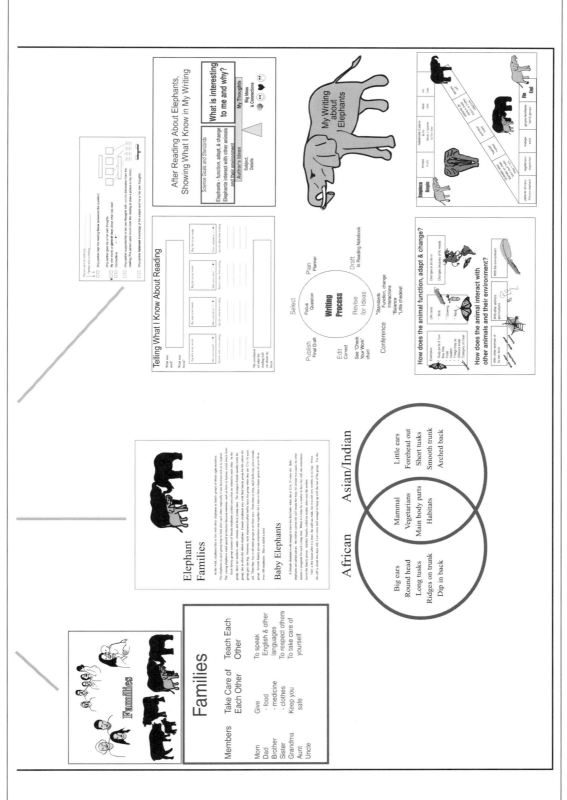

Figure 1.5. High School ESL Unit: Beginnings—New Classes, People, and Experiences

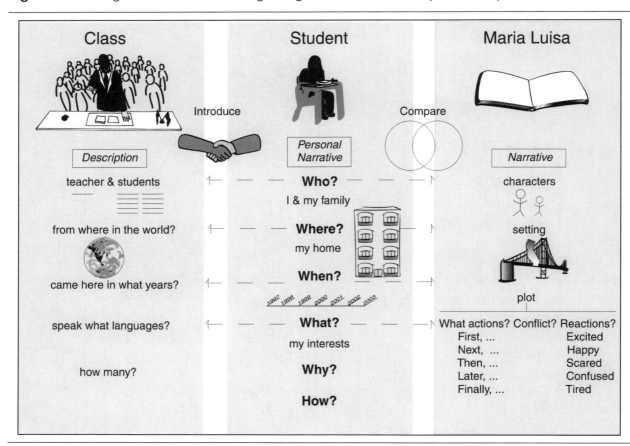

whether the work is focusing on the whole or on a part. A unit built to hone skills whose concepts have already been understood, such as increasing computation or writing skills, might best be served by support visuals, such as a graphic organizer. However, a UVF might have been used when the concepts underlying the skills were taught, in which case students would continue to reference, and possibly expand on, that UVF. An example of this can be found in Chapter 5, where an integrated science, reading, and writing unit began with understanding the features of a reading comprehension rubric used with written response. Because it was the first time students learned the comprehension features, the core UVF illustrated and developed the application of them.

UVFs are not for "units" that are loose collections of separate concepts or instructional components either. Consider the following two language units: If, after a dialogue or short reading about "a family birthday," a high school French class completes segmented grammar exercises—plurals, possessive adjectives/pronouns, and verbs in the present tense—that neither build on each other nor are cumulatively applied to discussing the topic, the "unit" is primarily defined by time and some common vocabulary encountered, but not necessarily learned, from exercise to exercise. This kind of unit, common in some language textbooks, is different from the progression of experiences that cumulatively lead to deep learning of clear targets that I described above.

Figure 1.5, in contrast to such loosely organized units, is a teacher draft of a UVF for a high school English as a Second Language (ESL) unit for beginning speakers starting their school year. In this unit, the students move from listening and responding with movement, to completing group, paired, and individual oral, reading, and incremental written work with the assistance of graphic organizers. The students developmentally use core vocabulary, simple sentences, compound sentences with "and" and "because," and basic question words in three different situations: (a) to describe their class, (b) to build a personal narrative about themselves and their beginning experiences in the school, and (c) to discuss literary elements of the novel *Maria Luisa* (Madison, 1971). They begin to get to know their classmates by introducing themselves and acting as peer support when writing and editing. They deepen their thinking and expand their ability to discuss their experiences by comparing their own experiences with those of the characters in the novel. Something like the UVF in Figure 1.5 is built with the students a little at a time, as they have the concrete experiences of the unit.

Now to the second part of the statement, "A UVF is a tool to manage a unit *together.*" UVFs are used when a unit of study is pursued as a shared learning experience by a whole class. That is, a class may have whole-group, small-group, and/or individual learning, but if the students' focus is the same, they can use the UVF to establish the focus and regularly expand their understanding of it by coming together for planning, review, debriefing of experiences that were done separately, and so on.

Examples of this are project-based and problem-based learning where the class has common instructional targets embedded in a common context they will pursue—either a problem to solve or a class project to complete. They create a plan together to complete the project or solve the problem and, thereby, meet the instructional targets. Work is often done individually or in teams; however, the class comes together frequently to monitor progress and ensure individual and class success. A UVF keeps the instructional targets and progress toward them visible. Figure 1.6 shows the draft core UVF for a science and language arts inquiry-based unit, where students help their community understand why there are so many skunks in the neighborhood and how they might coexist in ways that work for the people and the animals. Whether the inquiry for this unit is divided up or done as a whole class, the UVF can help the class stay focused and monitor their progress.

On the other hand, a UVF would not be used for individualized instruction where each student has different instructional targets and content. With some types of individualized sustained studies, the student and teacher might co-develop individual UVFs, if desired. Doing so, however, would be more realistic after students and teachers have had experience with class UVFs and were assisted by such software as Inspiration® (2000) or Kidspiration™ (2000). Because the teacher remains the more experienced learner who is

Figure 1.6. Teacher Draft UVF for Skunks Inquiry Unit

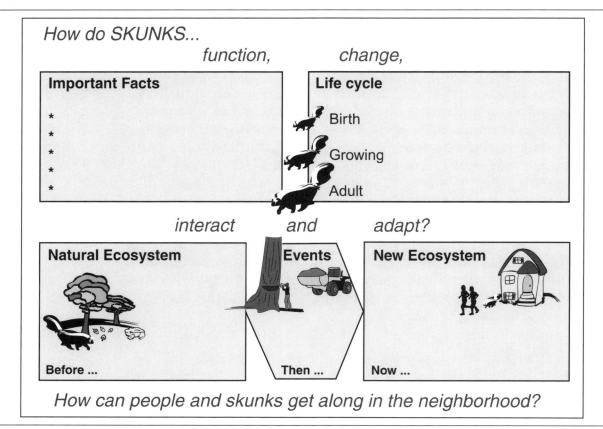

knowledgeable about curricular requirements, such individualized use of UVFs would require the same student and teacher co-development, or student-student collaboration with teacher monitoring, to help students meet the curricular requirements they choose to pursue through their interests.

The use of UVFs does not dictate the teaching; it does, however, require a willingness on the part of teachers and students to work the unit together, and an intent to unify separate learning endeavors toward cumulative understanding of clear targets, be the targets predefined or discovered as patterns highlighted throughout the unit.

WHO ARE UVFS FOR?

My use of UVFs in my own teaching, as well as the observations and reports from other teachers who have used them, indicate that UVFs work equally well for ESL and bilingual students as they do for native English-speaking students, for gifted students as well as learning disabled students, and with second-grade students as well as with graduate students. Moreover, these visual guides help diverse students work side by side or in flexible groups toward the same end goals. Even when groups of students have some different materials and some different experiences, their UVF helps them synthesize those into common experiences focused on common goals. Carol Ann Tomlinson, in *The Differentiated Classroom* (1999), explains:

> In a differentiated classroom, the teacher carefully fashions instruction around the essential concepts, principles, and skills of each subject.... Clarity ensures that teacher, learners, assessment, curriculum, and instruction are linked tightly in a journey likely to culminate in personal growth and individual success for each child. (Pp. 9–10)

Reports from students and teachers I've worked with have confirmed my awareness that UVFs overcome some of the challenges of auditory or language-intense methods, such as lecture and whole-group discussions, which otherwise force many students to be isolated or lost. Here is how some students put it, when evaluating the usefulness of UVFs to them:

- The picture and things gave me an idea of what we were talking about.

- It showed me the things I need to learn instead of making me read so much.

- If we just talked about it, I wouldn't understand it.

One teacher noted that the UVFs helped her deaf student connect the various learning events that were occurring in the classroom. She noted the same benefits for her English language learners and her special education students. She saw each of these populations following the lesson along with other students in the class. This may be because, as John Clarke (1991) puts it, "Visual organizers temporarily simplify complexities. Visual organizers simplify the thinking process, allowing access and understanding on the part of different students with different attitudes and abilities" (p. 534). Once new information is thus simplified, students and teachers can rebuild conceptual complexity together.

The need to keep students with the lesson and the lesson with the students is a basic component of any teaching/learning situation. Only by maintaining this alignment among clear learning targets, evolving student readiness and interests, and instruction and assessment will goals be met. Therefore, it has not surprised me to see the benefits of co-developing and using UVFs with K–12 learners as well as adults. Here are some examples:

- After a year and a half of using UVFs, a group of first-grade teachers reported that UVFs helped their students comprehend subject matter, demonstrate their knowledge, and write about what they had studied.

- Another teacher described the pride and wonder in an adolescent student's voice when, looking at her evolving UVF in her own notebook, the student exclaimed, "Look at this! Look at all we have going!" This student had obviously experienced "having all this going" before that moment. The difference this time was that the student apparently was more aware of the learning that was occurring and how it all connected and moved her forward to specific understandings.

In addition to using UVFs in K–12 teaching, I have used them to guide my workshops and graduate courses. This use has repeatedly shown up as a positive impact when participants submit evaluations. Graduate students have commented on how the recurring connection of the class experiences to the course UVF kept the material clear, deepened the learning, made accountability easier, and helped them demonstrate their learning.

HOW DID UVFS EVOLVE?

The answer to how UVFs evolved is rooted in my own teaching experiences. One of my earliest memories related to UVFs is of my second-grade classroom in Johnstown, Colorado. At the time, my class was made up of an even mix of students who spoke English as their first language and students whose first language was Spanish. I was teaching in what today is called a dual-language bilingual program. Because one objective of the class was academic achievement in two languages, some days I taught content-area material to all of the students in English and other days in Spanish, alternating the language of instruction, if not every other day, then with a regularity that made sense for what was being taught.

"What does this have to do with UVFs?" you may wonder. Well, it was extremely important that all students successfully participated in each lesson and that the lesson was responsive to the students' needs and strengths, no matter what language we spoke. Therefore, I wanted to document our learning path visually each day in ways that highlighted important concepts and relationships among them, making evident what we were holding ourselves accountable for in the unit.

I can still see the chart papers assembled across the room. For example, when we did a science unit on the water cycle, I elicited students' ideas in whatever language we were using that day, and added illustrations that made sense to us all. To make sure that the threads of important concepts and relationships were clear whether students were learning in their dominant or second language, I organized the text, illustrations, and use of color to build coherence and cohesion from day to day. The charts couldn't be random bits of information or activities; they had to build upon previous learning in a way that students could follow and reference when they were learning in their newer language. Each time we switched languages, we reviewed all charts (those written in English or Spanish) speaking the language of the day, but examining the developing academic content across the charts. Each review reinforced the visuals' ability to assist recall of the preceding learning experiences and paths. Little by little, we could discuss and use the science concepts in either language. The visuals and key text helped students acquire, expand, and demonstrate their content knowledge regardless of instructional language.

The bilingual unit charts were my early constructions of UVFs, co-developed with my students, growing organically as the unit progressed, and used in many ways throughout the unit. Those experiences introduced me to the value of a UVF to rivet attention in the midst of exploration and learning that span a period of time and that, in some cases, occur in more than one language. Bilingual teaching also taught me the requirements of consistent key text and illustrations to ensure cumulative and cohesive learning.

My thirty years in education have reinforced those UVF beginnings. This same need to help students and teachers stay focused on the central learning that will be assessed in a unit—whether the targets have been chosen by teachers, students, or both—motivated me to continue to develop UVFs. Influenced by such authors as Anne Shea Bayer (1990), I noticed that, regardless of the age of the learner, if I began a unit of study by eliciting students' own language and experiences, and captured these on chart paper in ways that organized the information to reveal and ready the class for new insights, two things happened. First, with the focus clear and centered, we stayed on target and together even as ideas multiplied. Second, over time students had stepping stones on which they could travel forward or backward to understand the development of ideas and increased levels of abstraction and formal language as they worked through a unit of study.

My staff development and consulting work continue to provide opportunities to test and refine the use of UVFs, as well as to verify their role in serving educators and students to achieve their targeted results. For instance, K–5 teachers in one district constructed draft UVFs when they developed new science, social studies, math, or language arts units. They found that designing a UVF forced them to be clear about their unit targets. After adapting and using these UVFs with their students, they were enthusiastic about the variety of ways students used them.

The significance of the role of UVFs was also reinforced for me after I had made thirty classroom observations. These observations indicated that when a UVF was used, the teacher more explicitly stated the focus and larger purpose of tasks and instruction. Furthermore, work with teachers and students in their classrooms indicated that UVFs not only facilitate the end learning result, but also can assist students and teachers to share power and leadership in teaching and learning. This shared power and leadership proved true both in classrooms that started with student interests or expressed needs and in those that began with curricular or teacher-chosen priorities.

Another precursor of this book was a set of prototype units illustrating instruction and assessment of state social science and language arts standards, *The Illinois Content-Based Assessment Exemplars* (Ewy et al., 1998a,

1998b, 1998c). The UVFs and related practices are some of the reasons why the units may be used with the general student population in ways that permit second-language learners to succeed with their peers. These cohesive visuals have also appealed to educators in the field of special education, as they have tried to help their students achieve state standards. A special education coordinator noted that, because of the visuals in the units, "you can see where you are, where you've been, and where you're going" in a unit of study at any given time.

WHY UVFS NOW?

In his book *Visual Tools for Constructing Knowledge*, David Hyerle (1996, pp. 18, 124) speaks of a merging of forces that partially account for our readiness for UVFs:

- The constructivist-cognitive revolution, which responds to students' needs to seek out and make connections and interconnections on their own
- The new visual technologies for accessing and displaying information
- Schools' much broader movement toward student-centered interaction, cooperative learning, and interactivity

We can add three more factors to Hyerle's list:

- The current compelling need for effectiveness and accountability
- The greater awareness of the diversity of our learners
- The increase, caused by the standards "movement," of impetus, training, and skill in teachers being able to decide instructional targets based on knowledge of students' readiness, interests, needs, and curriculum

The rest of this book will show how UVFs respond to all of the above.

WHY DO UVFS WORK?

I believe that using UVFs has tightened up my teaching and made what I teach more substantial, visible, and accessible. I feel that I am teaching so much more holistically with more meaningful results. It just feels like I am much more together this year, but I haven't sacrificed the creativity and ingenuity that I thought I'd have to. I'm able to stay with the big picture, but still have lots of spontaneity and open spaces.

I have the energy to look at things in terms of growing, getting bet-
ter, trying more and more things that may be a little risky. At the same
time, the UVF pins me to my underlying values and practices. It is a won-
derful mix of comfort and risk.

—Teacher

This teacher's reasons for why UVFs work for teachers overlap why they help students. A UVF and its related practices improve the accessibility, owner-ship, alignment, documentation, and effectiveness of a whole unit of study in ways that students, teachers, and classroom observers can see and under-stand. Why?

One reason is its visual nature. Hyerle (1996, p. 20) says that visual tools promote definitions that are relational, patterned, and context driven. Teachers who have been using visuals and generating charts in their class-room know this to be true. Furthermore, "visual" in a UVF encompasses pic-tures, text, and sometimes artifacts that are designed to evoke memory of concrete experiences, activating the multiple intelligences of which Howard Gardner (1992, 1993) has made us all aware.

Though these reasons are valid, we must think about more than UVFs' visual nature to understand why they work. When viewing the draft UVF in Figure 1.2, one teacher wondered aloud, "How can such a simple visual make a difference?" The answer, of course, is that it doesn't: It is the *process* of co-developing, expanding, and using the UVF individually and as a class that makes the difference. These processes have cognitive benefits:

1. Students and teacher have defined what's important using terms and pictures that they understand from their own experiences and knowl-edge base.

2. They have a common understanding to the degree that the concepts and principles have thus far been developed.

3. They have a readiness and basis for integrating new learning.

In addition, the class has formed a working team with each other and the teacher to apply their learning and monitor their progress toward their goals. This purposeful teamwork will continue for the duration of the unit. The fol-lowing are merely a few testimonies to why these are important:

Coherence in the curriculum involves creating and maintaining visi-ble connections between purposes and everyday learning experiences. (Beane, 1995, p. 7)

We cannot make real progress until we recognize that cognitive and social processes are neither separate nor separable—that learning is inherently social. (Institute for Research on Learning, 1993, p. 3)

We all want to go deeper into subjects that mean something to us, but we find it hard to do alone. We are social creatures; we need the support and interest of others. (Glasser, 1986, p. 77)

In summary, UVFs work for students because they begin with constructivist uses of advance organizers and utilize the strengths of graphic organizers and learning as a social endeavor to make and keep public the central focus of a unit and the evolving learning schema of a whole class. The previous sentence is as technical as I want to be in this book. The following section will strengthen its meaning, address some of the research supporting the use of UVFs, and reference other authors who have done masterful jobs of documenting related research.

HOW DO UVFS COMPARE WITH OTHER VISUALS?

Some readers may have found the previous information in this chapter sufficient to see both the similarities and differences of UVFs relative to other visuals. If so, I look forward to our continued interaction in the chapter summary, or whatever part of the book you choose to read next. Other readers may welcome the additional practical, theoretical, and research information that the following comparisons offer.

Advance Organizer

So why not provide the scaffold (of ideas) at the beginning (of the course)? Let the students in on the secret of the structure, including an understanding of how it continually emerges through further inquiry, so that the mind can be active as the course progresses.

—David Ausubel (1968; quoted in Joyce & Weil, 1996)

An *advance organizer*, as the term implies, helps students organize their thinking about something that is to come. It offers students a mindset or thinking structure they can use with the coming new material. That is one function of a UVF. Some UVFs use comparisons or metaphors, as Ausubel's works often contain. The UVF in Figure 3.5 evokes students' previous understanding of how a teeter-totter works to help them understand that a community works when it balances response to individual needs and the needs of the group. Other UVFs act as an advance organizer by previewing in a concise visual manner the work of the unit, the way the UVF in Figure 1.5 helps students see a structure from separate activities by placing them in the three contexts that they serve and link.

Advance organizers, therefore, help students more readily understand, integrate, interrelate, and distinguish old and new information and experiences. The *Handbook of Research on Improving Student Achievement* (Cawelti,

1995) references more than a dozen studies that support the benefits of relating past learning to present learning and alerting students to key points to be learned.

A UVF helps students anticipate and benefit from a whole chunk of learning—a unit of study or a series of units with the same underlying base—by creating an advance organizer for the unit or units. Because it organizes such complex learning, however, the UVF may be co-developed with students little by little, until the structure of all essential learning of a unit is previewed and organized, at which point the class has a "core UVF." The UVF serves as a cumulative advance organizer for the learning it precedes, connecting new learning to that which has already occurred.

According to Ausubel, whether or not material is meaningful depends more on the preparation of the learner and on the organization of the material than it does on the method of presentation. If the learner begins with the right "set" and if the material is solidly organized, then meaningful learning can occur (Joyce & Weil, 1996, p. 268). Thinking about that organization—of the material and how its structure might be made meaningful to the students—is part of planning UVF co-development, as Chapter 3 explains. Although Ausubel considered advance organizers appropriate for presentation forms of teaching (lectures and reading), they can serve diverse approaches, as the UVF examples already seen in this chapter and those to come will prove.

The most effective advance organizers are those that use concepts, terms, and propositions that are already familiar to the learners, as well as appropriate illustrations and analogies (Joyce & Weil, 1996, p. 271). In fact, Marzano, Pickering, and Pollock (2001) even attach an effect size to the use of nonlinguistic, or imagery, representation, which is reported and discussed in *Classroom Instruction That Works.* Suffice it here to say that when teachers help students generate nonlinguistic representations, the effects on achievement are strong. Marzano and colleagues emphasize that the goal is to produce nonlinguistic representations of knowledge *in the minds of the students.* Their research explains why UVFs are not predesigned posters, but dynamic representations co-developed with students to anchor prior knowledge, concrete experiences, and new knowledge and experiences as the unit progresses. The comparison chart in Figure 1.7 summarizes the similarities and nuances of difference between advance organizers and UVFs.

Graphic Organizer

I found out that a UVF is more than a graphic organizer, or you might say it's a complete graphic organizer that connects teachers and students, learning, content areas, and goals.

—Primary Teacher

This teacher acknowledges the fact that a UVF is literally a type of graphic organizer. *Graphic organizer* is a term for graphic representations that combine

Figure 1.7. Comparison Between Advance Organizer and UVF

Advance Organizer	Unit Visual Framework
1. Built around the major concepts and/or propositions of a discipline or area of study 2. May be in oral and/or visual form 3. Presented to students 4. Taught in its totality in the beginning of a study 5. Designed for presentation forms of instruction: lectures, discussions, films, experiments, or reading 6. Depends on knowledge of the students, of the discipline/area of study, and on well organized materials	1. Structures essential learning that will be taught/learned and assessed 2. Always multiple modalities: oral and visual evoking experiences and memories 3. Co-developed with students 4. May be built cumulatively a little at a time, until the structure of all essential learning of a unit is previewed and organized 5. Serves teaching/learning that has common learning targets for the class no matter the means to achieving them — presentation, inquiry, simulation, etc. 6. Depends on knowledge of the students, clear instructional and assessment targets, and a clear conceptualization of the unit(s) of study that will be pursued

Both:
➢ Create a structure to organize thinking about material to come
➢ Make organization explicit
➢ Relate prior knowledge to organizing structure
➢ Continually relate new material to organizing structure
➢ Promote active, critical approach to subject matter

linguistic means (words and phrases) and nonlinguistic (symbols and arrows) to represent relationships. Webs and Venn diagrams are examples of graphic organizers that have been seen on classroom walls and in educational materials for some time. Figure 1.8 compares UVFs with other graphic organizers.

David Hyerle, in *Visual Tools for Constructing Knowledge* (1996) and the subsequent *Field Guide to Using Visual Tools* (2000), provides a clear and comprehensive theoretical basis for the use of graphic organizers. He references works from very diverse fields, such as Fritjof Capra's linking of quantum physics, information theory, and systems thinking in *The Web of Life* (Capra, 1996, cited in Hyerle, 2000, p. 28). Hyerle describes Capra's resulting

Figure 1.8.   Comparison Between Graphic Organizer and UVF

Graphic Organizer	Unit Visual Framework

Format
1. Uses words/phrases and symbols, such as a web and Venn diagram;
   may use lines or arrows to link symbols, such as a concept map;
   may use illustrations and/or color cues, such as a mind map
2. May have prescribed structures: concept map has a hierarchical structure; mind map has labeled, linked lines radiating from a central idea, with infinite branches
3. May or may not visually anchor students' learning experiences and memories related to the content
	Format
	1. Always uses words/phrases, illustrations, and color cues;
	   may use symbols, arrows, and artifacts
	2. Built on negotiated structures that represent the learning in the minds of the students and teachers
	3. Visually anchors and evokes students' learning experiences and memories related to the content, using illustrations chosen by the students

Ownership
4. Sometimes constructed for students, such as a commercially prepared or commonly used graphic organizer of the writing process, or a partially completed concept map used for assessment purposes, that has the main concept;
   at other times constructed by/or with students, such as a concept map or mind map that individual students construct to show their understanding;
   may be constructed and used by individual students and/or cooperatively by classes
	Ownership
	4. Always co-developed by teachers and students as a class to reach common visions and understandings; individual students also use and expand their portable UVFs

Use 5. May be a support visual as one tool of a unit or task 6. May be used for only a portion of a unit of study, or at one time period during the unit — such as at the end of the unit	Use 5. Designed to be the core visual that focuses and maintains the integrity of a whole unit of study, or a common focus across units 6. Always used from the beginning through the end of the unit

observations about systems having organizational patterns and how those patterns cannot be measured or weighed, but must be mapped as a configuration of relationships, then relates how theories linking the brain, mind, and cognition concur with Capra's work. He notes that, because we learn in patterns, graphic organizers provide a way for students to think holistically rather than in the linear fashion that discourse often forces upon us (Hyerle, 2000, pp. 29–33). Discussing Howard Gardner's work with multiple intelligences, Hyerle further asserts that visual tools are foundational for sensing, thinking, and feeling across all of these intelligences (Hyerle, 2000, p. 35).

John Clarke, in *Patterns of Thinking: Integrating Learning Skills in Content Teaching* (1990), also cites studies from varied disciplines that support the diverse use of graphic organizers. He notes their benefits for giving an outline of the content and an expression of the kind of thinking that can be applied to the content.

The theories and research just mentioned attest to the fact that graphic organizers do more than organize information. In fact, one need only thumb through *Future Force* (McClanahan & Wicks, 1993) to see that graphic organizers can be used as potent tools for students and teachers to apply Deming's principles of quality to their classrooms, in ways similar to what businesses have done before them. To emphasize the diverse use of graphic organizers, Hyerle (1996, 2000) uses the term *visual tool.* This term reminds us to attend to both form (the way the visual looks) and function (its purpose and use) as we compare UVFs to some specific kinds of graphic organizers.

Concept Maps

Concept maps are attributed to Dr. Joseph Novak of Cornell University, and to Robert Gowin, who collaborated with him on some works (Novak & Gowin, 1984). The maps organize a web diagram hierarchically to show one's understanding of a concept or set of concepts.

Figure 1.9 is a concept map of reading comprehension that could be one tool in the sample unit Reading to Remember and Show What You Know, which will be discussed in Chapter 5. This concept map happens to be rather symmetrical. As with any conceptual tool, it could be redrawn differently by another person or by the same person at another time. In fact, like Ausubel's advance organizer (Joyce & Weil, 1996), it is meant to serve as a conceptual snapshot that will continually be revisited to see how new learning relates to or alters it.

A concept map arranges labeled geometric shapes, such as circles or ovals, into a hierarchy that is linked by lines to show relationships. The hierarchy begins at the top with the concept or concepts to be explained and proceeds down the page with progressively more specific information about the concept. Although the primary relationship shown in a concept map is the hierarchy of ideas about a concept, other relationships can be shown by links, as the arrowed links in the center of Figure 1.9 indicate.

Though concept maps are often used for single concepts or parts of a unit of study, the Content Enhancement Series (Lenz, Bulgren et al., 1994; Lenz, Marrs et al., 1993) uses a hierarchical map to organize large studies, such as courses and units. This series does an excellent job of showing how graphic organizers can help a unit of study be coherent and cohesive. In fact, when I discovered the series, I almost stopped writing this book because of the

Figure 1.9.   Reading Comprehension Concept Map

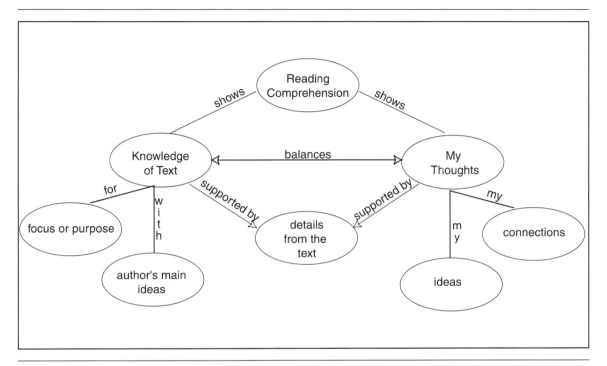

similarities and extensive explanations for using lesson, unit, and course organizers. The authors not only provide examples of their hierarchical graphic organizers, but also have developed clear routines that assist success. I highly recommend these materials in both their own right and as companion information to what is in this book. I wrote the book, however, because of the differences in the kind of visuals I present here, and I wanted to include examples of UVFs that support the achievement of state and national standards. Furthermore, I wanted to elaborate on how UVFs facilitate shared power by students and teachers, and enhance success by students of varied readiness, linguistic, and cultural backgrounds.

When a whole class constructs a concept map and revisits it for deeper meaning over time, similar to the way UVFs are used, the concept map's visual dependence on words and geometric shapes creates problems for some learners. Even if all students are total participants in designing a concept map, some students may have difficulty reconstructing the thinking when they return to it because the words and hierarchy may not elicit enough memory of the thought processes or learning experiences that produced it. This is apt to happen when the map has predominantly concept-specific vocabulary. Even with some more expressive vocabulary, second-language students may have difficulty recalling the meaning of the words that the class used as labels. With no illustrations, delayed or new readers may be unable to decode the words that

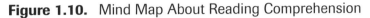

Figure 1.10. Mind Map About Reading Comprehension

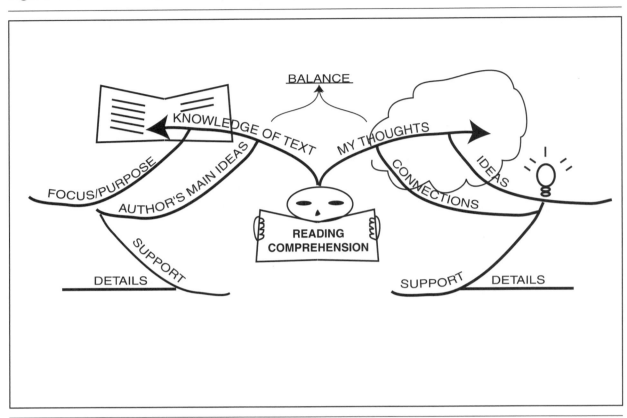

hold the meaning within the circles or on the links carrying important relationship insights.

Mind Maps

Tony Buzan developed mind mapping in the early 1970s as a form of nonlinear note taking (Wycoff, 1991). However, like most visual tools, they have also been used for generating ideas, developing concepts, and improving memory.

Figure 1.10 is a mind map version of the same content contained in Figure 1.9's concept map. Because mind maps are nonlinear, there is wide variation in their appearance. Nonlinear does not mean random, however. Notice that, as in the concept map, words and lines still link ideas, but the structure and visual aids are different. A mind map radiates out from a central image or idea. All words are printed in capitals, and single words are suggested for each line.

Mind maps and UVFs both use color to highlight and emphasize. Mind maps also often include some illustrations. Visual differences between mind maps and UVFs can be seen by leafing through this chapter. Additional differences in format, ownership, and use that exist between UVFs and other graphic organizers also hold true for mind maps. (See, for example, Figure 1.8.)

Joyce Wycoff (1991, p. 44) explains that each mind map is a unique product of the person who produces it. Similarly, each class's UVF will be unique, which is why a secondary teacher, who has more than one section of a particular subject, develops different UVFs for the same unit with each class. The resulting UVFs will have the same essential ideas and reflect the key structures and organization of the unit, so one class viewing another's will recognize the content; however, each UVF will reflect the students who co-develop it and their specific blend of prior knowledge and response to new knowledge and experiences. Furthermore, on their portable version of the class core UVF, individual students capture their own flow of ideas and experiences in ways that make sense to them, including using mind-mapping or concept-mapping techniques.

Concluding Statements
About Graphic Organizers

Hyerle (1996) advocates using a set of consistent graphic organizers that can be used across learning contexts. He has chosen eight that he calls *thinking maps,* because they represent eight types of thinking processes: (a) a circle map for showing context/frame of reference, (b) a bubble map for describing qualities, (c) a double bubble for comparing and contrasting, (d) a tree diagram for classification, (e) a brace map for looking at whole/part relationships, (f) a flow chart for sequencing, (g) a multi-flow for cause and effect, and (h) a bridge diagram for representing analogies. Hyerle recommends this consistency for the same reason that assessment experts extol the virtues of generic or global rubrics that can be used in multiple situations: With consistent use comes less confusion, deeper understanding, and more automatic use by students. Chapter 2 of this book discusses global UVFs in the same vein.

Hyerle (1996, 2000) cautions that the use of a different graphic organizer for each situation may overwhelm students. The very reason a UVF is used as the core visual for a whole unit of study is to decrease the possibility of being overwhelmed, helping students to separate out essential elements and organize for meaningful use an abundance of information and experiences. Additionally, Hyerle suggests that when presented with multiple graphic organizers, valuable time must be spent teaching each graphic organizer as well as the related content. Because UVFs are not presented *to* students, time is spent building the visual display experientially *with* them, and using it as an ongoing, collaborative tool for deep learning and the demonstration of content. The examples, comparisons of UVFs with other visuals, and descriptive information in this chapter have set UVFs apart from the kinds of graphic organizers Hyerle cautions against.

Chapter One
Visual Summary

Making Ongoing Sense of a Unit of Study

A Unit Visual Framework (UVF)

is an organic, collaboratively created, class display (on the wall, if possible) that focuses, supports, & documents a unit of study from its beginning to end.

What Teaching/Learning Situations Do UVFs Serve?

Unit(s) of study
that allow time for a progression of experiences, which cumulatively lead to deep learning of clear targets

Pursued Together
- Common learning targets for the class regardless of means to achieving them (presentation, inquiry, etc.)
- students and teachers work the unit together, and unify any separate learning endeavors toward cumulative understanding of targets.

The UVF begins as
a core visual, with pictures and key text representing the essentials of what is studied and assessed, overtly establishing focus.

Each student has a **portable core visual**.

Core Visual Example

Showing Reading Comprehension

Test

If student performance or products that demonstrate understanding of the UVF **also** result in achievement of the instructional targets, **then** the UVF design is effective.

The core visual grows into
an expanded display, organized by the core visual to show learning paths and evolving, cumulative understanding of the unit.

Expanded Display Example

Unit Visual Framework (UVF)

Test

If, throughout the unit, each student and teacher can ...
1. Successfully access & participate in unit learning
2. Establish, review, and trace learning paths
3. Observe & express cumulative understanding

Then the expanded UVF has been effectively co-developed, organized, visually depicted, & used

Focus 2

The Basis for Coherence and Cohesion

Success in school subjects depends on being able to scan large volumes of information and use a purpose to select certain items for more careful processing.

—John Clarke (1990, p. 68)

A middle school science teacher begins class talking about a specific topic. He invites class participation from his students. A boy asks a question and then makes an association with something else, taking the discussion in a different direction for about ten minutes. The teacher writes on the board.

Another student, Ana, takes notes the whole time. An observer sees that she has captured isolated vocabulary used by both student and teacher. When asked, she is unable to connect the vocabulary to express the points made by the teacher or student. The focus begun by the teacher, and returned to after a meandering discussion, is perhaps somewhere in Ana's vocabulary list, but she can't retrieve it because she didn't really see it. There is no cohesion among the bits of information filling the classroom, so this student, though attentive, is not yet engaged in learning.

Have you ever "been there" or "done that" as a teacher or student? It can be frustrating in either position. Though not all classroom scenarios are like this, we know that focus is important to all learning situations and is the center of cohesive teaching and learning. By cohesive teaching and learning, I simply mean that the varied events occurring in the course of a unit of study always maintain the same central focus, are meaningfully connected to it, and cumulatively lead to the intended purpose embodied in the focus.

Most educators would agree that cohesion is desirable, but we all know variables that make it tough to create—little things, like schedule changes, absences, interruptions, life happenings, and the actual challenge of finding the focus to begin with! Unit Visual Frameworks can help students and teachers establish and maintain focus even with the challenges presented by most of that list. The exception is the selection of the central focus itself, which must be decided before designing the UVF.

Because it visually anchors key concepts, experiences, and relationships, a UVF enables divergent thinking and learning experiences to occur without getting lost in activities, interruptions, life happenings, or the passage of time. Depending on when it is referenced, a student or teacher should be able to say, "This is what we said is important in this unit. Here's what we've done so far related to it. What we're working on now is related to that in the following way. . . . We'll show that we achieved what we wanted by doing. . . ."

Did you notice the "we" in that last sentence? In Chapter 1, I mentioned that a major reason I get excited about the use of UVFs is their function as a concrete tool for teachers and students to work together with wide open eyes to achieve the results they target for the unit. Some sixth graders I worked with called that "power." Not the kind of power, they explained, where you stand on chairs and do whatever you want, but the responsible power of co-developing and managing the learning that occurs. Please keep this priority in mind, because as we move into examples, it would be very easy to interpret some of them as recommending presentation-type teaching (i.e., the passing on of knowledge) exclusively. I urge you to be alert and to know that my reason for using the example is seldom about the visual itself, but more often about the possibilities for teachers and students that arise from co-creating and using something like it together.

GLOBAL VISUAL FRAMEWORKS

What? *Global* Visual Frameworks? Haven't we been talking about Unit Visual Frameworks? Yes, and we still are. A Global Visual Framework (GVF) may be thought of as a UVF that applies to more than one unit of instruction; in other words, a GVF is a global UVF. So, if they are still UVFs, why did I choose to use the second term? Because considering "global" versus "unit" helps us clarify our focus. The examples in this chapter will demonstrate how a UVF guides the specific unit and how a GVF can give that same focus a wider perspective so students can more readily recognize and apply their learning in other situations.

You may be asking why I introduced GVFs here. I have done so because the examples we will soon see, which people have chosen as most helpful when first learning about UVFs, have global applications. In addition, they solve another dilemma that practitioners have expressed. As I introduced UVFs to various educator groups, most people responded enthusiastically to the idea of what UVFs were and could do. The intimidating part to many was deciding what would go into a UVF. A teacher I respect explained, "It's hard for me to decide what's important in a unit of study."

I can identify with that. Deciding what we will hold our students and ourselves accountable for really takes deliberation, especially when we want to create a framework broad enough to encompass both curricular and student priorities. Therefore, when that teacher saw examples of GVFs that focus on standards written as broadly applicable generalizations, she breathed a sigh of relief. "Oh, this makes sense to me. I know the standards are important, and UVFs that help me and my students with the standards would be really useful." Now that you have my rationale for introducing a new term, let's see how GVFs and UVFs help establish focus.

ONE SOURCE OF GVF CONTENT— LEARNING STANDARDS

Co-Developing GVFs Enables Making and Understanding Generalizations

The National Council of Teachers of Mathematics (NCTM) expects teachers to be able to decide what aspects of a task to highlight, how to organize and orchestrate the work of the students, what questions to ask to challenge those with varied levels of expertise, and how to support students without taking over the process of thinking for them and thus eliminating the challenge (NCTM, 2001, p. 19). All of these teacher decisions require a clear focus, which the NCTM guides through the content standards they have identified.

Now, my experience is that we educators have a love-hate relationship with the kind of abstractions standards often demand. We like the idea of higher-order thinking, which requires abstraction, but we are also wary of the challenges that abstract ideas present to students. We know the sequence that assists students in succeeding with abstractions: first concrete, then abstract. However, even this sequence is not always evident to students, particularly when the sequence is done solely through oral means.

Consider, for example, when a teacher, confident that some students have had the prerequisite concrete experiences, asks knowledgeable students to relate their experiences to classmates as preparation for targeted abstract concepts. If *relate* means only "to talk about," two sets of students are likely to have difficulty gaining from the peer knowledge: students learning a new language and students whose backgrounds have not included the wide experiences required for academic success. For both groups, the oral discussion itself will be too abstract to follow. Co-developing UVFs can help. Over time, students and their teachers understand that the UVF helps them take the first step of abstraction: recalling and communicating their concrete experiences through their images and their own words. Therefore, oral discussions often involve the creation or use of a UVF or a related support visual.

Figure 2.1. Draft UVF for PreK–2 NCTM Geometry Standard

Describing Shapes

name	example	it looks like	it's made of	it does not look like ... because	symmetry
rectangle		*door* *ruler*	2 short sides = 2 long sides ≡ straight lines equal angles	...... only 3 lines ...... round lines ...... different angles	

Making, Finding, and Using Shapes

making	finding	transforming	using for ... because	
geoboard	what? where? which way? how far?		making a brick house	can stack them

To illustrate with NCTM standards, the co-development of something like Figure 2.1 would over time provide the needed support for teachers and their primary students to abstract from everyday experiences the NCTM geometry standard for PreK–2 students. With this support, students and teachers could share responsibility for questioning, thinking, and challenging varied levels of expertise toward success with the geometry focus.

Of course, *giving* young students a UVF like the one in Figure 2.1 would be too much. However, if such a visual were developed and expanded over time with students as they planned and debriefed primary activities—building with blocks or sorting them to put them away, using movement to form shapes and shape transformations, folding or cutting shapes to see symmetry or compose new shapes, and so on—then teachers would be highlighting and helping students organize their thinking about geometric shapes, structures, and relationships as they completed what might otherwise be separate, diverse concrete tasks.

If students consistently used the attributes illustrated across the top of Figure 2.1, they would move from expressive language about mathematics, as they described common objects that the shape resembles, to academic language, when they learned how to describe the shape's makeup. The UVF would provide visual cues for language patterns that native and non–native speakers of English could use at first, something like the following:

> This shape is a _____. Some examples are _____. A _____ looks like _____ because _____. The _____ is made of _____. It does not look like _____ because _____.

After students had described more than one shape using their UVF, they could compare the similarities and differences in the characteristics and properties of each shape, as well as the advantages and disadvantages of each for different purposes, taking the discussion toward the more abstract level of the NCTM standard, which is the focus. They could continue to expand and review their UVF, generating these types of specifics and generalizations about two- and three-dimensional geometric shapes.

This UVF could also have global applications, and the process of analysis might be reversed. For example, when students used geometry as part of integrated work and problem solving, such as when designing a model of their neighborhood in their study of community, questions spurred by the visual in Figure 2.1—particularly its bottom half—would help students recall and expand their knowledge of shapes and how they are used.

Learning for Forever

A primary teacher commented about UVFs, "The UVF is a tool for learning for forever—it will help bring out/back the learning in the future." This statement can be true of any UVF that is kept displayed, referenced, and used as a basis for new knowledge. Those visual frameworks co-developed for the broader generalizations (GVFs) are particularly designed for "learning for forever." (Practical tip: When sixth-grade teacher Ginger Benning noted that it was too bad there wasn't enough wall space to keep up all class UVFs throughout the year, we decided that an enlarged photo might serve that purpose, as long as the photo was accessible or on an overhead projector so the class and individual students could use it.)

The support we've just seen UVFs and GVFs provide for focus on generalizations at the primary level is available for all grade levels. To demonstrate, we can examine the content standard for science and technology as defined in the National Science Education Standards (NSES; National Academy of Sciences, 1995). Students in grades K–12 are expected to gain "abilities of technological design." As students progress in school, the complexity of the problems addressed and extended ways the principles are applied change. For now, we will consider the demands and supports related to this standard for middle school and high school students.

Students in grades 5–12 apply this standard in two ways: (a) to meet a need or solve a problem, and (b) to study the technological work of others.

Figure 2.2. Draft GVF for NSES Standard: Science and Technology

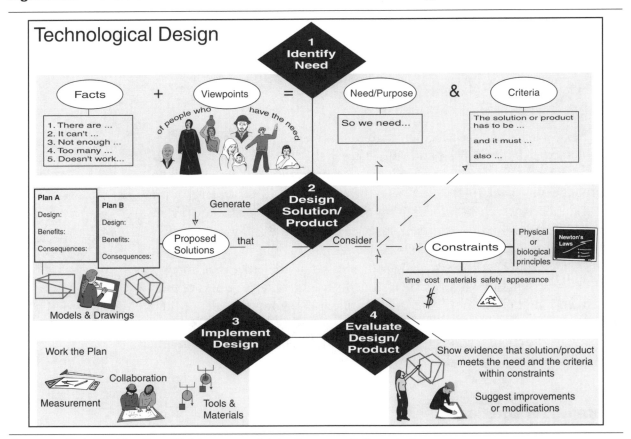

Consider the teacher draft GVF of this standard in Figure 2.2. Suppose that sixth graders co-developed a GVF similar to this as they designed a system to move dishes in a restaurant or production line, or high school students co-developed a similar GVF as they designed a machine that incorporated both mechanical and electrical control systems.

Once students have developed their core GVF, making their focus overt, they can repeatedly apply the whole process of technological design or only a part of it. That is, they can use and expand their GVF to create other products or solve problems, or they can study the technological work of others by examining full or partial design problems. For example, the sixth-grade class may compare characteristics of competing brands of skateboards, similar to the way the high school class analyzes the features of different athletic shoes. Because in both cases students will be analyzing products that have already been designed, students can reference their GVF to know what information they do and do not have and how to use the information they do have to better understand technological design.

Suppose, on the other hand, the sequence of learning events were reversed, and the classes first approached technological design through the study of others' works. Co-developing a GVF that at least provides a skeletal base of the whole process of technological design would still provide a focus that would unite the investigations. Then, when students analyzed constraints, such as those imposed by the sport, human anatomy, and materials, they would know how these constraints affect other parts of technological design. Rather than performing an isolated exercise, they would be establishing a basis for understanding the NSES standard.

Dream bigger. How many of you have been part of a committee that has tried to get lower-grade-level work articulated with upper-grade-level work—such as coordinating elementary, middle school, and high school curriculum—so students can see a progression of successful learning? Imagine if, during such articulation, teachers agreed on a draft GVF of a standard common to all grades, as the NSES science and technology standard is, and then co-developed a developmental GVF at each grade level that contained common, agreed-upon elements. If that were to happen, students would understand the process of technological design early and be able to progress in complexity, diversity, and depth of application and understanding as they got older. They would not have to figure out the focus over and over, but would rather apply the details of each learning experience to understand it more clearly and profoundly. Coherence and cohesion could cross grade levels and school systems.

GVFs Maintain Focus
at the Generalization Level

GVFs can be very helpful in seeing the forest as we walk through the trees. Illinois's Social Studies Goal 16 wants students to "understand events, trends, individuals, and movements shaping the history of Illinois, the United States, and other nations" (Illinois State Board of Education, 1997, p. 50) The standards document also gives as the rationale for the goal students' need "to develop an understanding of how people, nations, actions and interactions have led to today's realities" (p. 51).

When Illinois students focus on history through such diverse topics as the American Revolution, the Westward Movement, or past immigration patterns, they are pursuing the state's Social Studies Goal 16. However, it is easy for students to get lost in the details of these topics—the *who, what, where,* and *when* of the American Revolution, for example—and never get to the generalization of how the revolution shaped our nation and the world. Not having brought the learning about the revolution to the level of generalization required by the state goal, students are hampered later. When they encounter the topic again or another topic that could build on it, be the new situation an authentic learning context or a statewide test, they can't apply the previous learning to the new situation. A GVF, such as the one in Figure 2.3, can help. In fact, if something like this GVF were used every time students had a unit with a history focus, they would automatically frame their learning to attain this broader perspective.

Figure 2.3. Draft GVF for Illinois Social Studies Goal 16

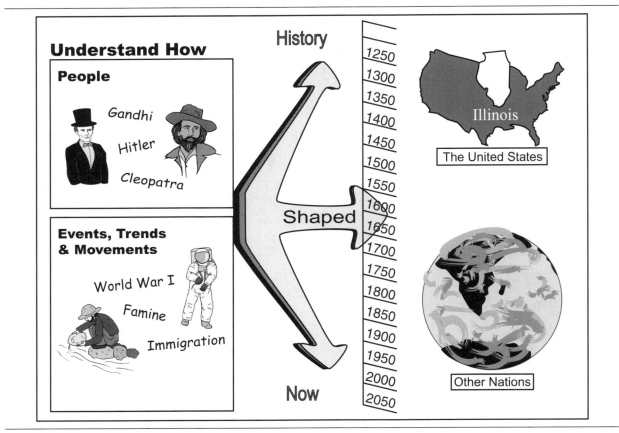

The GVF in Figure 2.3 illustrates generalizable knowledge that applies to more than one social studies unit. If used by more than one class, it would be important for each class to adapt or recreate the GVF to make certain that it was anchoring their experiences, comprehension, and requirements for accountability, just as a single class will do each time the class uses the GVF in a different learning context. Here are some classroom examples.

- The first time an Illinois class pursues a unit with the history goal targeted, the class might construct a GVF similar to Figure 2.3 to depict their understanding of what the goal is requiring of them. As they proceed through the first unit, the class can customize the GVF into a UVF specific to that unit's curriculum. The UVF depicted in Figure 2.4 shows a class beginning to do this with their study of immigration.

- Each time students and their teacher tailor the Goal 16 GVF to create a curricular-specific UVF, as was done again in Figure 2.5 for the study of the Westward Movement, they have to think through what the goal is asking them to understand as it relates to the specific topic of study.

Figure 2.4. Immigration UVF

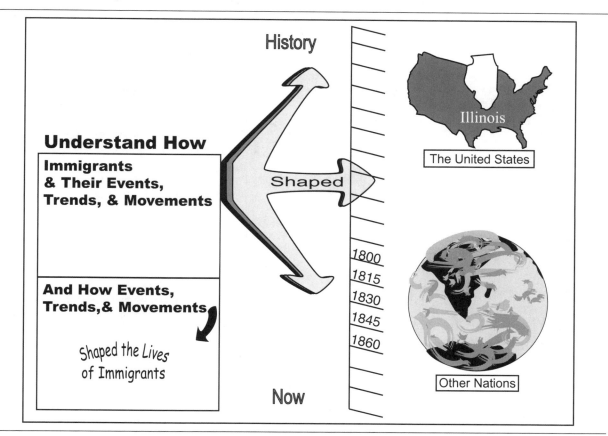

Consequently, they build on and deepen their previous understanding of the goal.

If the framework is already familiar from previous use, the UVF may also be used as a preassessment tool or as a graphic organizer to preview content. Figure 2.6 combines brainstormed prior knowledge with an initial survey of the text to organize a fifth-grade class's thoughts at the beginning of a unit on the Westward Movement. This initial unit overview will be verified or modified as the unit proceeds, and the learning experiences or expanded information needed to make these labels meaningful will be visually connected to the UVF to anchor concrete understanding.

So far, the examples have been units that begin with a targeted standard. Practitioners know that units of instruction don't always begin that way. In fact, the reverse is also true. Sometimes the students have an interest that mobilizes them toward a particular area of study. Other times, a teacher may have a favorite unit that has been taught and loved by students, and this becomes the beginning point. In either case, an adapted GVF may help

Figure 2.5.   Westward Movement UVF

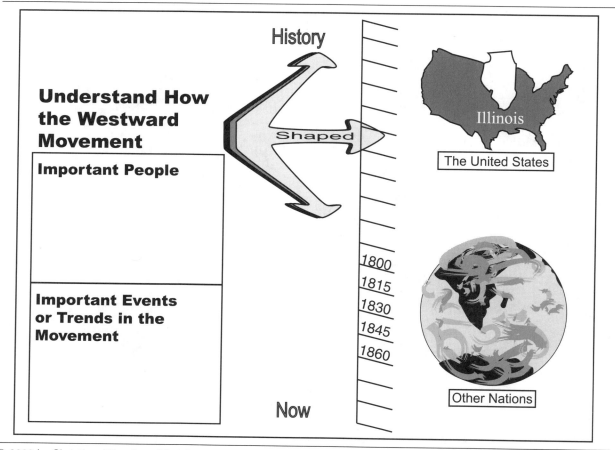

students and teacher ensure that they apply the rich details they enjoy to broader levels of abstraction or perspective, like those of Goal 16. For example, in Figure 2.7 we again see the Westward Movement theme, but it was approached through a study of the pioneers.

There is a teacher draft of the pioneers core UVF on the left side of Figure 2.7. This UVF contains the two critical questions that guide student insights into the pioneers of the Westward Movement and current times: "What were the characteristics of the pioneers?" and "Do today's pioneers have the same characteristics?" In pursuing the first question and learning about the events of the journeys pioneers took as part of the Westward Movement, students address the following instructional targets:

Illinois Social Studies Standard 16D Understand Illinois, United States, and world social history

- *Benchmark 16.D.2a* Describe the various individual motives for settling in colonial America.

Figure 2.6. Westward Movement UVF Reflecting Unit Preview

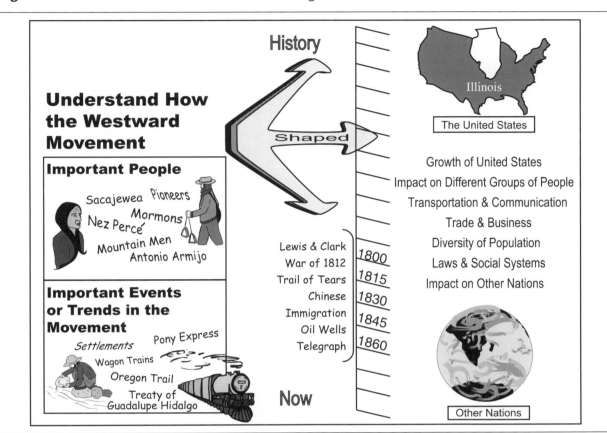

- *Benchmark 16.D.2b* Describe the ways in which participation in the westward movement affected families and communities. (Illinois State Board of Education, 1997, p. 54)

The second question asked in Figure 2.7 is a broad one that invites students to identify current pioneers of their choice, including themselves if they so choose, and to use history to analyze the present—and vice versa.

Through the pioneer UVF, students step back from the details about pioneers and formulate a picture of one group of people involved in the Westward Movement. This specific UVF, in turn, is placed in the context of the tailored Goal 16 GVF, which helps students to consider how pioneers, other people, and the Westward Movement shaped the United States and other nations. The teacher leads students to do the same with the second group, the modern pioneers; as students provide evidence that their chosen group or individuals are pioneers, they describe the effects of these modern pioneers on the U.S. and/or other nations.

Students, therefore, take the benchmark and standard-level knowledge to a broader level of generalization to achieve the specific social studies goal. In

Figure 2.7. Westward Movement Through "Pioneers" Study

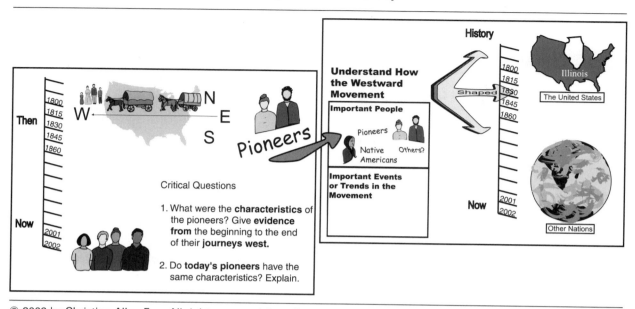

co-developing and connecting these two visual frameworks, students also store their knowledge of pioneers in memory in a way that will support integration of future, related curriculum or interests, such as other aspects of the Westward Movement or of United States history.

Figure 2.8, which adds a UVF to Figure 2.4's adapted GVF, is one more example of a GVF's ability to elevate theme-specific learning to broader perspectives. Figures 2.7 and 2.8 serve units of study about specific people—in the case of the latter, immigrants. A class using the Illinois Content-Based Exemplar *Immigration Stories* (Ewy et al., 1998b) connects the detailed parts of their UVF in those materials to the adapted Social Studies Goal 16 GVF. The UVF gives visual support for students to learn about and document their understanding of immigrant experiences and patterns, including the impact of immigration on the United States and the world. The GVF helps students relate that specific knowledge to a broad historical perspective that they eventually come to recognize as common to all of their studies of history.

In addition to eliciting historical perspective, the GVF in Figure 2.3 or its adaptations over time becomes both a storage device and a prompt for the multiple examples students have placed in this perspective. This cumulative storage of what was concretely learned and visually represented can then be more easily recalled and explored in holistic ways. For example, students who have successfully participated in the pioneers and immigration units can make new discoveries by comparing the experiences of each group, the time periods and patterns of each movement, and their respective impact on the United States and the world. Such comparisons force deeper thinking, keep learning cumulative, and make connections for cohesive learning.

Teacher Concerns

Knowing these benefits, teachers have described to me their difficulty in taking students to the level of the Goal and Standard. As one teacher has said,

I've never done this—the global and the unit. It requires higher-level thinking. Parents don't converse with students at home in ways that help students do this in school.

Usually, it is I who do a graphic organizer, not the students. It seems hard to bring it out of the students; many students don't have prior knowledge, maybe. If I go to the Standards, I lose my kids. How do I bring them back to the whole?

There seem to be four concerns expressed by this teacher. First, there is the difficulty of making the level of the standard a clear, understandable focus for students, so that "going to" that level doesn't lose students. Second, there is the problem of engaging and sustaining the type of participation necessary to form generalizations when working with students who have different background knowledge from what is needed for this topic. Similarly, students who are inexperienced with the type of conversations that lead to academic generalizations may have trouble participating. Finally, there is the challenge of ensuring that students with emergent levels of language development or acquisition of the English language can also succeed.

This chapter, hopefully, has answered some of these concerns. First, all the sample GVFs have shown how to make generalizations contained in standards the explicit focus of a unit. In addition, Figures 2.7 and 2.8, along with the discussion of them, have demonstrated how to scaffold from the more concrete or specific learning to the standards' level of generalization.

Of course, one can't elicit something from students if they don't have the background. So what do we do when students don't have the background knowledge? I can hear the mental reply that most teachers would automatically say when they're not in the midst of instruction and are able to think carefully about the question: We create the experiences. One of the reasons the pioneers unit is found in many classrooms is that there is such great literature at many different reading levels, and literature is one source of background knowledge. Simulations are another. As Chapter 4 will elaborate, the sequence of co-development of a visual framework, therefore, is clear: Begin with concrete experience, talk about the experiences in developmental language, and illustrate the class understanding of the experiences—documenting the language and conceptual knowledge about the focus.

The teacher's concerns above about conversational norms and degree of language development available to express generalizations are both understandable. There is research that many students of low socioeconomic status (SES) have different types of conversations in their homes than students from middle and upper classes have (Mehan, 1991). Instead of school-like discussions at home, conversations in low-SES homes often are more focused on

Figure 2.8. *Immigration Stories* UVF With Adapted Goal 16 GVF

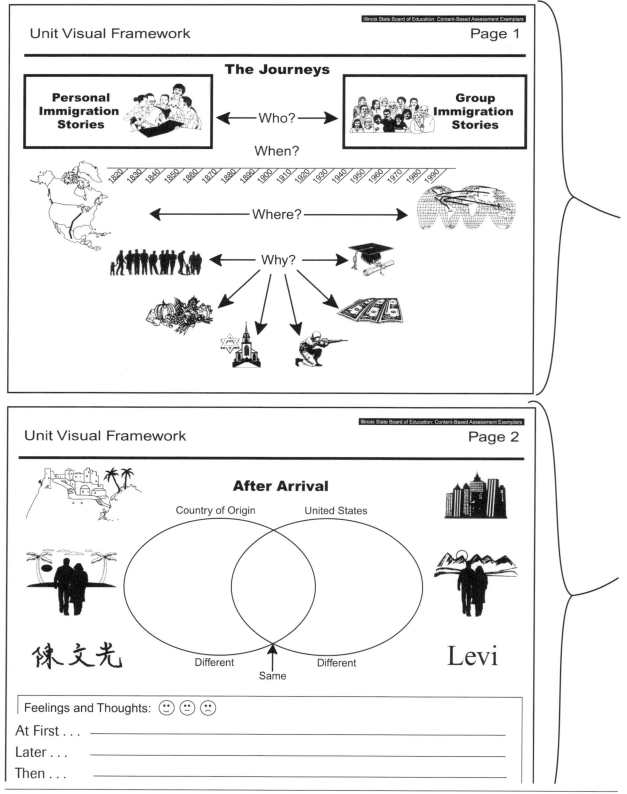

From *Immigration Stories* (Ewy et al., 1998b). Reprinted with permission of the Illinois State Board of Education.

Figure 2.8. (Continued)

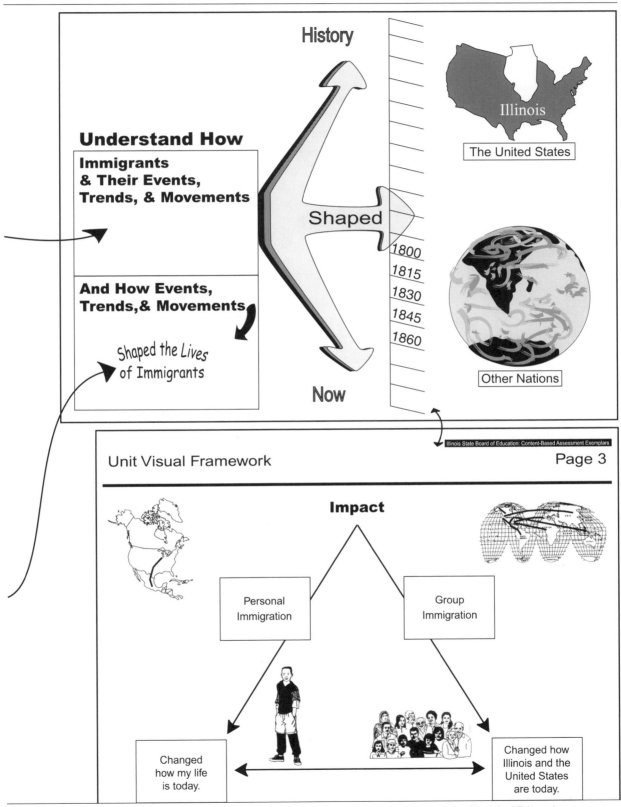

From *Immigration Stories* (Ewy et al., 1998b). Reprinted with permission of the Illinois State Board of Education.

immediate and real occurrences, like chores that need to be done or a family member that needs to be visited. Therefore, students in such homes are not accustomed to the abstract, oral discussions that elicit generalizations. Other children, for varied reasons, do not have extended conversations at home, or have them in languages that they aren't able to use at school.

English Language Learners

Teachers ask how students who have limited command of the English language can have discussions at the generalization level. Previous paragraphs, plus the type of visual cues contained in the NCTM geometry example, answer that question. Instead of an oral, abstract discussion, students and teacher scaffold orally *and* visually with their visual frameworks. For example, as students study the pioneers, they use vocabulary and sentence patterns acquired from studying the details of the pioneers' journeys to formulate generalizations, expanding their UVF with lists and evidence from the actual events they study. These expanding visuals give meaning to the term "characteristics."

The two questions, supported by the illustrations and timeline on the UVF, stimulate higher-order thinking regarding the concrete information they are learning about pioneers. As students consider and document their responses to each of these with the details along the way, they build linguistic and conceptual competency to synthesize this information a little at a time. Thus, each step prepares them to move on to the GVF or broader generalizations.

After students have expanded their pioneer UVF, they will be better able to say how the pioneers were important to the Westward Movement. They will also be able to express some ideas about how the Native Americans were important. With the ability to express ideas about those two subjects and the actual events of the Westward Movement that they used to offer evidence of characteristics and importance, they can venture hypotheses about how the Westward Movement shaped the United States. We see, therefore, that when students co-develop a GVF, they do not have an abstract conversation until they have built readiness for it. Students concretely discuss one experience and then another. When they compare or synthesize the two, they must go to another level of discussion for which they already have some vocabulary and structure.

Meaning From Abstractions

In summary, this chapter's emphasis has been on how the co-development of core visuals can assist focus, including focus at the level of generalizations, and how sustained focus engenders coherence and cohesion as students build understanding throughout the unit. A teacher needn't debate whether to label a particular visual display "UVF," "global UVF," "GVF," or "visual framework." The distinctions between "unit" and "global" are most helpful to the teacher in the planning stages, when determining the instructional targets, because it is just as accurate to say, "Let's look at our UVF [or visual framework] for our math standard," as it is to say, "Let's look at our GVF." What is important, however, is that the evolving visual display alleviate teacher concerns and student challenges with abstractions. When students and teachers work together to represent their experiences meaningfully via an expanding UVF or global UVF, the abstract should become meaningful, memorable, and useful.

HONEST AND POSSIBLE

As I shared my ideas and examples of UVFs, three types of "yes, but" responses surfaced from administrators and teachers. They are worth addressing before getting into the actual steps of planning and using UVFs, particularly because I want to ensure that Chapters 1 and 2 have been useful without creating misperceptions. The concerns went something like this:

1. It's good stuff, but teachers aren't going to do that. Due to time or other circumstances, they grab the textbook or curricular guide and teach from it; they don't design units themselves. They're not going to take the time to plan for a UVF, especially since many texts or materials on which they depend don't always make the focus as clear as it needs to be to create a UVF.

2. I like the idea of UVFs a lot, and would like to begin using them. However, as I look at the examples you have, they seem to require a lot more advance thinking about what will occur in the units than I generally do. I probably wouldn't be able to do it as comprehensively as the examples seem to show.

3. It's hard to know what's important in a unit, so I don't know how I would do something like this.

Source of Units

There seem to be several parts to the first concern. One is an apparent misperception that UVFs may only be used with teacher-designed units. In reality, the source of the unit does not matter. Furthermore, any teacher who previews a textbook unit or curriculum guide for its intended goals, and adapts it according to his or her knowledge of the students, is, in effect, redesigning a unit.

Teacher Planning

Another skepticism is the question of whether teachers will take the time to plan for a UVF, and the frank answer is that sometimes they will, and sometimes they will do what they can in the time that they have, "planning" or adjusting as they go. The unit examples in Chapters 4 through 6 give examples of how units went in both cases. The most crucial planning is related to the concern raised earlier in this chapter and appearing again in the above list: It's hard to know what's important.

If the materials themselves don't make the intended goals clear and, therefore, one must decide for oneself, Clarke (1991) suggests asking the following question: "As I look at this content, what central facts, ideas, arguments, processes, or procedure do I want students to understand?" To ensure student representation in deciding "what's important," I also recommend asking something like, "What does this material lend itself to teaching all of my students well, given their interests, readiness, and needs related to required curriculum?" These basic preparations, necessary for teaching a unit as opposed to simply "covering" or "exposing" the unit material, serve to make the unit clear to the teacher. Chapter 3 will elaborate on this type of questioning, which facilitates planning and can guide thinking when planning is done "on the run." Chapter 3 also suggests that, when time allows, a teacher design a draft UVF before approaching the class for co-development. Designing a draft UVF checks and reinforces the teacher's clarity and prepares possible ways for students to acquire a similar clarity about "what's important."

The saving grace is that classroom UVFs are actually co-developed in real time—that is, in the classroom while pursuing the unit. In addition, student clarity is a crucial part of the co-development process itself; students and teacher work *in partnership* using their experiences to design core and expanded UVFs as tools that *everyone* owns, understands, and uses to achieve their goals. This partnership has time advantages as well as others, as Ginger Benning notes,

> I'm going deeper personally and with the students, without feeling overwhelmed. I don't have to do a lot of research about lots of different things; students can do it. The UVF has kept me focused, so I can keep the students focused.

Desire to Get It Right

The second concern in the above list is a hesitation to "get started" or to share with others one's beginning implementation of UVF use because of our desire as teachers to "do things right." An immediate response to this concern is the fact that, with students and teacher acting as both the designers and consumers of the UVF, the "perfect" visual is unnecessary.

It is true that, for the UVFs to serve each student and for all of the students to achieve their goals within the unit, the teacher facilitates the co-development process. The teacher serves as the experienced learner who mentors the students in both the content and format of the UVF. (Chapter 3 will elaborate on content and format.)

However, as I pondered this concern in preparation for writing this chapter, I kept hearing in my mind, "Be sure they know that it's a messy process."

Figure 2.9.   UVF in the Classroom

What I mean is that creating and using UVFs is messy and organic, just like teaching and learning are. Now, the word *messy* has multiple connotations, but I think that some teachers *want* teaching to be messy or creative or, as I mentioned above, organic, and, in fact, designing, co-developing, and using UVFs reflects the teaching and learning experiences that occur. Figure 2.9 perhaps makes my meaning more concrete.

Unlike the computer-generated examples used before, this picture shows a UVF in the classroom setting. Though the photo doesn't allow you to read exactly what is on the UVF, you can see that neither the print nor the illustrations are perfectly formed. The yellow chart—the evolving UVF—has only the co-development that has occurred to that point, and the visuals supporting and anchoring learning experiences are irregular sizes. They were connected and attached to the yellow UVF in a purposeful but pragmatic way, given the space in which we were able to work at the time. In addition, the unit took us in many directions that I had not predetermined, and as it did, we connected and reconnected those experiences to the UVF by adding visuals to anchor them and discussing the new connections with the previous ones.

I feel compelled, however, to reinforce the point that the *message* or meaning conveyed in the core and expanding UVF must not be messy; that's the part that we work hard to keep clear and cumulatively organized. That clarity begins with an understandable focus communicated through a core UVF—the subject of this chapter. Subsequent chapters will discuss how to keep that clarity through visual consistencies, purposeful review, and repeated use, as the generative process builds the expanded UVF.

Invitation: Just Get Started

My last response to the "yes, buts" comes from a knowledge that the demands of a teaching position often make it difficult to do what we would like with every unit we teach. I, therefore, offer the advice given to me many years ago by one of my mentors, Dr. Robert Pavlik: "Do what's honest and possible." Begin where you can begin to get a UVF drafted and then co-developed: Work with a unit you know well, and learn what works best for you and your students. For added encouragement, here are a few student and teacher voices that confirm some of the benefits of spending time on a UVF.

Student: It [The UVF] helped me know what was the focus and the title plus the direction of what we should do.

Teacher: It's easy to go off in a direction and come back, so I've given information more systematically than in the past, while still having flexibility for students and me.

Teacher: The UVF makes my normal use of review at the beginning of each day's work easier.

Chapter Two
Visual Summary

Focus, The Basis for Coherence & Cohesion

A Unit Visual Framework (UVF)

visually anchors key concepts, experiences, and relationships, allowing divergent thinking without getting lost in activities.

The UVF begins as a **core visual**, which establishes a unit and/or global focus. Each student has a **portable core visual.**

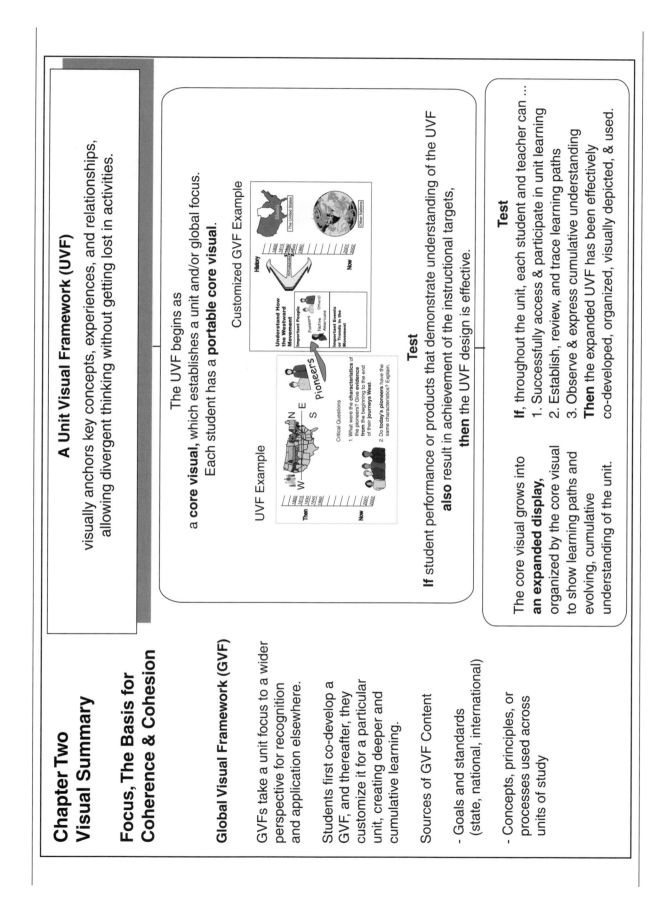

UVF Example

Critical Questions

1. What were the **characteristics** of the pioneers? Give **evidence from the beginning** to the end of their **journeys West.**

2. Do **today's pioneers** have the same characteristics? Explain.

Customized GVF Example

Test

If student performance or products that demonstrate understanding of the instructional targets, **also** result in achievement of the UVF **then** the UVF design is effective.

Test

If, throughout the unit, each student and teacher can …

1. Successfully access & participate in unit learning
2. Establish, review, and trace learning paths
3. Observe & express cumulative understanding

Then the expanded UVF has been effectively co-developed, organized, visually depicted, & used.

Global Visual Framework (GVF)

GVFs take a unit focus to a wider perspective for recognition and application elsewhere.

Students first co-develop a GVF, and thereafter, they customize it for a particular unit, creating deeper and cumulative learning.

Sources of GVF Content

- Goals and standards (state, national, international)

- Concepts, principles, or processes used across units of study

The core visual grows into **an expanded display,** organized by the core visual to show learning paths and evolving, cumulative understanding of the unit.

Getting Started 3

The first step in teaching with Unit Visual Frameworks is the same as for any complex task—identifying priorities. Priorities lead to a clear conceptualization of the unit or units and to the focus that will be reflected in the UVF (see Figure 3.1). From knowledge of the students and of the unit, the teacher identifies a clear instructional and assessment focus to be depicted by the UVF. The teacher also surveys or thinks through the unit for challenges and resources to inform choices of UVF content and design. The optional next step is to design a teacher draft core UVF, which can result in a clearer conceptualization of the unit, as well as advance notice of challenges and resources. With the priorities in mind, and with some ideas about a UVF from the focus and the design of a teacher draft, the teacher plans the initial teaching/learning experiences to begin co-development of both the unit and the UVF with students in the classroom.

GETTING TO KNOW THE UNIT

The core UVF at the beginning of the unit will be an advance organizer of the unit essentials to be taught and assessed. To know what the core UVF will organize, then, we first survey or think through the unit. We're looking for bottom line or big picture focus:

1. Its purpose—what the predesigned or planned unit was designed to achieve

2. The teacher's and students' purposes—how to use the unit to achieve what is most useful for our students

3. What all students will need to demonstrate—criteria that will be used to determine if students have achieved these purposes

Figure 3.1. Getting Started With Unit Visual Frameworks

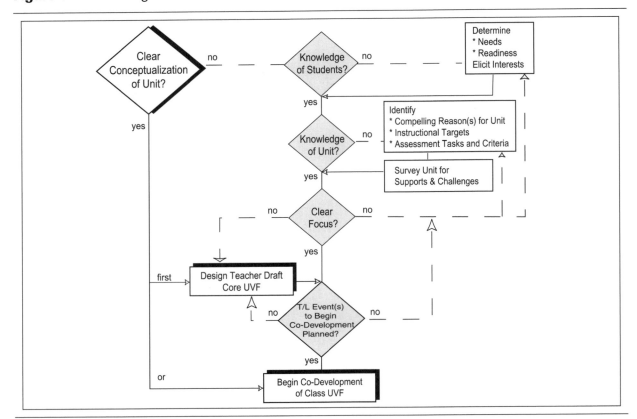

Some units may focus on curricular content. In Chapter 2, one example was the Illinois history goal: When the students study the Westward Movement (or other historical topics), all students are expected to demonstrate that they know how this movement, its events, and key people in it influenced the history and current events of the state, nation, and world.

Other units may focus on skills and processes that students need to be self-directed, independent learners, such as how to use a workshop, inquiry-based, or problem-based learning approach to pursue both individual and class goals. In one Chapter 7 example, each student needed to be able to identify, succeed in, and lead the work of each part of the workshop approach—planning/mini-lesson, working the goal-achievement process for their individual goals, and sharing/reflection—that the class was using for its student-directed learning.

In either case, everything begins with the learning and assessment focus.

Previewing the Unit for Priorities and Focus

Figure 3.2 offers some questions to stimulate your thoughts about priorities and focus as you preview unit curriculum and materials. Many of the

Figure 3.2.   Previewing the Unit for Priorities and Focus

General Brainstorming	**More Precisely with Standards**
As I preview the unit with my students' interests, readiness, and needs in mind,	
■ If my students and I learn all this unit offers, "so what?" What underlying goal makes it worthwhile?	■ What is the <u>compelling reason</u> that makes this unit worthy of my students' and my time?
■ How will the unit help my students and me do something that matters to us individually and/or as a group?	■ What in this unit will enable my <u>students</u> and me to meet our own <u>goals</u> or interests as part of pursuing the curricular targets?
■ What does this material lend itself to teaching all of my students well?	■ What <u>content goals and standards</u> will I hold students and myself accountable for in this unit?
■ If students don't learn anything else in this unit, I want every student to walk out of the classroom knowing (or knowing how to) …	■ What <u>core curricular</u> concepts, processes, and/or <u>ideas</u> will I hold students and myself accountable for in this unit? (Goals and standards in particular content & developmental context)
■ As I look at this content, what central facts, ideas, arguments, processes, or procedure do I want students to understand? (Clarke, 1991)	■ What tasks will <u>assess</u> students before, during, and at the end of the unit?
■ What bottom line learning will students complete in what context?	■ What <u>criteria</u> will be used to determine if students have achieved the unit's and their own goals, standards, and core curricular targets and distinguish the quality of <u>student performance</u>?
■ What should all students come out of the unit being able to demonstrate?	
■ For what will I hold all of my students and myself accountable?	■ What <u>criteria</u> will be used to determine if I have achieved the unit's and my own goals and standards to see the quality of <u>my performance</u>?
■ The knowledge, reasoning, and communication students should demonstrate are …	**If using engaged learning principles:**
■ What do students need to clearly see and be confident with, so assessment tasks aren't "gotchas"?	■ What <u>meaningful context</u> will engage the whole class collaboratively in the unit priorities, and provide a model and means of support for individual goals and/or projects?
■ What is central to the evaluation criteria?	
Many of the questions in this column are variations of another, meant for the reader to choose according to personal preference.	*Each question in this column is distinct, meant to give different information.*

Test: Does the focus support achievement of all priorities? Is the focus (all components of it) worth the time it will take to teach and continually assess to ensure that we all achieve it?

questions in the left column are variations of one another; you might select the few that work best for you. The set of questions in the right column works well when standards achievement is important.

There is also a question in the right column for teachers who are using engaged learning principles to build their unit. This question not only supports that excellent way of teaching and learning, it also serves as a placeholder for other specific components that might be planned into a unit. For example, where technology is an integral part of instruction, one might also ask such questions as, "How will technology be used as a cognitive, communication, management, and/or production tool in this unit?"

The "test" at the bottom of the list in Figure 3.2 is a reality check. Our priorities and the resultant focus are what we commit each member of the class and ourselves to achieving, if teaching is meant to achieve those results. These priorities determine how we will spend our time. Therefore, when we synthesize the answers to the questions we ask in previewing the unit, we want to make sure the focus supports achievement of all priorities. Moreover, we want to ensure that the focus (and all its components) is worth the time it will take to teach and continually assess.

Figure 3.3 contains the resulting layers of information generated by using the questions in Figure 3.2 to plan a unit called People and Places in Community (see Ewy et al., 1998c). The more layers that you are able to review or to anticipate, the better able you will be to capture in the UVF the heart of the unit and its demands. However, heed the "honest and possible" advice given in Chapter 2 and remember that the core UVF will be supplemented as it expands to reflect the work of the unit. Therefore, even if you haven't been able to be quite as thorough as you'd like, go ahead and begin when you think you have the focus in mind based on what you know about your students and the unit.

The layered list for the People and Places in Community unit communicates the focus in multiple ways. All that it contains will be taught in the richness of the unit, but the simplest way to tell the central focus is to read over the performance tasks and criteria at the bottom of the list. There, we see alignment between the tasks and the compelling reasons. We also see the way the geography and other social studies targets will be integrated: The primary unit focus is for students to know how to meet their needs and help make their community work, requiring their understanding of the community as an interdependent social system. The geography knowledge serves students in better understanding the physical characteristics of their community, its resources, and representation tools, like maps and models, which help them both in learning about the community as well as meeting their needs.

If you'd like to look ahead to Figure 3.5, you might see that the UVF depicts this focus and the relationships, or integration, of the instructional components in this particular unit. You might keep in mind, though, that the additional details to come about UVF design will make this clearer in the following sections before we shift to other unit examples.

Figure 3.3. Example of Resulting Priorities/Layers of Focus

People and Places in Community

COMPELLING REASONS FOR THE COMMUNITY UNIT

So students can know how to...
- Meet their needs within a community
- Be contributing community members

The compelling reasons create real reasons for students to learn
- The interdependent roles of individuals and the whole group to make a community work for everyone
- Community resources
- How maps or models can help them find or tell about resources

SOCIAL SCIENCE GOALS & STANDARDS

Goal 17 Geography and its effects on society.
Standard A Locate, describe and explain places and features.
Benchmark A.1b Identify the characteristics and purposes of geographic representations and be able to locate the specific places using each, including maps, globes...

Goal 18 Understand social systems, with an emphasis on the United States.
Standard B Understand the roles and interactions of individuals and groups in society.

CORE CURRICULAR CONCEPTS AND IDEAS

Concepts: community, community helpers, resources, needs, viewpoints, maps

Ideas
- "Community" can describe a place or a group of people.
- A community works well when the community helps each person meet individual needs and each person helps community meet the group's needs.
- A feeling of community exists when people in the community feel they matter to the rest of the people and they feel the rest of the people matter to them.
- Understanding differing viewpoints helps meet individual needs and group needs.
- Community workers help people meet specific kinds of needs.
- Maps and models can help people find what they need in communities and show what their community is like.

PERFORMANCE TASKS AND CRITERIA
- Communicate how to meet a need they or their family have. Tell how the community works or doesn't in the process of meeting the need and whether a map is useful in meeting the need.
- Evaluate whether the community in which they find themselves at any given time is or is not working and why. Must show benefit to individual and whole.
- Represent experiential knowledge of the community in a map, mural, or model. Must orient viewers using age-appropriate geographic terms, and communicating needs that can be met by major resources there.

From *People and Places in Community* (Ewy et al., 1998c). Reprinted with permission of the Illinois State Board of Education.

—◉—————————————

Previewing the Unit for Student Challenges and Supports

Once the focus is clear to the teacher, answering the following questions can reveal how clear the focus will be to the students in unit events and materials, and how to make it clearer through a UVF, if warranted:

1. Is the unit focus evident to students when they begin the unit?

2. Is the structure or organization of the unit clear, so students know how to think through each part of the unit and how it will relate to the rest?

3. What supports and challenges do the methods and materials have? That is, what seems to make it harder or easier for students to focus on the essentials of the unit as they proceed through the unit and use materials to access information and/or to complete their tasks?

When the teachers designed the People and Places in Community unit analyzed in Figure 3.3, they knew they had both concrete experiences and materials to support students in learning the primary-level geography component of the community unit. For example, students would take photographs on their walk through the community, and later use them to describe places and features. They would study maps and models, and use the photos and concrete materials to understand representation and locate places in their own community. They would use these same materials to examine the effects of geography to the degree feasible with the local community under study and the developmental level of primary students. The teachers also knew that there were many visuals of community helpers and community places that would help students become familiar with community resources and explore the roles of people in the community.

The challenge in this unit was to make the seemingly abstract idea of the community as a system comprehensible to primary students. Because this was a new element in their unit design from previous units, the teachers had no piloted learning experiences or materials to support the understanding or application of this goal.

These realizations about the supports and challenges of the unit informed the UVF design. The task of the UVF would be to organize the supports—the visual reminders of the community helpers and geography experiences—in a way that helped students understand how all those worked together as a system, or well-functioning community.

DESIGNING THE CORE UVF

Once teachers have a clear focus that has been informed by knowledge of the students and of the unit, there is a decision to make. They can next design a teacher draft core UVF, or they may go directly to initial teaching/learning

Figure 3.4. Pros and Cons of Teacher Draft Core UVF Versus Immediate Co-Development

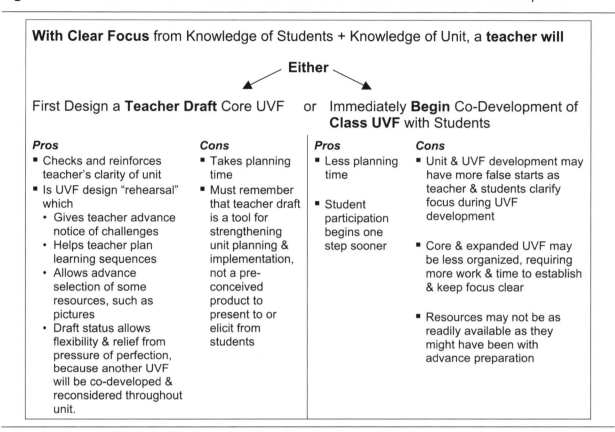

With Clear Focus from Knowledge of Students + Knowledge of Unit, a **teacher will**

Either

First Design a **Teacher Draft** Core UVF   or   Immediately **Begin** Co-Development of **Class UVF** with Students

Pros	*Cons*	*Pros*	*Cons*

■ Checks and reinforces teacher's clarity of unit
■ Is UVF design "rehearsal" which
  • Gives teacher advance notice of challenges
  • Helps teacher plan learning sequences
  • Allows advance selection of some resources, such as pictures
  • Draft status allows flexibility & relief from pressure of perfection, because another UVF will be co-developed & reconsidered throughout unit.
	■ Takes planning time
	■ Must remember that teacher draft is a tool for strengthening unit planning & implementation, not a pre-conceived product to present to or elicit from students
		■ Less planning time
		
		■ Student participation begins one step sooner
			■ Unit & UVF development may have more false starts as teacher & students clarify focus during UVF development
			
			■ Core & expanded UVF may be less organized, requiring more work & time to establish & keep focus clear
			
			■ Resources may not be as readily available as they might have been with advance preparation

events for co-development of the core UVF. Figure 3.4 lists the pros and cons of each choice. Over the course of a year, teachers will probably begin both ways, depending on the planning situations preceding a unit of study. Chapters 4 and 5 show the evolution of units that began with a teacher draft, and Chapter 6 exemplifies beginning immediately with student co-development.

Both teacher drafts and classroom-developed core UVFs have two design features, *content* and *format*, both of which are influenced by the *scope of the focus*. The UVF content is the unit's focus communicated through key text and accompanying images. The format is the organization of the text and images to show the content of and relationships in the unit. Scope of focus tells us if the focus of the UVF is unit-specific, has more global application, or is unit-specific but will later connect with a Global Visual Framework, as the Pioneers UVF did with the history GVF. Anticipating these connections or future applications helps teachers and students design the core UVF.

To choose the text and images for the core UVF, one considers how the focus may be depicted using student knowledge and experiences, as well as any helpful supports seen in the unit materials. Are there illustrations, graphics,

Figure 3.5.   Community Core UVF

People and Places in Community

Our community helps us.   We help our community.

We Make Communities Work
for

Every one
matters in a
community.

Is your community working?
Can you find
helpful people and places
in your community?

Everyone
matters in a
community.

slogans, or key phrases in the materials that capture or assist understanding of the focus? If so, which ones might it be useful to incorporate into a UVF to evoke unit learning and materials and to guide tasks?

If you look at the class core UVF in Figure 3.5, you'll notice the key text used to translate the unit's central focus, "We Make Communities Work." This text was selected for several reasons. First, the text brings attention to the central understanding to be learned and applied in the unit. Second, it succinctly says the same thing as, "It takes everyone to make a community work for individuals and the whole." Third, when students explain this phrase to someone or apply it to any given situation, they pursue other targets in the Figure 3.3 list. That is, they must draw on their knowledge of community helpers and places, and describe how they work together or serve the community.

The format of the UVF brings attention to this central focus. "We Make Communities Work" is made prominent by the larger print and the size of the accompanying image, the teeter-totter. The enabling ideas also have familiar images and simple text chosen to represent and elicit key geography and social concepts, and they are placed near the teeter-totter to show the interdependent relationships of the individual and whole. The questions at the bottom of the UVF prompt students to apply all of these ideas to achieve the geography and social system's goals.

Although the Community UVF is a unit-specific depiction of state Goal 18, listed in Figure 3.3 as one of this unit's targets, the UVF design anticipates future applications of this generalization about social systems. When the teeter-totter symbol for balance (or the actual one students use when co-developing the unit in class, if different from this teacher draft) is used again in UVFs for studying other systems that depend on balance or interdependence to work, it will prompt student recall of insights learned about systems in this unit.

CORE UVF CONTENT: KEY TEXT AND IMAGES

We now examine the design of some UVFs previously seen, as well as some new ones. This additional information about content and the section about format are included because teachers have requested them. However, readers needn't be nervous about either. The guiding principle for designing a UVF is that it makes ongoing sense of the unit *in the minds of students and teachers*. Therefore, whatever UVF achieves that purpose will be perfect.

Both images and text are used in UVFs because one or the other by itself does not always convey enough meaning. Primary teachers see this source of confusion after emerging writers use pictures to "tell a story" but can't remember "the story" when they come back later to the picture. Secondary teachers often see the same thing happen in reverse: Students take brief written notes that don't carry enough meaning when they are revisited for study or new application. Because a UVF is a working display that is returned to over and over again, the images and text must team up to hold meaning consistently each time they are revisited. Furthermore, the text will be a combination of students' expressive, everyday language and key content-specific terms. These two types of text are recommended because, like the combination of text and images, the different types of text are separate comprehension aides that may each help students recall the learning experience or may work together to do so. Furthermore, students will be able to demonstrate achievement of the instructional targets only if they are able to comprehend and use key content-specific language, not just expressive language, so including them in the UVF gives students repeated opportunities to do that.

The teacher draft UVF in Figure 3.6 for a unit on skunks shows why we want to elicit the three types of aides to meaning—expressive language, content-specific language, and images—to assist comprehension. The two critical questions guiding the inquiry exemplify the two types of text. The first is taken from a science standard that the students will encounter in multiple units and that, therefore, uses the standard's formal language. The screened boxes help students understand this formal language. Each box also combines the formal

Figure 3.6. Teacher Draft UVF for Skunks Inquiry Unit

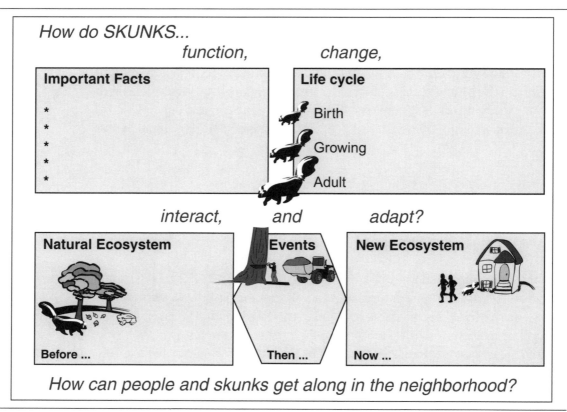

or content-specific text with expressive language and/or images to further assist meaning. The more formal "Important Facts" is accompanied by a set of asterisks as a cue that "facts" are often a list of information. The asterisks may be replaced by numbers in the classroom UVF when students compile facts to illustrate the ways skunks function, but the list will bring sense to the terms *important facts* and *function* for future recall of the real classroom experiences captured in the UVF. "Change" has the formal language *life cycle*, as well as the more expressive terms for each stage and the accompanying picture of skunks in different sizes. The three boxes at the bottom also use specific terms, such as *natural ecosystem*, combined with images, and expressive text. Each group of images in these three boxes contain enough items to review both *interact* and *ecosystem*, and the common terms (*before, then, now*) cue the pictorial sequence that adds meaning to the term *adapt*. The students will use all of these to problem-solve answers to the second critical question.

CONSIDERING STUDENT CHARACTERISTICS

It is important to include the three elements mentioned above—expressive and content-specific text and representative images—in all UVFs, regardless of the

Figure 3.7. Draft UVF for PreK–2 NCTM Geometry Standard

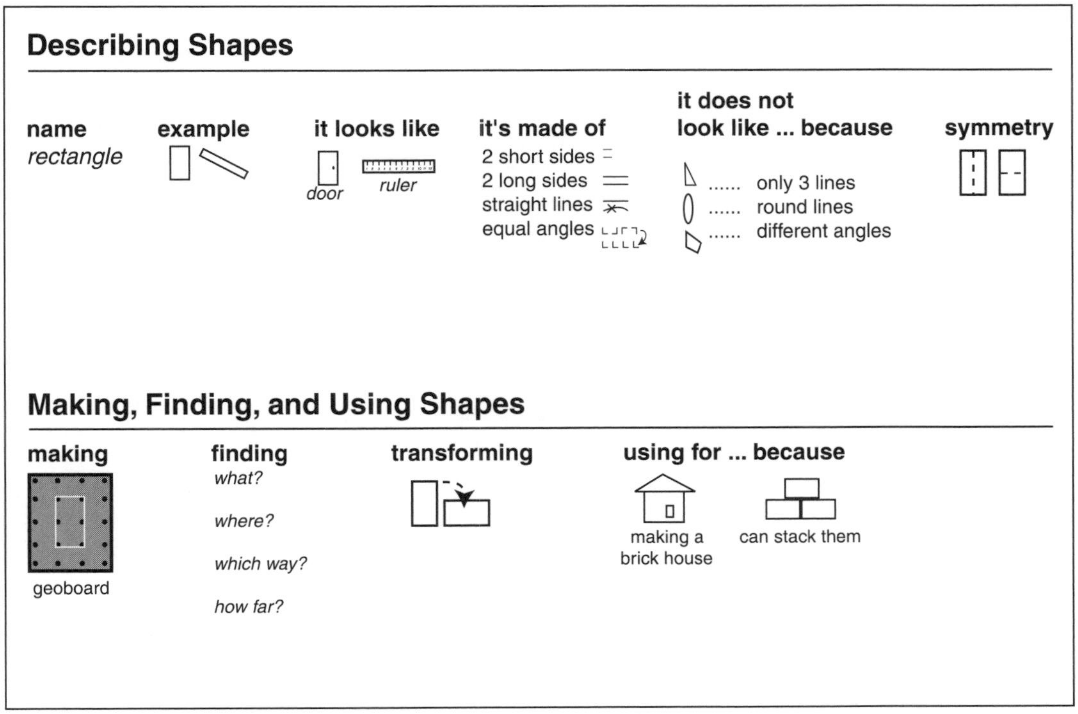

age of the children or characteristics of the student population. Although older students might use more text in their UVFs, primary teachers shouldn't shy away from the two types of text. Primary students, older nonreaders, and English language learners will learn to use all three elements the same way they learn to "read" predictable books if the UVF is consistently used as described in this book. For example, when building a UVF such as the geometry draft in Figure 3.7, students may depict and learn to read one characteristic at a time. As they study a shape, they might create the first label "name," and place a representation of it on their chart with the label "example." When ready, they could review those two and add the label "it looks like" with images of objects they think of that have that shape. Next, they might review those first three descriptors and add "it's made of" with representations of its lines, curves, and angles. Alternatively, if students first build most of the parts under "describing shapes" for rectangle and triangle, the next time they add a shape, they will review those parts for rectangle and triangle, and then be ready to describe the new shape.

Though older students may use more text on their UVF than primary students might, they will still use both expressive and expository text, accompanied by as many images as are necessary to convey the meaning of the text. Figure 3.8 shows contrasting amounts of text used in the teacher drafts of the Pioneers core UVF and the history GVF for intermediate students.

Figure 3.8.   Westward Movement Through "Pioneers" Study

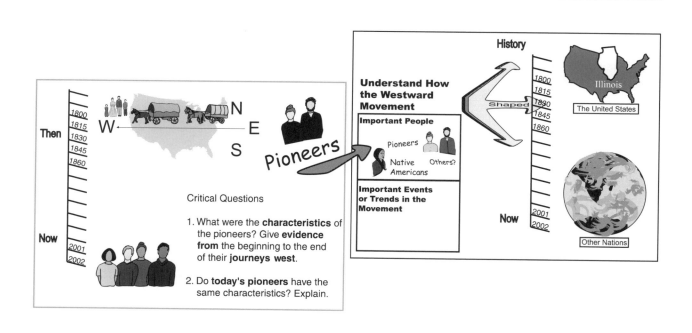

The core UVF, seen here as Figure 3.9, was designed as a teacher draft for secondary students. It has a larger quantity of complex concepts and contains mostly text. The actual content of this UVF will be more understandable later in this chapter when we discuss the correlation between its format and the way it is developed with students. However, it is a good illustration of a heavier text load than most UVFs have, so here we'll examine some reasons why that text load is possible.

The amount of text is not because of the students' age, but rather because the UVF is built with students in modules, and each module is supported by visuals, as you see in Figure 3.10. For instance, the adolescent couple that illustrates interpersonal conflicts on the UVF is also used in the separate support visuals that illustrate "viewpoints" and "primary and secondary sources." Therefore, the few visuals on the UVF and the text become a type of shorthand that evokes the more extensive visuals. Of course, because Figure 3.9 is only a teacher draft, the text/image ratio may be very different when students co-develop a classroom UVF for this unit.

Quantity of text has been mentioned twice above. Because of my emphasis on using relatively small amounts of "key text," I have been asked, "How much text should be on a UVF?" My rule of thumb is this: There should be enough text to combine with the images to convey and anchor meaning without

Figure 3.9. Core UVF

Unit Visual Framework							Illinois State Board of Education Content-Based Assessment Exemplars
Conflict and Resolution		**Interpersonal**		**& Political**			
Social Sciences Scoring Rubric	**Model for Conflict Resolution**	**Drama Example**	**Personally Important Current Conflict** Task One 	 **American Revolution** Task Two-A	Task Two-B	Task Two-C	 Task Three
				Prewar through Boston Tea Party, 1773	Boston Tea Party to Close of First Continental Congress, 1774	First Continental Congress to Lexington & Concord 1775	Lexington & Concord to Yorktown & Treaty
Knowledge	**Get the FACTS** Actions & Reactions						
	Get the VIEWPOINTS						
	List What Each WANTS						
Reasoning	**Brainstorm POSSIBLE ACTIONS** All Types of Resolutions						
	Consider Best, Worst, Short-term & Long-term OUTCOMES of Each Action						
	Choose/Decide & ACT						
Communication	**Examine Short-term & Long-term Impacts & Use Criteria to EVALUATE Effectiveness**			Use primary and secondary sources to ensure accuracy of information.			Impacts on USA Impacts on Lives

From *Conflict and Resolution: Interpersonal and Political* (Ewy et al., 1998a). Reprinted with permission of the Illinois State Board of Education.

making the UVF a major reading task. I'll also repeat my message from the beginning of this section: The guiding principle for designing a UVF is that it makes ongoing sense of the unit *in the minds of students and teachers.* Therefore the simplest check on quantity of text is to see if all students can use the UVF to make sense of the unit. If not, the UVF should be modified.

CORE UVF FORMAT

Two more questions, posed by Clarke (1991), can inform decisions about format:

1. What pattern or organization holds the material together and makes it meaningful?

2. What kind of visual organizer will show students how to think their way through the content?

Figure 3.10. Support Visual

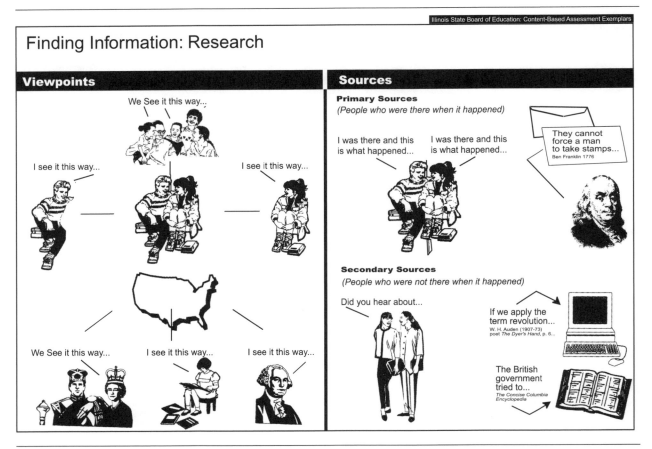

From *Conflict and Resolution: Interpersonal and Political* (Ewy et al., 1998a). Reprinted with permission of the Illinois State Board of Education.

The following query, which came from a teacher who had begun using UVFs in her classroom, is an example of why this section is included:

As a teacher, I'm getting stuck with the very usual web. The frameworks that I see in your examples are much more dynamic, with logical reasons for their flow from one area to another. I wonder if there are a dozen or so that would help a teacher springboard off of or even use in broad, general terms.

The teacher's awareness will help her explore different formats with her students. This book contains more than "a dozen examples" to help her do so. A reader may adapt a UVF whose format is helpful, even if its content is not the same or if the reader intends to use it with an older or younger student population. Whether adapting examples from this book or designing your own UVFs, there are a few basic types of core UVF formats. Some examples in this book exhibit recognizable graphic organizer bases; others use metaphors or basic forms that teachers and students found meaningful for their purposes.

The "logical reasons for the flow" are fundamental to the UVF format, as this teacher noticed. The web, for instance, has often been used to depict either a concept or descriptive pattern, and would not be as useful for a different purpose, such as representing a cause-effect relationship or a relationship better served by a metaphor. Figure 3.11 compares the Community UVF seen in Figure 3.5 with a UVF that has a web as its base. Though the focus and concepts are all there, the web is more abstract. Students have to work harder to understand the meaning of individual concepts as well as the relationships among them because everything is a separate idea. As the next chapter will elaborate, the teeter-totter was an actual experience students had of something that worked for each side if there was cooperation. Therefore, that metaphor visually recalls the concept of a working interdependent relationship, and the additional images and text are placed around the teeter-totter and connected to it in ways that help students transfer their experiential knowledge to understand communities. The "logical reasons" for format design result from the desire to find visual representations that carry meaning for the students, to successfully anchor their experiences and insights, and to maintain focus on the particular unit's essentials.

Formats Based on Graphic Organizers

If there is a discernible common pattern that organizes a unit and can represent its focus, it is very helpful to depict that in the core UVF design. *Classroom Instruction that Works* (Marzano, Pickering, & Pollock, 2001) has graphic organizers for six common patterns into which the authors have found information can be organized: descriptive, time-sequence, process/cause-effect, episode, generalization/principle, and concept patterns. You may also recall from Chapter 1 that Hyerle's books *Visual Tools for Constructing Knowledge* (1996) and *A Field Guide to Using Visual Tools* (2000) are good sources of graphic organizers for patterns.

A core UVF may use one or more of these patterns, as seen in Figures 3.10 and 3.11. For example, the left side of Figure 3.12 shows how a flow chart was used as a base to depict the process of technological design. The right side of the same figure shows how a cause-effect pattern simply and age-appropriately communicated the history goal, while additional images and text elaborated so students could look for important details of each cause and effect. One of the elaborations was a time line, often used to signal a time sequence pattern.

Note that UVFs use image and text cues for the patterns. On the left side of Figure 3.13, a Venn diagram used for compare/contrast patterns elicits some details in one part of the UVF for the Immigration Stories unit (see Ewy et al., 1998b). The same UVF uses the text cue words *at first, later,* and *then* for a sequence pattern. The right side of Figure 3.13 shows a UVF based on a tree

Figure 3.11. Comparison of Metaphor-Based and Web-Based UVFs

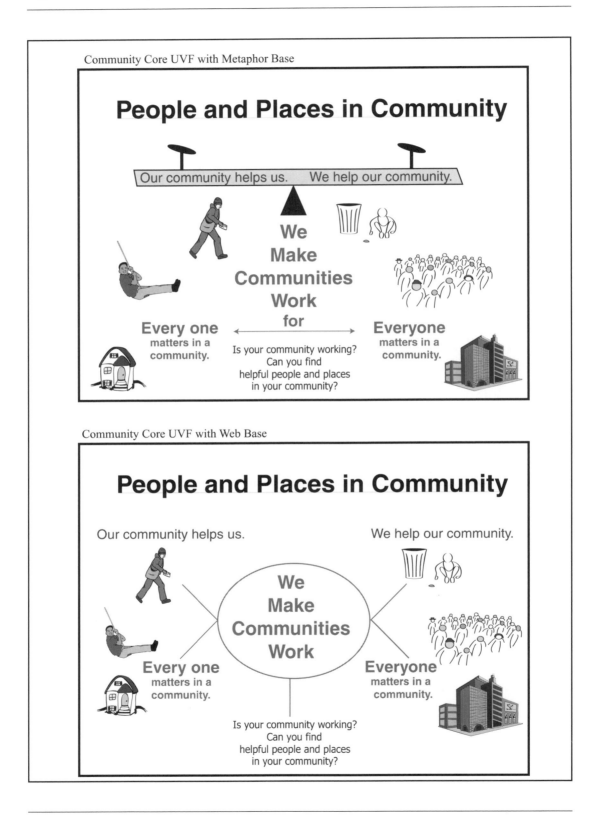

Community Core UVF with Metaphor Base

People and Places in Community

Our community helps us.   We help our community.

We
Make
Communities
Work
for

Every one
matters in a
community.

Everyone
matters in a
community.

Is your community working?
Can you find
helpful people and places
in your community?

Community Core UVF with Web Base

People and Places in Community

Our community helps us.

We help our community.

We
Make
Communities
Work

Every one
matters in a
community.

Everyone
matters in a
community.

Is your community working?
Can you find
helpful people and places
in your community?

diagram, which generally shows a hierarchy of ideas. In this UVF's case, the main focus is machines and their positive and negative impact, captured by the phrase "Machines Can Solve and Create Problems." *Machines* is subdivided into "design" and "effectiveness," which are in turn subdivided, respectively, into "simple" and "compound" machines and the "principles" and "evidence" needed to determine effectiveness. "Impact" emanates from the word *and* to prompt the examination of problems solved and created by machines, and is subdivided into cultural, political, and economic impacts.

Making these patterns overt and helping students recognize and use them in multiple situations add to the tools students have for constructing and representing knowledge. The more aware students become of these kinds of patterns, the quicker they will suggest and use them as they develop their core and expanded UVFs.

Metaphor Base

Some UVFs may not be based on graphic organizers, but may either use a metaphor familiar to students or another display that makes sense to the students and teacher. We've seen the teeter-totter metaphor in Figure 3.5 in a social studies context for primary students, and a scale in Figure 1.2 that captured student's prior science experience with "balance" and applied it to a language arts context. Figure 3.14 uses a more involved version of the scale in a science context for intermediate students.

Visually Depicted Critical Questions

In some cases, key text may actually determine the organization or format of the UVF. To illustrate and anchor the two critical questions that guide the Pioneers unit, the UVF in Figure 3.8 uses a time line for a time/sequence pattern, plus other symbols, text, and illustrations that students recognize. The timeline, cued by the words *then* and *now*, shows students at a glance the two time frames of each critical question. The bold-faced print in the first critical question, "journeys west," is elaborated with images at the top of the UVF. Students easily go from the large-print title and the illustration of the pioneers, reading from right to left because they recognize the compass rose and note its arrow to the left that leads them to follow the wagons across the map of the United States from east to west. The second critical question is also signaled and illustrated with a time cue word, the years on the timeline, and people that the students choose to represent today's pioneers.

Basic Shapes and Forms

Basic shapes and forms that are used for other purposes may also organize the content of a UVF. We can see that three shaded rectangles in Figure 3.15

Figure 3.12. Examples of Flow Chart and Cause-Effect Patterns in UVFs

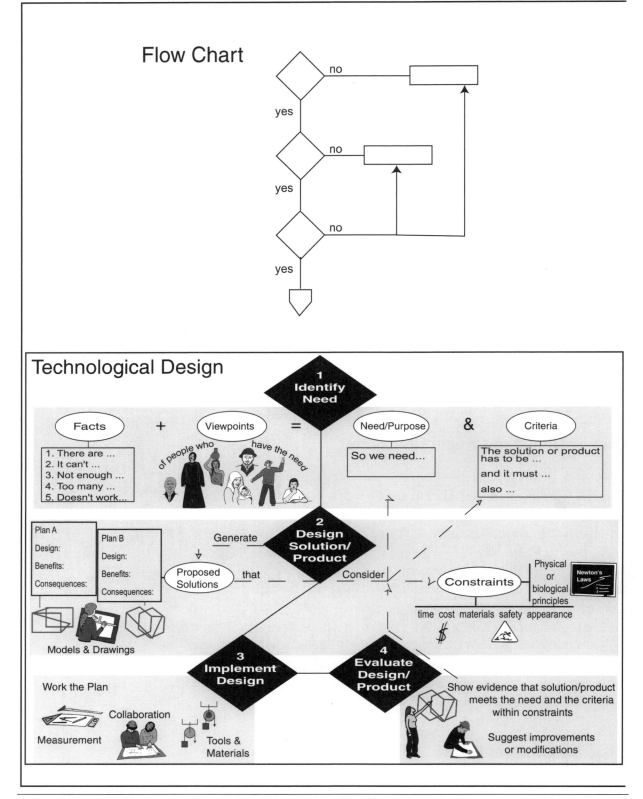

Figure 3.12. (Continued)

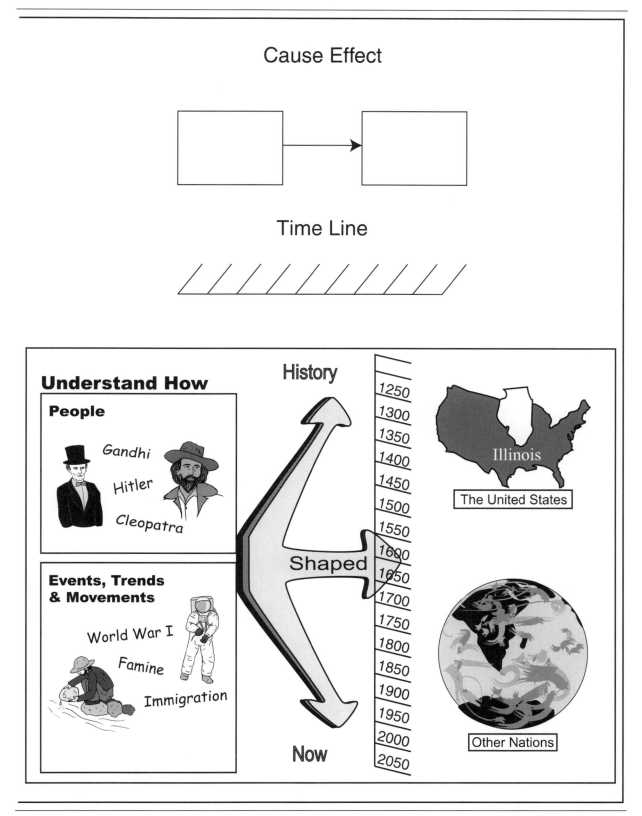

Figure 3.13. Examples of Compare/Contrast and Tree-Shaped Patterns in UVFs

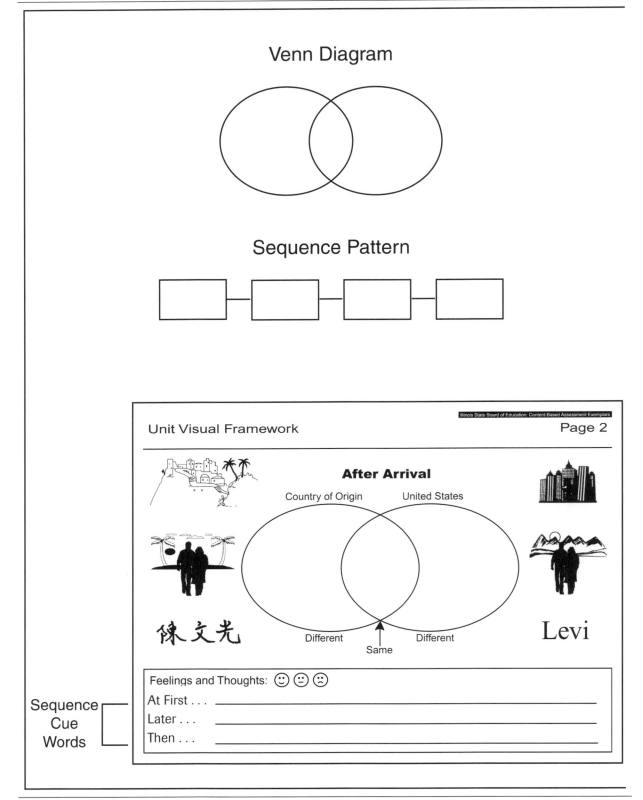

Figure 3.13. (Continued)

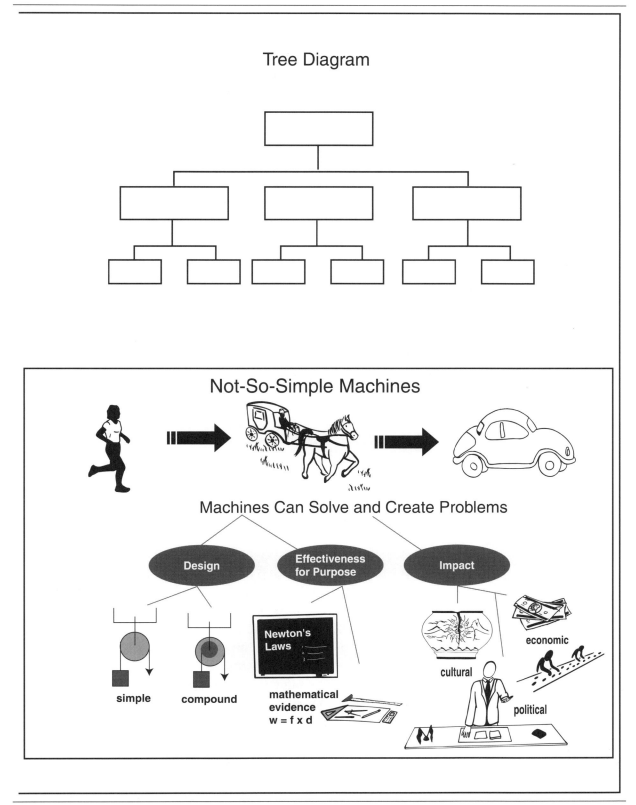

Figure 3.14. Draft Core UVF: Balance in Ecosystems

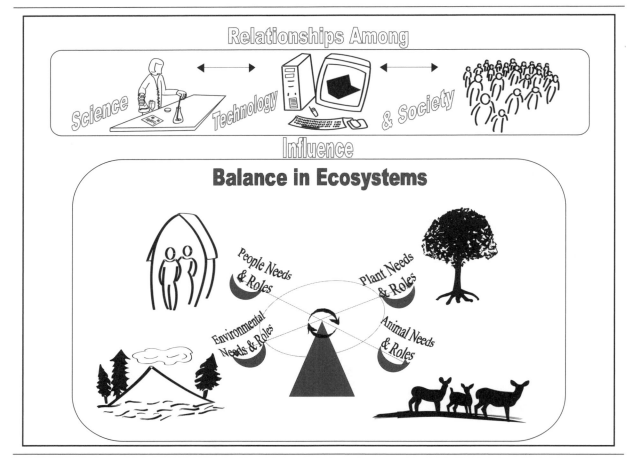

distinguish the three contexts about which ESL students speak and write, and the symbols, illustrations, and text elaborate and connect the three.

Figure 3.16 uses a circle, which is a common symbol for a cycle, especially when arrows form its perimeter. The circle is used in this visual to depict the process of scientific observation. This visual may be a core UVF if it prompts students for all they will need to demonstrate in the unit, which may be the case when students are first learning the process. The figure in the center of the circle and the two-sided arrows indicate another ongoing step used throughout the process. The same structure, a circle made of arrows with a step noted in the center that occurs throughout the cycle, is widely used to illustrate the writing process, as seen in Figures 5.20 and 5.21 of Chapter 5.

Neither a metaphor nor a basic shape, the organizing structure of Figure 3.17 is a table. We have seen this draft UVF twice before in this book, and will now spend a little time understanding it to see how this table format and its specific content enable a concise view of a complex, integrated study. Secondary teachers and students often face such a challenge with increasing amounts and complexity of material in their curriculum.

Figure 3.15. High School ESL Unit: Beginnings—New Classes, People, and Experiences

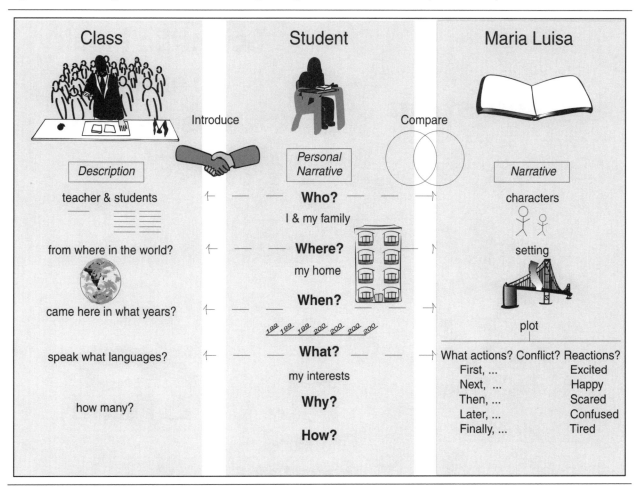

The Conflict and Resolution unit (see Ewy et al., 1998a), which this UVF serves, was estimated as a five- or six-week unit when designed. Piloting teachers said that estimate was conservative. This integrated unit targets history through the study of the American Revolution, health through the study of the process of conflict resolution, and language arts through attention to oral and written communication in each task. The table format of the UVF is due to its multiple purposes for the older students it serves (Grades 6–12):

1. Curricular clarity: Students are learning a conflict resolution process simultaneously in two contexts—the interpersonal seen in a dramatization of conflicts they actually face, and the political context of the American Revolution

2. Structure/organization of the unit: Its tasks and subtasks and how they all relate to the conflict resolution process

3. Accountability features: Knowledge, reasoning, and communication, which the unit rubric will assess

Figure 3.16. Observation UVF

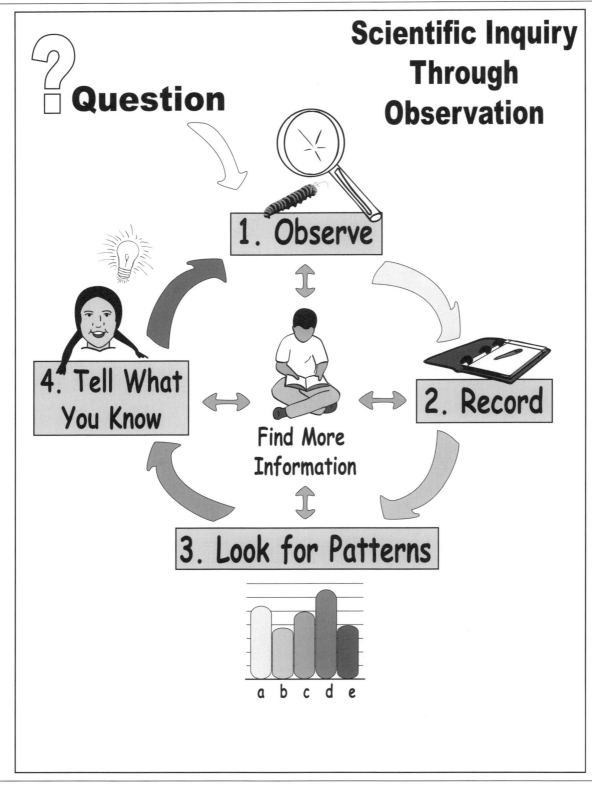

The teacher and students build this core UVF in modules after concrete experiences. Here's a brief look at the lesson sequence, so you get a feel for the way the UVF is built and used, and why it is, therefore, designed as it is:

1. Little by little, students build columns one, two, and three—"Social Sciences Scoring Rubric," "Model for Conflict Resolution," and "Drama Example."

    a. First, students witness a dramatization of a conflict pertinent to their age group and document the facts, the characters' viewpoints, and what each person in the conflict wanted. When they compare their individual notes in small group and whole group, they learn about the "knowledge" feature of the rubric.

    b. With the facts documented, students brainstorm ways of solving conflicts and how they would solve the one they've witnessed. From this brainstorming, students extract a conflict resolution process they agree on (like the one in column two of Figure 3.17) and also transform it into a graphic organizer (like the one in Figure 3.18). This graphic organizer will become part of the expanded UVF to support repeated applications of their conflict resolution process. Students are also introduced incrementally to the "reasoning" and "communication" rubric features during this work.

2. Students read about and/or do other types of research on the first part of the American Revolution noted under "Task Two-A" of Figure 3.17. As they do, they compare personal conflict and resolution with political conflict and resolution. Students test and adjust their conflict resolution process and graphic organizer.

3. Having established a consistent conflict resolution process and examined its application to interpersonal and political conflict, the students complete the rest of the core UVF as an advance organizer of the remaining tasks in the unit

    a. The class studies the rest of the American Revolution incrementally in whole group, in small groups, and individually (see the last four columns of Figure 3.17).

    b. Students work on their "Personally Important Current Conflict" projects (see column four of Figure 3.17), which may be an interpersonal or political conflict they individually or in cooperative groups choose to pursue.

As with the Community UVF, this example shows how an integrated unit is depicted in a UVF based on its central focus and incorporating all targets. The title and each task emphasize the health goal—consistent application of a

Figure 3.17. UVF

Unit Visual Framework							Illinois State Board of Education Content-Based Assessment Exemplars

Conflict and Resolution		**Interpersonal**		**& Political**			
Social Sciences Scoring Rubric	**Model for Conflict Resolution**	**Drama Example** 	**Personally Important Current Conflict** Task One	**American Revolution** Task Two-A — Prewar through Boston Tea Party, 1773	Task Two-B — Boston Tea Party to Close of First Continental Congress, 1774	Task Two-C — First Continental Congress to Lexington & Concord, 1775	Task Three — Lexington & Concord to Yorktown & Treaty
Knowledge	**Get the FACTS** Actions & Reactions						
	Get the VIEWPOINTS						
	List What Each WANTS						
Reasoning	**Brainstorm POSSIBLE ACTIONS** All Types of Resolutions						
	Consider Best, Worst, Short-term & Long-term OUTCOMES of Each Action						
	Choose/Decide & ACT						
Communication	**Examine Short-term & Long-term Impacts & Use Criteria to EVALUATE Effectiveness**			Use primary and secondary sources to ensure accuracy of information.			Impacts on USA Impacts on Lives

From *Conflict and Resolution: Interpersonal and Political* (Ewy et al., 1998a). Reprinted with permission of the Illinois State Board of Education.

conflict resolution process across multiple types of conflicts and multiple stages within a conflict. Therefore, the UVF uses a type of table format to align each task with the conflict resolution process across the display. In applying the process to the American Revolution, students fulfill the history goal—learning important details about the war and analyzing its impact and effectiveness on the U.S., Great Britain, the world, and their own lives. Something like the history GVF seen on the right side of Figure 3.12 would be a useful additional tool during the American Revolution unit. It would work well as a reflective tool used periodically for students to synthesize the details in which they've been engrossed, especially when working with only modules of the conflict, to the broader generalization more readily evoked by the GVF. The GVF would then be a part of the expanded UVF as a support tool for the American Revolution section of this table-formatted UVF.

Figure 3.18. Graphic Organizer Support Visual

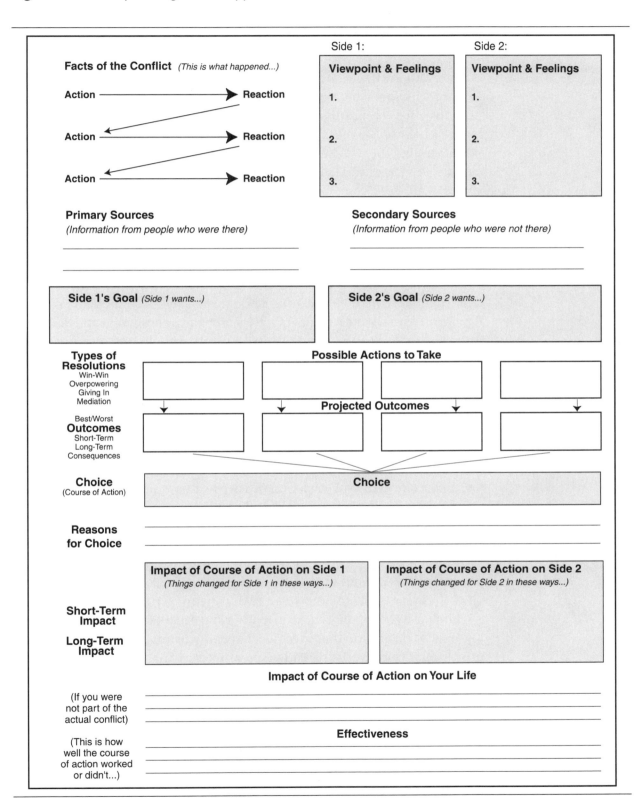

From *Conflict and Resolution: Interpersonal and Political.* Reprinted with permission of the Illinois State Board of Education.

UVFS WITH UNITS
THAT INTEGRATE COMPLEX
STUDIES OF MULTIPLE DISCIPLINES

As the examples have shown, UVFs may be used for units with a single subject focus or with units that integrate multiple subjects. The UVF follows common principles for integrating units. That is, the core UVF provides a central focus—an umbrella—for what will be learned and assessed across all the disciplines, uniting them. When a unit integrates complex studies of multiple disciplines, there are also likely to be either multiple expanded UVFs—one in each subject area with complex learning—or one expanded UVF with clustered support visuals to clarify the complexity of each learning area.

Multiple expanded UVFs for each subject area are likely to evolve when a team of teachers is working on one unit in separate rooms. Figure 3.19, a draft core UVF that was previously analyzed for its format, is part of such a unit. Based on a middle school, integrated unit originally designed by a teacher team in Illinois, this UVF and its unit bridge state and national standards. As a final team performance, students solve a problem by designing and building a Rube Goldberg device (a complicated invention to do one or more simple things). Designs are submitted to an engineer and a Healthworld representative for judging. With their own design and in the studies of other machines that will enable this team performance, students address the areas signaled by three ovals on the core UVF.

Each class will launch their specific study from this core UVF (or something like it developed with students) and will expand it with the specifics relevant to their particular subject area. The core UVF will help them link the learning from all the subject areas. In science, the emphasis will be on understanding the processes of technological design to solve problems. Therefore, in that class they may use the GVF on the left side of Figure 3.12 as a support visual and expand the UVF with related detail about technological design. Their expanded UVF would also reflect their attention to simple and complex machines. Throughout their work in science, they will relate their learning to all of the areas in the common core UVF in Figure 3.19.

Similarly, the expanded UVF in math will reflect the time they spend learning how to determine the work, mechanical advantage, and application of principles of work to possible designs or prototypes, considering all of the areas of the core UVF. Likewise, the language arts and social studies expanded UVFs will have more detail in their areas of emphasis as students read about, interview people about, and plan conditions of work. They will investigate and project the cultural, economic, and political impacts of their proposed device and others they study.

The Not-So-Simple Machines example illustrates how, even though work is being done in separate classes, students maintain the focus of the integrated unit. They can actually take their individual, portable UVFs from one class to

Figure 3.19. Draft Core UVF for the Not-So-Simple Machines Unit

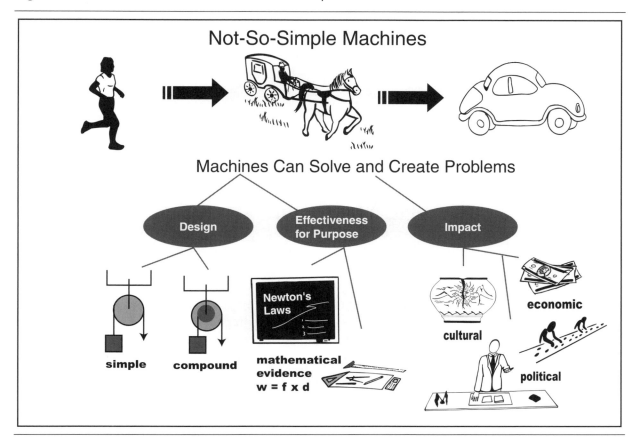

another and should have no trouble using one to help with the other. The recognizable core UVF unites the learning reflected in each expanded subject-specific UVF.

In cases where the various subjects are taught either by the same teacher or by a team in the same room, the specialized knowledge may be physically integrated into one connected, expanded UVF. For ease of handling by students, there may be multiple portable UVFs for each area of the core UVF—design, effectiveness, and impact—or in other ways that make sense as the expansion occurs.

Whether in separate rooms or one, the intent is for the core UVF to help students always see the focus of the integrated unit and how the content-specific knowledge connects with and helps them achieve the unit's larger purpose or purposes. Thus, coherence and cohesion across the integrated unit can accompany coherence and cohesion within each subject area. (See Consistency in Integrated Units in Chapter 5 for additional points using a language arts example.)

RESOURCES

A hand-drawn sketch is enough for a teacher draft of a core UVF, and the actual classroom core UVF will be constructed with students using their images or ones provided or copied from the materials students will be using. However, Appendix C describes software and hardware that may be helpful in drafting and using core UVFs and related support materials. Information is also provided about an available CD containing full-page color versions of the examples in this book.

BEGINNING UVF CO-DEVELOPMENT WITH STUDENTS

Okay, planning has yielded a clear focus. What's next? The teacher is ready to co-develop the unit and UVF with students, so, as the flow chart in Figure 3.1 indicates, that's when a teacher chooses initial teaching/learning events. Note that co-development of *both* the unit and the UVF is occurring, so the first consideration is how to engage students in the unit, with the focus at the core of this engagement. Additionally, Chapter 2 stated that the sequence of co-development of a UVF is to begin with concrete experience, talk about the experiences in developmental language, and illustrate the class understanding of the experiences—documenting the language and conceptual knowledge about the focus. Therefore, the second consideration is how to elicit and visually portray student prior knowledge and interests to reveal the focus explicitly.

Naturally, there are unlimited numbers of ways to begin a unit with students. The difference when we are also developing a UVF is that we are always eliciting images from students and helping them capture those images, and related language, in the visual display. Therefore, when we are choosing teaching/learning events, we are asking ourselves, "What experiences will elicit images, key text, and student language that show our view of the focus now?" The next three chapters show how different teachers, each in different subject areas and at different grade levels, took these first steps with their students and then expanded UVFs as they continued on with their units.

Chapter Three Visual Summary

A Unit Visual Framework (UVF)

visually anchors key concepts, experiences, & relationships through the use of at least three elements: students' own words, content-specific text, & images.

Getting Started

1. Identify curricular & assessment essentials to depict in UVF, based on
   - knowledge of students
   - clear concept of the unit

2. Decide if the focus lends itself to a UVF only, or will be connected to a GVF

3. Survey instruction, materials, & assessment tasks for challenges & supports

4. Consider key content & logical formats revealed from planning & surveying

5. Decide whether to design a teacher draft or immediately begin co-development with students

6. Plan initial teaching/learning events to co-develop unit & UVF

The UVF begins as a **core visual**, which establishes the unit focus through its content & format.

Each student has a **portable core visual**.

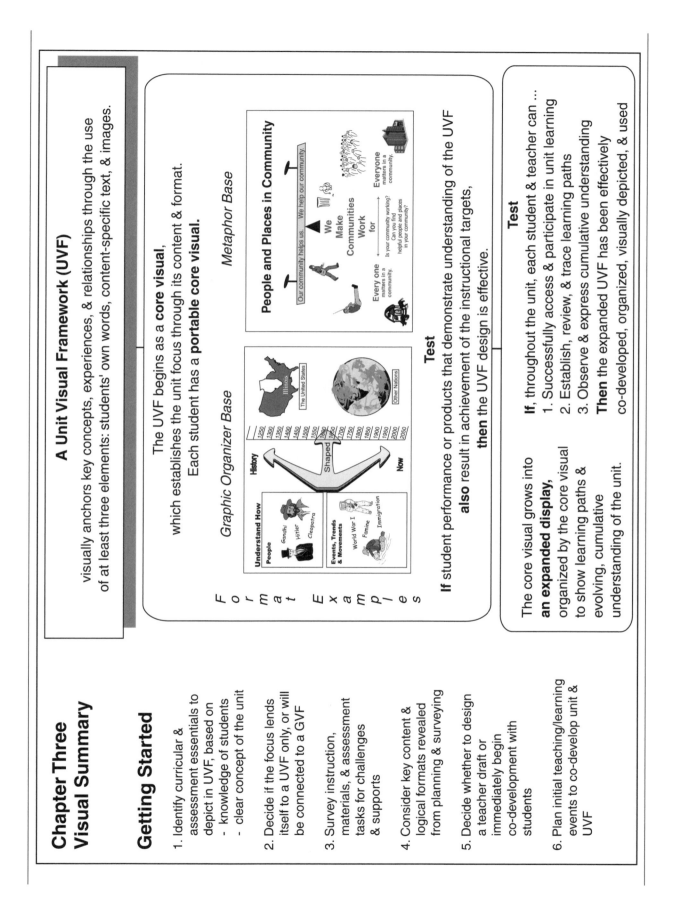

Graphic Organizer Base

F o r m a t

E x a m p l e s

Metaphor Base

People and Places in Community

Test

If student performance or products that demonstrate understanding of the UVF **also** result in achievement of the instructional targets, **then** the UVF design is effective.

The core visual grows into **an expanded display,** organized by the core visual to show learning paths & evolving, cumulative understanding of the unit.

Test

If, throughout the unit, each student & teacher can …

1. Successfully access & participate in unit learning
2. Establish, review, & trace learning paths
3. Observe & express cumulative understanding

Then the expanded UVF has been effectively co-developed, organized, visually depicted, & used

Co-Development and Ownership 4

Essential Requirements

People get attached to their own UVF, because it's what their kids added and reflects the relationship with the kids.

—Middle School Teacher

To support the claim made by this chapter's title about Unit Visual Frameworks, one could make a case that visuals are most useful to the persons who design them, at least until others understand the visual equally as well as the designer did. In fact, in this book you may have experienced frustrations when you looked at some of the examples and tried to get the same meaning as was being described in the text. In these instances, we are trying to figure out something that has been *designed by someone else* based on *their* knowledge, thinking, and experiences, and expressed in *their* words and images.

We could also argue that even though there are times when you, others, or I view a visual created by someone else and readily understand what it is communicating, those times do not suffice; we don't want *some* students to understand the visual display *some of the time.* It must be understood, expanded, and knowledgeably used by *all* students throughout the unit if it is to be a worthwhile tool.

Although these points are well taken, if you recall from Chapter 1 the reasons why these core visuals are effective classroom tools, it's the wrong case to be making. It is true that if we presented a UVF to a class, students would have to labor to figure it out. Instead of the UVF assisting students in understanding and using the unit to achieve their goals, the UVF would be another unit layer—one more abstraction requiring more time and effort. However, more importantly, when we debate whether or not a teacher draft UVF can be presented to and understood by students, we misinterpret what a UVF is. Co-development and ownership are essential requirements because, as Chapter 1 explained, a UVF is not a single visual or graphic organizer, but rather a visual display of a mental image shared by students and teacher as they pursue a unit of study.

APPLICATIONS OF THIS CHAPTER FOR TEACHERS OF OLDER STUDENTS

Because this chapter uses a primary social studies example, I want to mention some reasons why the chapter's points apply across grade levels and subject areas. As in the following primary unit, teachers of all age groups might begin a unit by open-ended brainstorming as one way of activating prior knowledge, eliciting ownership, and beginning co-development of the unit and UVF. As teachers of older students follow the same steps of the co-development process herein described, they, too, will use multiple modalities to include all learners, engage in "really talking" with their students, and maintain the key role of making the UVF obvious through student contributions. In fact, although this chapter uses a primary social studies example, each chapter subheading highlights the ideas that are generalizable across grade levels and disciplines, as does the chapter's visual summary. If teachers of older students still want additional ideas closer to their own teaching situation, perhaps the following chapters will help as they show examples in other subject areas with third graders, sixth graders, and adult learners.

CO-DEVELOPMENT PROCESS

After initial planning for the unit, the teacher begins the unit with one image, based on curricular targets and how the teacher thinks those mesh with student readiness, interests, and needs. To have a *shared* mental image, the teacher will continually elicit the students' images of the unit and will work together with the students to display their common understanding of the unit in a class UVF. This continual cycle of moving from elicitation to purposefully organized display is the essence of the co-development process.

It is important to note that the elicitation, like the visual display, ideally involves multiple modalities—pictures, objects, movement, focused freewriting, oral discussion—for reasons well documented by brain research. In addition, these varied stimuli help students at all points of the English acquisition continuum to participate fully. Moreover, they help the teacher avoid confusing the students' knowledge of the *subject* with knowledge of the *English language* if instruction is not done bilingually.

At the beginning of a unit, the teacher is primarily seeking understanding of prior knowledge, experiences, thinking, and language related to the unit, though a new, common, concrete experience may be used to bring these to mind. This elicitation accompanies another beginning-of-the-unit task: setting the context with students to answer the questions "What will we be learning and for what purpose?" "What will the learning and the demonstration of learning look like?" and "Who will the audiences be for the demonstration(s) of learning?"

That word "messy" keeps coming back in my head, because in my mind setting the context and eliciting prior knowledge work together without occurring in a set sequence. Moreover, experienced teachers know that eliciting prior knowledge will often occur in stages, through multiple events, and over time, and that this is a part of powerful, responsive teaching.

The unit introduced in Chapter 3, People and Places in Community (see Ewy et al., 1998c), uses this multistep process. It first suggests ways to elicit, through varied types of stimuli, student knowledge, experiences, thinking, and language about the concept of "community" and later their knowledge of the specific type of community they are studying. (This 20-hour unit has options for studying home, school, or municipal communities.) Suggestions for finding out about community from students include asking students verbally, reading one or more short books with illustrations, showing students pictures of communities from around the world, and taking a brief tour or showing a videotape of a community.

The following narrative of the implementation of the People and Places in Community unit in a primary class shows one way that teachers co-develop a UVF. Please note that the actual sequence of events in this unit is not the emphasis: Every unit will evolve differently each time it is taught and the co-development of the UVF will reflect these unique sequences of teaching/learning events. Chapters 5 and 6 will give other examples of complete units for contrast. The steps listed in Figure 4.1, however, are the common elements of UVF co-development across all units of study.

Eliciting Student Images

The teacher had the targeted curriculum and draft UVF in Figure 4.2 in mind when she announced that the class would be studying about community. Before eliciting and sharing the compelling reasons she envisioned for such a study, she began finding out about the students' understanding of the concept itself. Figure 4.3 shows how co-development began in this class.

The teacher wrote the word *community* in the center of a large piece of paper and asked students what they could tell her about it. Because this was the class's first use of a UFV, the teacher was the recorder, modeling how to organize and highlight student ideas on a large piece of butcher paper according to the essentials of the unit. After a beginning chart was evident, she asked students to state where they thought she should put each new piece of

Figure 4.1.   Co-Development of a Class UVF

**Elicit
Students' Image of Unit**

Use multiple modalities
Seek representation
of class diversity
Bring forth experiences, knowledge,
thinking, and language
Create shared understanding

**Display
Students' Image
Organized to Show Unit Focus**

Use students' own words
Agree on illustrations
Arrange visually and highlight
to show key unit ideas &
relationships

**Expand
Students' Image**

Build on student ideas with new
experiences, knowledge, thinking, &
language specific to unit

**Update
Displayed Image (UVF)**

Repeat process of eliciting
& displaying student
understanding of unit
Connect new experiences &
reasoning with previous ones
Connect content-specific wording &/or
images to student wording
& previous images

Figure 4.2.   Priorities and Teacher Draft UVF for People and Places in Community UVF

Compelling Reasons for Unit
So students can know how to:
Meet their needs within a community
Be contributing community members

Social Science Goals & Standards
Goal 17 Geography and its effects of geography on society.
Standard A - Locate, describe and explain places and features.
Goal 18 Understand social systems, emphasizing the United States.
Standard B - Understand roles & interactions of individuals & groups in society.

Concepts: community, community helpers, resources, needs, viewpoints, maps

Core Ideas: feeling of community, what makes it work, using maps
                    and models for representing a community

Figure 4.3.   Eliciting Prior Knowledge About Key Unit Concepts

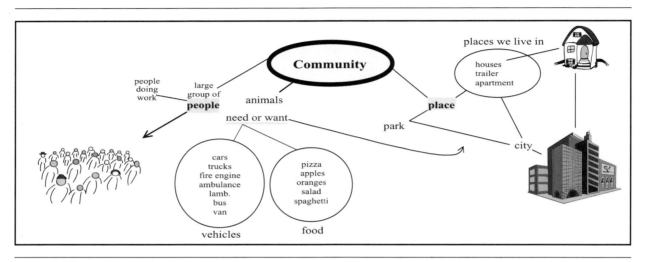

information they volunteered and to give their rationale for placing the new information where they suggested. She sometimes asked them to explain terms they used, like "trailer" and "vehicle," to ensure that the whole class stayed with the discussion. When the class reacted to a seemingly strange contribution, such as "pizza" or "Tokyo," the teacher invited the contributing student to tell the group the connection he or she had made with "community" to suggest the item. The teacher's assumption that students *had* made connections acknowledged and encouraged divergent thinking, while always relating it back to the focus.

The teacher thus was doing what Belenky, Glinchy, Goldberger, and Tarule (1986) describe as "really talking":

> "Really talking" requires careful listening; it implies a mutually shared agreement that together you are creating the optimum setting so that half-baked or emergent ideas can grow. (P. 144)

The shared agreement active in "really talking" is also present in the co-development of a UVF. That's one reason why the teacher wrote down the same words the students used and invited their illustrations as they talked. Their thoughts, words, and images would be used to help make the unit understandable, relevant, and culturally fair. Students could recognize these first steps on the learning path as their own visible entries into the unit of study. If, after days or weeks of study in the unit, students got lost in the thick of the academic terms or abstract concepts, they would be able to backtrack through the evolutionary stages of the framework to their own expressive language and previously known concepts.

Because these individual responses were to build a *shared* mental image by all students in the class, the teacher probed to ensure that the UVF represented the diversity in the classroom. She recorded the more formalized knowledge of *community,* such as "a large group of people," as well as the surface associations like "pizza." She made sure to write down "trailer" and "apartment," as well as "houses." Her questioning students on what they meant and asking them to elaborate when they offered a contribution ensured that she and other students knew what was meant by the picture or text placed on the chart. As students piggybacked on each other's thought processes, they generated content and language that would be used to help them infer the principles of the unit.

Organizing and Highlighting Student Contributions to Show Unit Focus

Because they were hearing "student talk," it was easier for students with less knowledge or weaker English language skills to understand and to help each other understand the content. Likewise, when bilingual students translated for each other, the language was less difficult than "teacher talk" or "book talk" would have been.

However, although student talk is often easier than book or teacher talk, it may also be a source of confusion, as Ana showed us in the scenario that opened Chapter 2. When student talk gets complicated because of language structure or content, or when associations are not obviously connected, it can be a detour from which a student with little background knowledge or English language skill might not return unless the teacher reframes the discussion.

Therefore, to keep the students with the unit focus, the teacher clustered student-generated lists with their assistance ("Where do we put 'trailer'?"), and elicited labels for these groups ("So, when we list 'pizza,' 'apples,' and 'spaghetti,' we're saying that people in communities need what?"). If students didn't know all the words in the group, they could use known vocabulary within the cluster to follow the conversation about community; likewise, if a student wasn't familiar with a group label, such as "vehicle," the student could use list items, such as "cars" and "trucks," to help understand.

Knowing that making the unit framework obvious was her major role, the teacher arranged the clusters and all of the students' ideas to show key concepts and relationships; random recording would not help students focus. She organized students' ideas in the following ways:

- The central concept was in large print and associated with the color yellow.
- Yellow highlighting of "people" and "place" linked the central concept with these two major ideas, which represented the instructional targets of social relationships and geographical concepts.

- Highlighting "need" and "want" connected the student lists to other major areas and laid the groundwork for a performance task in which students showed how to meet a need or want that they had.

- Pictures anchored student thoughts. Some were pictures that students found helpful from among the set the teacher had generated with her draft core UVF.

This first chart was the class's beginning description of community. By making a mental comparison of that to instructional targets and the teacher draft core UVF, the teacher knew the students had to go deeper into how communities work. Therefore, she continued to elicit prior knowledge.

The teacher invited small groups of students to fill three pieces of chart paper with visual and textual examples of the following:

1. How they help their community

2. How other people help them and the rest of the community

3. Places that help them and their community

The teacher then facilitated the attachment of the pages to the first wall chart, overtly linking them to students' specific original ideas, as seen in Figure 4.4. She used the yellow highlighting and the visual linking to keep the big ideas obvious and to reinforce the respective areas of social/people and geography/place.

This organized display of connected student ideas was moving their prior knowledge toward the larger generalizations. However, before students could go to that generalization about social systems, the teacher had to ensure that they were seeing the two elements involved in the system—the part and the whole.

Moving Prior Knowledge Toward Unit Generalizations

With the two charts at the top and the one at the bottom right of Figure 4.4, the class had expanded the display in Figure 4.3. The teacher led students to revisit their ideas to see the whole-part relationships in their visual display. She probed students about the connections and distinctions between the house (trailer/apartment) and the city, as well as those between "us" and "the community." The teacher helped students distinguish the difference between "every one" as individuals and "everyone" as a group or larger community, and added a picture of a student swinging to contrast with the crowd picture that represented "everyone" (Figure 4.4). Whether students ultimately remembered the difference in spelling was less important than if they remembered the concepts of individual and system. She used these distinctions to introduce a unit slogan, "Every One and Everyone Matters in a Community." This slogan, used throughout the unit, would be both auditory and visual

Figure 4.4. Eliciting Additional Prior Knowledge About Unit Principles

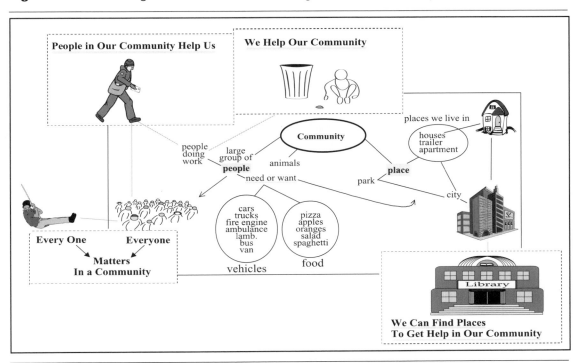

support to understand and remember the concept of community and how it works. By asking students at various times how their actions or decisions related to the slogan, she would induce application of the concept and principle.

To further assess and establish as key the generalization about how social systems work, the teacher decided to test out the metaphor she had chosen in her draft core UVF to see if it made enough sense to the students to add to the class UVF. On the playground, they explored connections between the teeter-totter and what they'd discussed to date about community. They felt, watched, and talked about balance and how the teeter-totter looked when the students on each side did or did not cooperate. They specifically discussed how each student had to make the teeter-totter work for both of them.

The Class Core UVF

Returning to the classroom, students and teacher followed the same process of anchoring this last experience in a chart. However, because this teeter-totter experience completed initial examination of all unit essentials, the teacher wanted to display a more cohesive and overt student image of the unit than the open-ended brainstorming had revealed. Therefore, as they anchored the teeter-totter experience, the teacher asked students to synthesize their

Figure 4.5. Synthesis Into a Core UVF

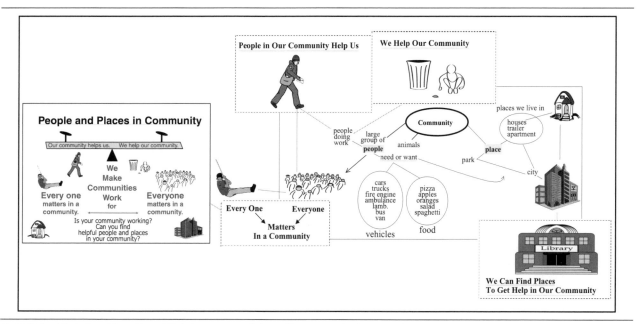

accumulated knowledge. She led students to create one simple visual—a core UVF—that focused on the unit's core ideas and two main instructional targets. To create this visual they

- Drew a picture of a teeter-totter

- Placed pictures and the slogan from previous charts near the teeter-totter picture in ways consistent with their playground and class discussions of the teeter-totter

- Added a new refrain, "We make communities work."

- Asked two questions that expanded their focus on places, reminding everyone to focus on the primary-level geography concepts and preparing students for their assessment tasks

- Observed the relationship between the unit title, "People and Places in Community," and their own highlighted words in the first chart, which they now knew were the areas of focus in the unit

Figure 4.5 shows how the core UVF pulled from previously displayed work. Figure 4.6 is an enlargement of the core/portable UVF itself.

With each step, the teacher checked the choice and understanding of text, visuals, and placement with the class to ensure that they owned the new

Figure 4.6.  Core UVF

People and Places in Community

Our community helps us.   We help our community.

We Make Communities Work

for

Every one
matters in a
community.

Is your community working?
Can you find
helpful people and places
in your community?

Everyone
matters in a
community.

chart, understood where in previous charts it was coming from, and understood the implications of their new placement.

In this case, the class core UVF worked out to be quite similar to the teacher draft pictured in Figure 4.2. Perhaps it was because the teacher used previous knowledge of the students to choose the individual images and text for her draft. Another reason might have been that, during elicitation of prior knowledge, the pictures were connected with the more inclusive representations of students' own situations. For example, by the time students synthesized their ideas into a core UVF, the fairy tale–type house was just a symbol for house, trailer, apartment, and other "places where we live." The concepts and relationships of the class core UVF had been cumulatively built from student experiences and prior knowledge—a very different process from "covering" material or trying to get students to understand a predetermined visual. Most important, the teacher was willing to let go of the draft and develop something new with her class.

The Portable Core UVF

The class had completed the co-development of the core UVF for the unit People and Places in Community. As part of their evolving display, they could look at its relationship to previous charts and trace their learning more easily than if it were elsewhere in the room. The teacher also reproduced and distributed copies of the class core UVF (Figure 4.6) for each student's portable use.

For the portable core UVF to be useful, each student had to own it as a representation of his or her ideas. Furthermore, the portable UVF had to be as meaningful as the large, class charts that they had built incrementally and cumulatively. Therefore, the teacher asked students to pair up. Each pair was to refer to the large class charts, recall for each other the concrete experiences they had had, and tell each other what the portable UVF meant to them. Thus, each partner was helping his or her peer self-assess unit understanding using the portable UVF. To clarify or strengthen individual understanding, the teacher encouraged students to add representations and/or text that made personal sense.

During this paired work, the teacher circulated to ensure the following:

- That students realized the portable was a reproduction of the co-created class UVF

- That students saw a representation of the concrete ideas they had expressed in their own words and images

- That they understood the core unit ideas and relationships depicted on the UVF

- That any personal adaptations they made were elaborations, not distortions, of the meaning of the core ideas represented on the core UVF

The teacher was verifying that each student shared the same understanding of the unit, even as they had the opportunity to personalize this visual tool in ways that served them.

The portable core UVF brought the unit focus up close for individual and team work in the classroom and at home. For instance, when students compared two communities, they had visual and textual representations of three major features to compare: (a) how community members helped the community, (b) how the community helped its members, and (c) whether or not the community was working for the individuals and for the whole. Students had this same support for two tasks they did at home. Their UVF helped them interview their parents about their views and experiences of their current community. Students and their parents also made a new version of the UVF to reflect another community the family knew, or had experienced previously, and discussed how well it worked.

Another benefit of the portable UVF was its assistance to nonverbal and English language learners, helping them communicate with their peers and teachers within their classroom and from other classes. In one case, two classes, who called themselves *buddy classes,* met once a week to work on collaborative tasks central to the unit they each studied in their separate rooms. One of the classes received bilingual instruction and one was studying the same unit using only English. These classes used their portable UVFs not only as described here in their homerooms, but also to summarize and expand their learning with each other when they worked together weekly on unit tasks.

Expanding and Updating the UVF

Figure 4.7 is a partial view of the class's expanded UVF. The class used and expanded their core UVF throughout the rest of the unit, keeping all wall charts displayed. Each new experience was discussed, added to capture the cumulative knowledge visually, and organized in the context of the unit's focus. The model that students constructed was physically located in the library, but, to keep its presence in mind, the class made a sign inviting people to go to the library to see the model. The sign also allowed students to map the model on the class UVF back to the students' original ideas about places in the community. Other charts, similarly connected, helped students keep track of and recall print and other resources that expanded their ideas.

As the class UVF displayed the learning of the whole class, students were asked to revisit and expand their portable UVFs. Some students elaborated differently from the class UVF, creating, in effect, individual mind maps of their own learning. Other students found the class representations sufficient for their own use.

The teacher continued the same practice of having students work with peers to review their learning via their portable UVF, as they had done when they first received it. However, the type of review varied. For example, as a "three-minute pause" to help students process what they were working on, the teacher might ask student pairs to use their portable UVFs to tell each other how their current learning event related to the rest of what they had learned to date. On another occasion the teacher might pose a problem, and ask students to confer with each other to solve it using their portable UVFs to support their thinking. In either case, if students weren't able to do the task, or found a conflict in their views of the unit material, they could (a) go to the class UVF and trace the learning backward, comparing with their portable UVFs and/or (b) request help from a neighboring peer team or the teacher. This peer work gave students and the teachers an opportunity in class to verify that their modified portable UVFs continued to strengthen their unit learning, so that when they used it on their own, with students outside the class, or with parents at home, they worked from accurate information and understanding.

These expanded class and portable UVFs guided and chronicled the journey to achieve the instructional targets. At the beginning of each lesson, students would use the UVF to recap what had been learned to date and where the class, group, or individual students were working that day. To introduce a new

Figure 4.7.   Expanding the UVF

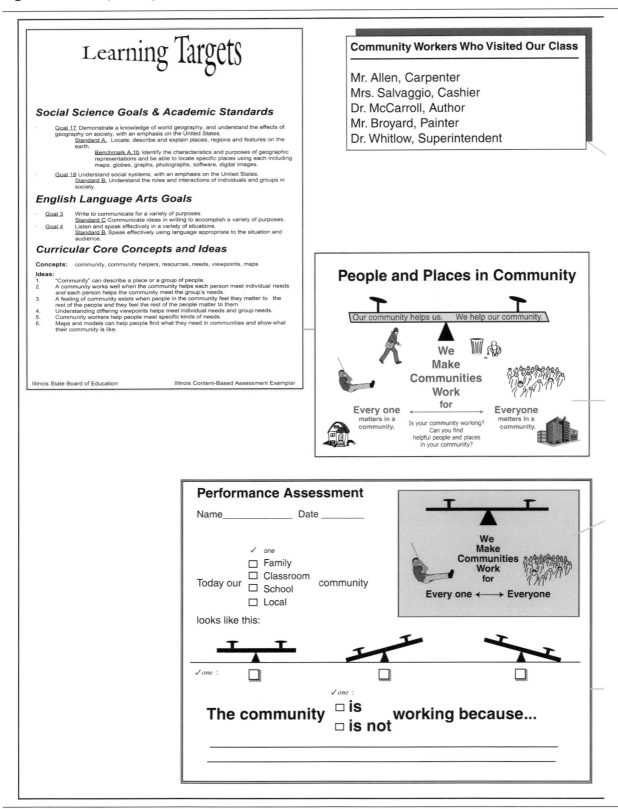

Figure 4.7. (Continued)

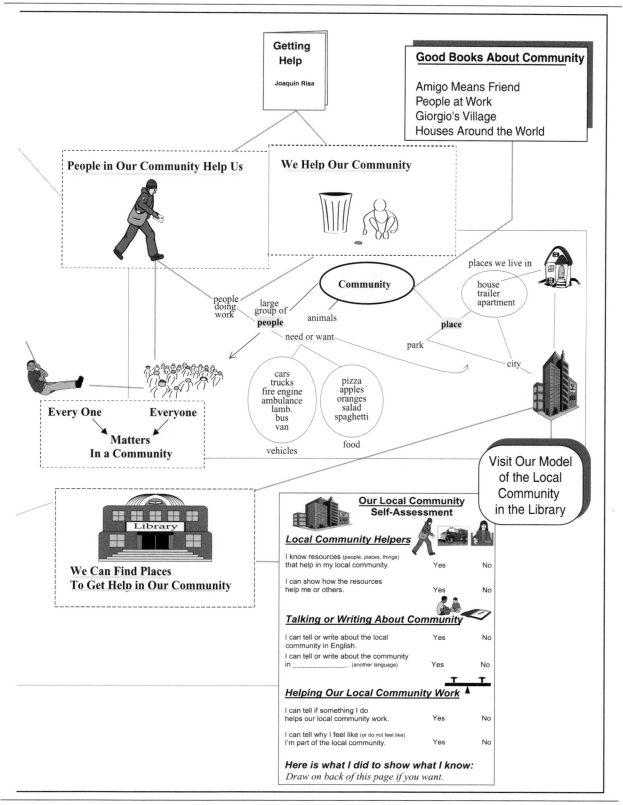

task, the teacher used the UVF to provide context, showing the relationship of the new task to previous learning. Students retraced their learning path to find their original words and original ideas to clarify new terms or abstract ideas. At the end of a learning task, the students used the UVF to debrief, articulate deeper understanding, or report progress.

One instance of supporting transitions and cumulative learning was the use of the UVF to make the unit learning from skits obvious, in preparation for a written project. The class dramatized some skits as a concrete rehearsal for individual booklets they would create, telling how they would meet a real need in the community.

The day after the skits, students first used an artifact to recall what had happened in a particular skit. Then, volunteers went to the class UVF to explain unit concepts related to what had occurred. One student pointed to the left side of the teeter-totter and named the community helper that was part of the skit. Another student pointed to the "Places" chart, telling what community places were involved in meeting the need. A third student used the moveable replica of the teeter-totter and asked classmates if the community worked in the skit, and if so why. With each of these interactions the teacher playfully asked, "Why was that important?" each time eliciting the refrain, "Because everyone matters in the community." This UVF-supported skit recall and analysis enabled students to transition from the concrete dramatizations to the project work that began that day.

A CURRICULAR, TEACHING/LEARNING, AND ASSESSMENT RESOURCE

Figure 4.7 shows some of the performance and assessment tasks, as well as how they were linked on the class UVF to the ideas that students were being asked to apply or assess. Let's look a little closer, first examining the task illustrated in the lower left corner, labeled "Performance Assessment."

At different times during the unit study, the teacher would ask the students to pause and use the teeter-totter image to show what the community looked like in the particular situation in which they were engaged; the students might be on the playground, in the classroom, or in the cafeteria. The teacher would ask the students to show the teeter-totter's position to indicate if the community was working for that individual student and the group of which he or she was a part at the time. The student would also explain his or her reasoning related to that judgment. Sometimes, this was done orally with the child using his or her hands or a cardboard teeter-totter. At other times, students would write on a page like the one in Figure 4.7. A sample written version was part of the expanded class UVF to show students its link to the slogans, "Every One and Everyone Matters in a Community" and "We Make Communities Work," supporting their performance.

The written assessment task mentioned in the previous section was to create a booklet called "Getting Help." As Figure 4.7 shows, a template of the booklet was placed on the right, upper half of the expanded UVF and physically connected to two of the early prior-knowledge charts students had generated. This placement cued students to use the information on those charts to complete the task.

To create the booklet, each student stated a real need or desire, such as "I want a puppy." On the first page of the booklet, the student brainstormed a list and/or drawings of community resources she or he might use to get a puppy. To do this step, the student could use the multiple pictures and text of the expanded UVF as immediate resources. They also had visual reminders of additional resources, such as the books read by the class, the list of community helpers who had visited the class, or the model of the actual community they had re-created. In like manner, the class and portable UVFs supported the student with the remainder of the steps of this task:

- To communicate the resource she or he would choose, and explain the choice

- To tell whether a map would be useful in the process of obtaining the puppy and why or why not

- To reflect on how the community works in this process—how the student's getting a puppy can help both the student and the community

VISIBLE FEEDBACK AND ACCOUNTABILITY

As students co-developed the UVF throughout the People and Places in Community unit, they had to be active participants in constructing and monitoring their learning. They had to supply *their* words and images for the learning that was occurring. Each time they reviewed, added, and connected ideas to expand the visual, they had to reexamine the unit focus and check their new understanding and performance related to it. The teacher, in turn, had this ongoing information as to how closely the students were progressing with the unit targets and whether the teaching/learning events were working for the students.

This visual display of a unit's work and student understanding, therefore, can serve students, teachers, and all stakeholders in learning and in accountability. Using the UVF, students learn to monitor with their teacher the learning targets informally represented on the display. The more formal form of these targets, such as the actual goals and standards students are pursuing, may also be posted and connected to the UVF, giving students, teachers, and visitors two visible means of judging the alignment of targets and teaching/

learning events as the unit progresses. However, without co-development and ownership, little of this will make sense to the students.

FORMAT REVISITED

The core UVF in this unit uses a metaphor base—the teeter-totter. On the other hand, the expanded UVF is basically a web, which may often be the case. It is important to reiterate that the connections forming this web are not random. As teachers facilitate UVF expansion, they might ask such leading questions as

- What does this new information/experience most connect with in our core UVF?
- What learning and/or language already displayed does this build on?
- How can we show that connection?

Such questioning honors student ownership and thinking processes, and makes distinctions for them between brainstorming and building understanding through connections.

MANAGEMENT CONCERN: PHYSICAL SIZE OF THE EXPANDED UVF

This unit has shown an ideal situation, in which the class UVF is displayed for the duration of the unit on a wall where there is enough space to accommodate it from its beginning through its expanded completion. Obviously, not all classes have this luxury.

Some teachers are able to post the core UVF, but must hang and take down the expanded components each class meeting. Other teachers don't even have a dedicated place to keep the core UVF posted, and must dismantle and reassemble all components when working on the unit.

Two principles are relevant in these situations:

1. Effective implementation requires the UVF, in its cumulatively evolving state, to be visible every time the unit is pursued—otherwise the results will be less than their potential.
2. The more students participate in this task of keeping the display visible, the more consistent its use will be with its collaborative nature and cognitive benefits.

The type of student participation may vary. A teacher may sometimes put up the beginnings of the UVF when setting up for class and then elicit volunteers during class time to reconstruct the rest as a means of review and retracing learning. Other times, a student pair or team might reconstruct the entire UVF before or during class.

In cases where the UVF is taken down and reassembled for display, a digital camera can be helpful. A quick picture of the UVF at the end of the class, or after each expansion, will help teacher and students be able to reconstruct it. A picture is also helpful to show how it was before rearranging it with total class approval on occasions where a class discovers a more effective arrangement as their ideas evolve.

Again, the advice of "honest and possible" serves us. Students and teachers who work together can invent many creative solutions.

Chapter Four
Visual Summary

Co-Development and Ownership of a Class UVF

Elicit

Students' Image of Unit
Use multiple modalities
Seek representation of class diversity
Bring forth experiences, knowledge, thinking, and language
Create shared understanding

Display

Students' Image Organized to Show Unit Focus
Use students' own words
Agree on illustrations
Arrange visually and highlight to show key unit ideas & relationships

Expand

Students' Image
Build on student ideas with new experiences, knowledge, thinking, and language specific to unit

Update

Displayed Image (UVF)
Repeat process of eliciting & displaying student understanding of unit
Connect new experiences & reasoning with previous ones
Connect content-specific wording &/or images to student wording & previous images

A Unit Visual Framework (UVF)

visually anchors key concepts, experiences, & relationships through the use of at least three elements: students' own words, content-specific text, & images.

The UVF begins as a **core visual**, which the class co-develops to establish a shared image of the unit focus. Each student has a **portable core visual**.

Test

If student performance or products that demonstrate understanding of the UVF **also** result in achievement of the instructional targets, **then** the UVF design is effective.

Class Core UVF

Portable Core for Individual Use

The core visual grows into **an expanded display**, organized by the core visual to show learning paths & evolving, cumulative understanding of the unit.

Test

If, throughout the unit, each student and teacher can …

1. Successfully access & participate in unit learning
2. Establish, review, & trace learning paths
3. Observe & express cumulative understanding

Then the expanded UVF has been effectively co-developed, organized, visually depicted, & used

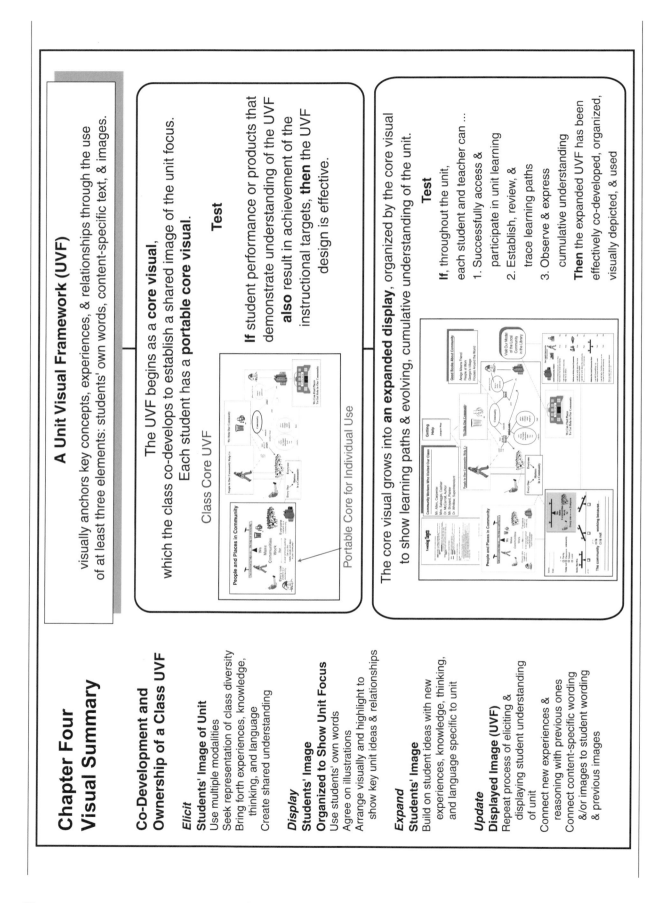

Visual Consistencies 5

Cohesion Building Blocks

When I review without a visual framework, students often think it's new material.

—Middle School Teacher

hapter 4 gave an overview of the step-by-step process of co-development and use of a Unit Visual Framework over the course of a sustained unit. This chapter reinforces that process and highlights the role of visual consistency in building cohesion.

Figure 5.1 shows how Chapter 4's case study contrasts considerably with the one in this chapter. For one thing, this sample didn't begin as a unit at all, but actually began as "brief strategy lessons." (Have you ever had a unit just sort of grow without previous planning?) It is this serendipitous nature of the sample unit that will demonstrate the importance of visual consistency when co-developing a UVF.

The unit emerged in the midst of already ongoing work. Therefore, the class UVF had to share with other demands for wall space, and its display was more disrupted than the one illustrated in the previous chapter. In addition, student portable UVFs were housed in portfolios that expanded as the class UVF expanded. These circumstances brought out the critical role of consistency in illustrations, color, and text in the UVF and all other unit materials to maintain coherent and cohesive learning. The retelling in this chapter highlights these visual consistencies and pauses to add hindsight observations and recommendations that would strengthen the cohesion. There is also a sense of the length of each phase of the unit and UVF development.

Figure 5.1. Comparison of Sample Units in Chapters 4 and 5

Chapter 4 Sample Unit, People and Places in Community	Chapter 5 Sample Unit, Reading to Remember and Show What We Know
1. Primary focus: content	1. Primary focus: process skills & content
2. Only social studies instructional targets highlighted to limit the variables in this first view of UVF co-development & use in a complete unit	2. Integrates reading, writing, & science
3. Chosen and presented to have few confounding issues	3. & 4. Shows the bumps & twists found in many units, especially one that is not preplanned
4. Preplanned by a team of teachers, and piloted before being taught	4. Shows how the UVF brought cohesion to the first-time use of a unit that evolved from strategy lessons:
5. Computer-generated figures assist author retelling of unit	*Phase I*—strategy mini-lessons in preparation for statewide tests
	Phase II—application of strategies in thematic unit, shifting from testing to everyday learning context
	Phase III—game-based celebration to which students invite guests from outside the classroom as an authentic reason to demonstrate their learning
	5. Photographs and quotes from students, parents, & teacher give in-classroom view & supplement author voice

Figure 5.2 is an overview of this chapter's case study as it eventually evolved. If preplanned, the integrated unit—as a whole and in its parts—would have been stronger in many ways. Nonetheless, as we witness its actual evolution, we see the UVF's significant role in (a) uniting each phase of the unit, and (b) illustrating for students how the three subject areas in the unit actually worked together.

SAMPLE UNIT'S ORIGINS

The unit originated from seemingly good intentions. I needed student work samples for staff development at a time when Paula Bullis's third-grade

Figure 5.2. Unit Overview: Reading to Remember and Show What We Know

GOALS, STANDARDS, & UNIT-SPECIFIC CURRICULUM	CONTEXT	TEACHING/LEARNING EVENTS & INDIVIDUAL ASSESSMENT TASKS
Language Arts Goal Read with understanding and fluency 　**Standard** Comprehend a broad range of reading materials 　**Unit-Specific Curriculum** Utilize state reading rubric features to demonstrate comprehension of narrative and expository selections **Language Arts Goal** Write to communicate for a variety of purposes 　**Standard** Communicate ideas in writing to accomplish a variety of purposes 　**Unit-Specific Curriculum** Apply the reading rubric features to communicate in writing information learned from reading science selections **Science Goal** Understand the fundamental concepts, principles, and interconnections of the life, physical and earth/space sciences 　**Standard** Know and apply concepts that explain how living things function, adapt and change 　**Standard** Know and apply concepts that describe how living things interact with each other and with their environment 　**Unit-Specific Curriculum** Know how elephants function, adapt, and change during their lifetime, and how they interact with each other and with their environment	**ISAT Reading Responses** 　**Engaging the Learner** 　Questioning regarding times when students want to show what they know, including ISAT (statewide assessment) **Content-Area Reading** 　**Engaging the Learner** 　• Jigsaw with narrative and expository selections 　• Elephant game 　• Guest Day. Students invite guest(s) of their choices – friends &/or family – to attend an afternoon of sharing, learning, and celebration. Using their UVF portfolios and products, students explain their learning process during the unit, read their written expository piece, and play the elephant game with their guests. Students and guests provide oral and written response to the events.	**Phase I, Application to ISAT Performance** • Context – showing what you know in math, social science, reading, writing, etc. • Co-develop UVF: metaphor, 　　　**K of S　MT** 　key text, and color-coding 　Details ▲ Connections • Before strategy – diagram/illustrate prompt for clear focus. During – graphic organizers, color underlining or highlighting, note taking • Narrative genre: Ruby the Copycat • Review & use of models – scored/unscored papers **Phase II, Application to Elephant Study** • Co-develop core & expanded UVF with Before, During, and After strategies • Family Groups visual, add strategies to UVF • Adapt and connect writing graphic organizer • Revisit narrative & expository strategies on UVF • Jigsaw: 1) read, 2) oral share, 3) self/peer assess • Ruby teacher simulation of self/peer assessment • Elephant Jigsaw #2, written response, oral share **Phase III, Application for External Audience** • Introduce elephant game, portfolio use with guests • Mini-lessons on writing conclusions & using science standards visual, adapted core UVF • Elephant writing as learning aid for guests • Guest day invitations, process, & preparations • Evaluations: learning, enthusiasm, GVF/UVF use **Individual Assessment Tasks** 1. Pre/post Phase I: written response to ISAT prompt 2. Pre/post Unit: written response Wolves/Elephants 3. Saguaro written response 4. Elephant synthesis of learning from two narrative and two expository selections

students were preparing to take their statewide reading assessment (the Illinois Standards Achievement Test, or ISAT), which included written, open-response questions to the test's reading selections. Paula and I agreed that I would introduce students to the ISAT reading comprehension rubric features and create an awareness of this rubric's similarity to rubrics used in math and writing. I would also lead a few mini-lessons to help students understand their task and to introduce some strategies for the reading assessment and its written response expectations. Because the strategy lessons would not be a full-blown unit, I would facilitate co-development of a very basic Global Visual Framework.

Though less than what we would have done if preplanning a unit, these strategy lessons seemed like a win-win situation for the circumstances. For ease of reference, we will call these strategy mini-lessons for the statewide assessment context *Phase I*, which took about seven hours spread over two weeks.

Figure 5.3. Draft Cross-Curricular Comprehension GVF

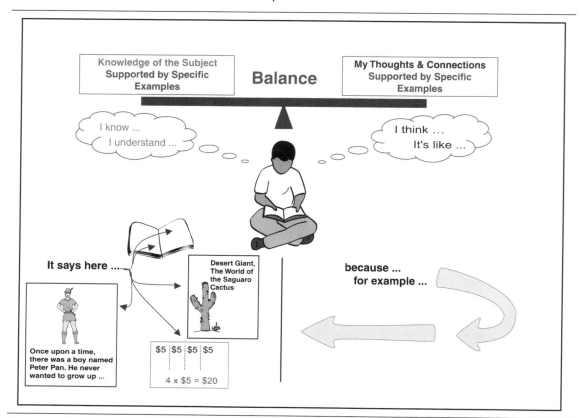

ELICITING STUDENTS' IMAGE OF THE UNIT

As indicated in the middle column of the unit overview (Figure 5.2), we began by asking students to think of times when they wanted to share with others what they had learned from reading or from other sources. Because students were recalling their own experiences, most of them were able to contribute. This brainstorming established a broader context for the strategies students would learn, beyond just the current anticipation of the statewide tests.

To focus on the rubric's features for demonstrating comprehension, we drew on two teacher draft GVFs (Figures 5.3 and 5.4). We explored the use of a balance as a metaphor for two reasons: (a) the students had used balances in their science studies and were already familiar with them concretely and conceptually, and (b) the rubric for the reading response questions actually used the word *balance*, seeking both student interpretation and text support. We wanted to elicit student recall of the first and relate it to the second.

Students had no difficulty recalling their prior science knowledge with balances. *What* was being balanced was the part students had to think about in this context. We first asked them about the situations they had brainstormed,

Figure 5.4. Draft Reading Comprehension GVF

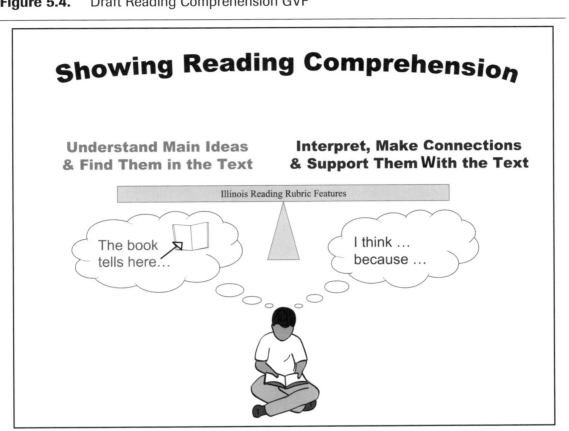

noting, for example, that when they told someone about a TV program, they both gave information about the program (that is, they demonstrated their knowledge) and shared their own thoughts about it. Next, we showed the students the teacher draft in Figure 5.3 and talked about how they needed to give a balance of the same two things—knowledge and their own thoughts—in their school content areas assessments. We used examples from various subject areas, eliciting evidence of knowledge of the subject and "my thoughts."

DISPLAYING STUDENTS' IMAGE ORGANIZED TO SHOW UNIT FOCUS

On the second day with students, we began co-development of a basic GVF. I again elicited from students the context of our work together, as I would do at the beginning of most sessions thereafter. Reinforcing that we were focusing on one type of reading purpose only, we formalized this purpose in the title Reading to Remember and Show What We Know (Figure 5.5)

Figure 5.5. Initial Class Core GVF

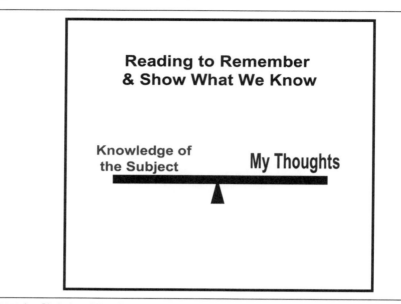

**Reading to Remember
& Show What We Know**

**Knowledge of
the Subject**   **My Thoughts**

When I asked what we had compared reading comprehension to, students readily recalled the balance as our metaphor and named "knowledge" and "my thoughts" as the two sides of the balance. Their term "knowledge" was not the complete concept needed to guide their future work, so, I persisted through questioning to elicit "knowledge *of the subject.*" We wrote this specific concept on the class GVF to be consistent with the examples they had analyzed and discussed and to distinguish it from prior knowledge, which would go on the other side of the balance as one example of their thoughts, as well as those that would form during and after reading.

We used two different colors to show the items on each side of the balance, providing both text and color cues for students. Blue was kept on the right side for "my thoughts" and red would be associated with knowledge of the subject. Because these were supposed to be only a couple of mini-lessons, and because I had given the classroom teacher a copy of the draft GVFs, we merely captured this class GVF on a blank overhead transparency.

The right column of Figure 5.2 outlines the remaining teaching/learning events for Phase I. With each teaching/learning event, students referred to the core GVF and used its metaphor, key text, and color coding. For instance, as they analyzed models of scored student responses or looked at anonymous samples from their own initial written responses (listed as "Individual Assessment Task #1 at the bottom of the first column in Figure 5.2), they used red and blue to highlight which statements in the responses were mostly showing knowledge of the text and which were interpretation or "my thoughts." They then held their arms out fully at their shoulders and moved them up or down to show if the response was heavier with knowledge of the text or the writer's

Figure 5.6. Comparison of Scores Before and After Strategy Application

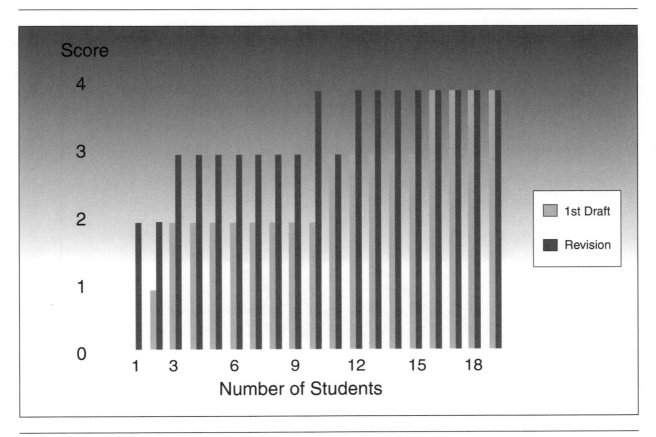

own thoughts. They looked for overall balance of text and interpretation in the response, and checked to see if the response gave enough evidence that the person had read and understood the selection. This use of color and metaphor to analyze their writing reinforced their use of the class GVF to revise their writing.

Figure 5.6 compares their first draft scores with those of the revision in which they had applied their new understanding of the task and strategies. Based on student results and their ability to discuss the class GVF, the mini-lessons seemed to have achieved what was possible in that amount of time. Students had a visual tool that strengthened (a) their understanding of the task's requirements, and (b) their ability to demonstrate reading comprehension in this isolated context of standardized testing.

At that point, the students, their classroom teacher, and I wanted to go on. It was clear to us that the *immediate* reason for students to learn the comprehension rubric features had been performance on their statewide test. However, the *compelling* reason was what we had discussed the very first day—that they could use these features to demonstrate reading comprehension in any situation important to them any day of the year. We had felt justified taking

Figure 5.7. Beginning Class Core UVF

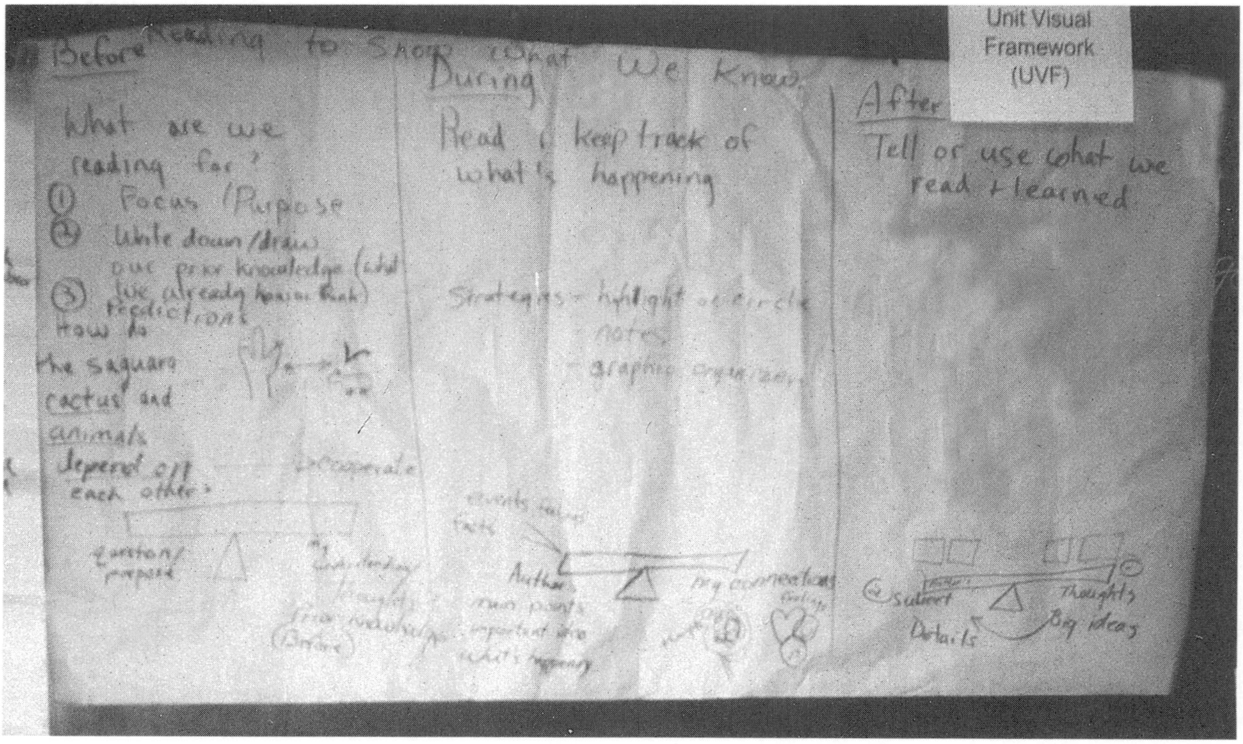

time for focused strategy lessons for the statewide test. Next, we wanted to continue to get a feel for the promised broader applications.

As we proceeded to what became Phases II and III of the unit, I continued to plan the work with Paula Bullis's input and to serve as guest demonstration teacher. Paula and her students completed some tasks when I was not in the classroom. Because of this arrangement and the unexpected evolution of the strategy lessons into a complete integrated unit, I was scheduled in the classroom when previously planned class events and my schedule allowed. The whole unit took approximately 45 hours, spread over two and a half months.

FROM GVF TO EXPANDING UVF

With student input, we began Phase II by choosing the study of elephants as our content, and the science learning standards as our focus. Because we were now going to have a sustained unit, we began the process of co-developing a UVF. We constructed a visual display of what we had experienced in Phase I and supplemented it with prior knowledge students had from other learning (Figure 5.7 is an actual classroom photograph; Figure 5.8 is a more legible reproduction with additions we later captured).

Figure 5.8. From GVF to Expanding Class UVF

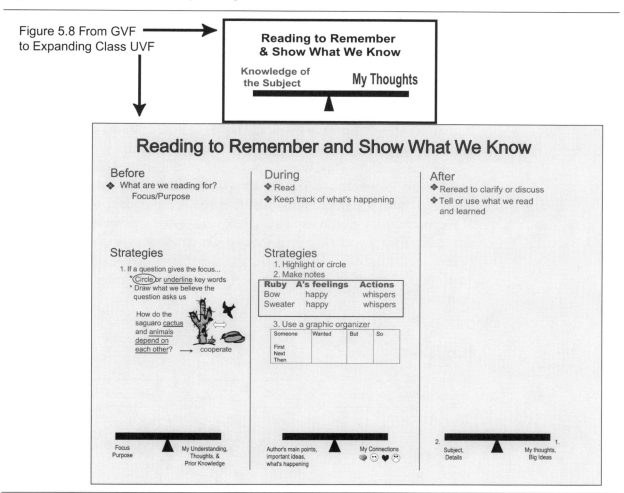

Figure 5.8 From GVF to Expanding Class UVF

On a large piece of yellow butcher paper, we wrote the title we had used previously for the focus and broader context of our study, Reading to Remember and Show What We Know. Thereafter, when I asked students to recall what we were studying and why, I also asked them to show us on the UVF how they knew that this was our focus and context, expecting them to at least reference the title.

We transferred to this new chart the GVF metaphor we had used in Phase I. However, to emphasize that the balance of interaction between author's message and reader's thoughts occurred throughout the reading process, and to display the strategies students used throughout as well, we made the "Before," "During," and "After" reading stages overt on the chart. As we discussed each stage of the reading process, we interpreted "what knowledge of the subject" and "my thoughts" meant during that stage. We noted that, during reading, some connections we make are thoughts and others are feelings.

Because students were studying the human body in health at the time, they decided that a picture of the brain would represent thought connections and that both the heart and faces showing different emotions should represent feeling connections.

After the core GVF was displayed in each reading stage on the chart, we recalled and recorded strategies we had used in Phase I. We included some graphics to remind us of the actual experiences we had had with those strategies, such as samples of the actual notes we had taken when reading Peggy Rathman's story "Ruby the Copycat," from the ISAT training materials. With Phase I experiences anchored, we began to build on them.

A Phase I strategy had been to make sure we understood the prompt or test question before we read so that we would have a clear focus while reading. We discussed the fact that, though students weren't reading for a test in this study of elephants, they would still be reading for a specific purpose, which would determine their focus. Therefore, the two terms *focus* and *purpose* were written next to each other. Strategies for "During" and "After" were similarly recorded. Thus, over a couple of class sessions, a core UVF was created on this yellow chart paper.

Hindsight

Visual Consistency	Observations/Recommendations
Title	Keep labels of "Knowledge of Subject" and "My Thoughts" on top of the balance, as in the GVF, and add new ideas below
Balance image as metaphor	
Placement of "Knowledge of Subject" and "My Thoughts" information on each side of balance consistent with original	Keep color coding from the GVF for information on each side of balance
"Strategies" text and images are directly from previous experiences in Phase I	Caution: Students who are color blind may see the writing on the UVF and the red/blue distinctions on the GVF as distinct colors, but the red and green might appear to be tan. The UVF's lighter writing in red and green may not even be discernible on the yellow background.
Images for "My Connections" recall health studies of body to represent thought and feelings	

EXPANDING UVF INTEGRATES CONSISTENT SUPPORT VISUALS

In order to create a real reason for students to demonstrate what they learned from reading about elephants, we used a jigsaw structure: The class was divided into two groups, each group reading different materials. Therefore, students would have to share with each other what they had learned. For instance, one group read a teacher-written narrative called "A Day's Work" focusing on the interdependence of a village and the elephants they used to help them accomplish work. The other group read an expository selection focusing on the similarities and differences between African and Asian elephants. When finished reading, students broke into pairs made of one student from each group to exchange information. After sharing in pairs, the work culminated in a whole-class meeting to debrief and evaluate their experiences. This sequence took two to three class sessions for each pair of selections read. The groups alternated the genre they read, so each group explored strategies for both narrative and expository selections. The UVF guided whole-class, small-group, and paired work and reflection.

"Before Reading" Support Visuals

The UVF expanded as experiences were documented and support visuals were added. For instance, before both groups were to read different materials about the importance of family groups in elephants, we used the visual in Figure 5.9 as a class. The visual activated prior knowledge about family groups and elicited key vocabulary students would encounter in both selections as they read about bull, cow, and calf elephants. The visual and the discussion it generated also gave English language learners more equal prereading readiness with their native English-speaking peers who already knew these terms as they applied to cattle. We captured students' brainstormed knowledge on a white chart page which we titled "Families." On this prior-knowledge chart, we attempted to use the same color coding we had used previously—blue for their "big ideas" about family and red for the details that supported those big ideas.

After this brainstorming, we added the following strategy to the "Before" column of the UVF: "Write down or draw our prior knowledge/what we already know or think." Students used this prior knowledge to predict what they might be learning in their reading, and we recorded that previously acquired prediction strategy to the "Before" column of the UVF. In addition, an excerpt from the "Families" prior-knowledge chart was written on the UVF to support the strategy description. Thus, when the UVF became a portable and the support visuals that were attached on the class UVF were collected in the portfolio, the support visuals would be recalled to assist comprehension of the strategy description.

Each student had a copy of the Family Groups visual, which they could use first as they read the separate materials and again when they exchanged information in pairs. Figure 5.10 shows Alec in a later whole-class session revisiting the visual and brainstormed chart to recall their purpose before reading, and to explain how they had been used during and after reading as well. Thus, visuals supported students throughout their unit, each picking up illustrations, text, and color bearing meaning from previous use, and each being incorporated into the expanding UVF.

Figure 5.9. Family Groups Visual

"After Reading" Support Visuals

The value of this visual consistency and cumulative cohesion is also evident in the application of the "After" reading strategy to "tell or use what we read and learned." We developed two tools for this strategy.

Planner

The first tool was my adaptation of a graphic organizer that students had been using to plan their writing pieces. In this case, they would use it as a planner (Figure 5.11) to organize their thoughts about the selection they had read, in preparation for oral or written sharing.

The red and blue color coding carrying the same meaning from their initial class GVF was used to show where students would write their own thoughts and where they would note details from the text to support their interpretations. The symbols they had used on the UVF for connections were also on the planner in appropriate places to prompt student inclusion of these. During discussion of the selection, we reinforced the meaning of these symbols; students pointed to the heart and facial expressions when someone expressed dismay about elephant poaching, and to the illustration of the brain

Figure 5.10. Alec explains how he used the support visuals when reading

when another child thought of a connection between the current selection and something read in a previous selection.

Initially, we believed students would easily recognize this planner and the class writing graphic organizer as the same tool, because they looked very similar. When students used the planner the first time for oral sharing only, this seemed to be the case. In addition, student reactions when they did some brief writing supported our belief:

> The writing was challenging but fun because we put what we believe and what the author thinks.

> The planner was easy—you had ideas in your mind, and you could look back in the story.

> The charts on the wall helped writing.

> The color coding on the charts helped make it easier.

We were, however, wrong. As we examined their writing more closely and as Paula compared it to writing they had previously done, we realized that students were using the planner superficially, as often happens when someone other than the end user makes a graphic organizer. Though very similar, the graphic organizers for writing and reading response had purposely been varied. For instance, instead of the three boxes as placeholders for important ideas on the writing graphic organizer, four were used in the new visual to emphasize that there was no set number required. This difference, the color coding,

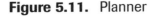

Figure 5.11. Planner

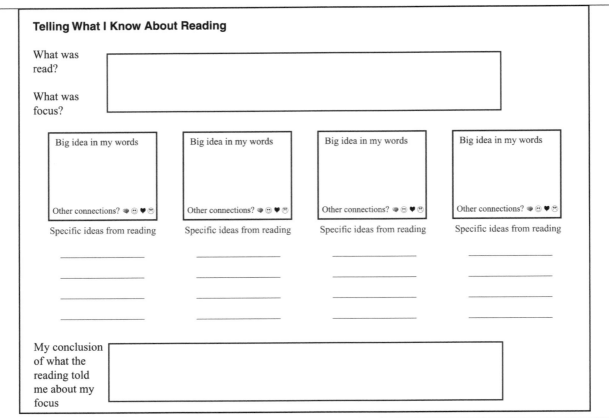

and the fact that another teacher—not their homeroom/writing teacher—gave them the graphic organizer were enough for students to think this was something totally new, thus preventing transfer.

We regrouped. We physically connected the two planners, placing the writing graphic organizer next to the class UVF where the planner had been displayed in the "After" column. Paula worked with the students recalling how they had used the graphic organizer in writing, and she elicited how those writing experiences and skills related to the planner being used in this reading response context (Figure 5.12). With these connections made, students more readily applied their learning from the writing context to this new context of reading response with content material (Figure 5.13).

Checklist

The second tool that students used with the "After" reading strategy of "sharing what they had learned" was a checklist to maintain the unit focus (Figure 5.14). When students met in pairs to share what they had each read, they used the checklist first to self-assess and then to get peer feedback on their use of the reading rubric features to show their comprehension. The color

Figure 5.12. Paula Bullis connects the class writing graphic organizer with the planner

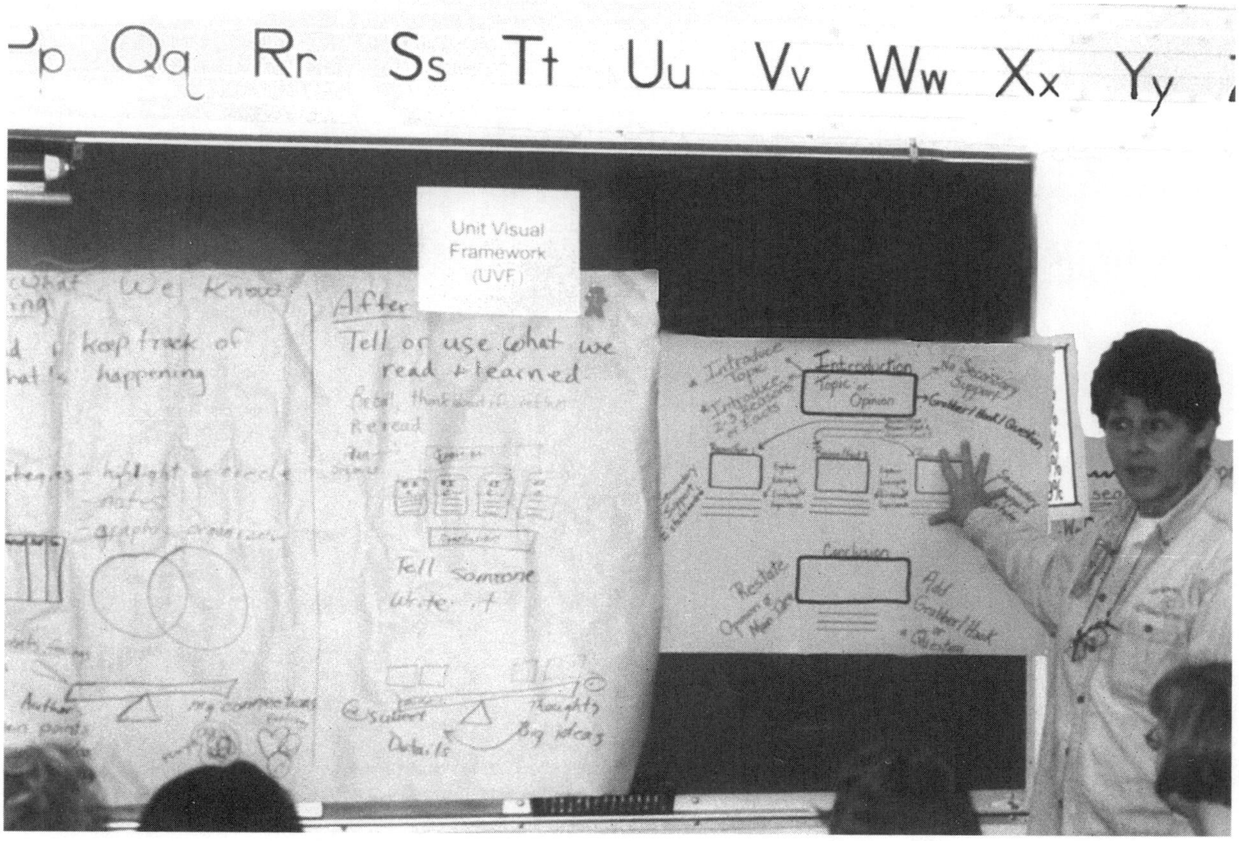

coding, key text, and illustrations on the checklist were very familiar to students from their work since Phase I of the unit, for they had seen them on their planners and on the UVF. Therefore, students needed to understand only how these were laid out on the page and how to use the checklist for meaningful assessment feedback. These are student plus/delta evaluations of the class sessions (+ = what worked well; ▲ = what could be improved) when they used the checklist:

▲ The checklist was a little confusing at first. It helped when you came around and helped us with them.

+ The example [simulation of its use] helped us know how to use the checklist better—we're not just checking it off now because they're our friend, we're thinking about how well we each did.

+ When we talk about why we checked it or didn't, it helps us understand and get better.

+ [After a second reading selection and use of the checklist,] I got better from doing it this time and it was easier.

Figure 5.13. Hannah explains connections

Figure 5.14. Self/Peer Checklist for Showing Reading Comprehension

Person who is listening _____

Person who is telling _____

☐ ☐ I/my partner kept the reading **focus** (answered the question)

I/my partner gave his or her own thoughts

☐★☐ My own words or **general** ideas about what was read

☐ ☐ Connections 🧠 😊 ❤ 🙁

☐ ☐ I/my partner supported his or her own thoughts with **specific** information from the reading (The person used **details** from the reading to draw a picture in my mind.)

☐ ☐ I/my partner **balanced** knowledge of the subject and his or her own thoughts.

Hindsight

Visual Consistency	Observations/Recommendations
Between Families Prereading Chart and the GVF/UVF • Color coding from the GVF carried through on the Families prior-knowledge chart generated by students • Excerpt from the Families chart written on the UVF to support the strategy description Among GVF, UVF, Planner, and Checklist • Color coding • Image for balance • Symbols for feeling/thought connections on planner and checklist • Drawing of the planner on the UVF and checklist • Image of two students talking/ sharing on the UVF to anchor the strategy and recall the use of the checklist	Teacher assumptions that visual consistency alone would allow students readily to use the tools made by teachers was proven wrong. • It would have been more effective to take the previously generated planner students had been using for writing and to elicit from students its application in the current context, incorporating the same type of visual consistencies the teacher used. • Students would also have had more comfort with the checklist's format if it had been developed *with* them— instead of *for* them—in keeping with UVF philosophy and effective assessment practices.

PORTABLE UVF

Because the unique scheduling of this unit's work resulted in my not being with the students on a daily basis, I prepared the portable UVF for them (Figure 5.15), rather than have the students make their own. When I gave them each a copy, I asked them to compare it with the class UVF (Figure 5.16). They noticed that a few of the experiences that had been orally reflected upon in the whole group were already recorded on the portable UVF. For this reason, and for those mentioned in the section on portable UVFs in previous chapters, the class broke into pairs or small groups (Figure 5.17). They assessed each other's ability to use the portable UVF and helped each other recall the experiences and related learning, as needed. The portable UVF was used in two ways in this unit: for students in their own work and as a tool for students and visitors on Guest Day.

Figure 5.15. Portable UVF

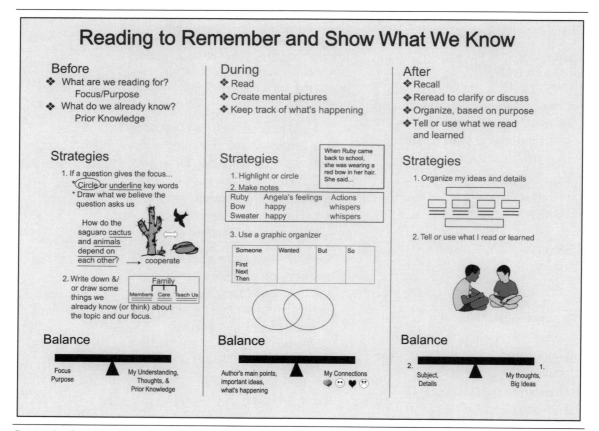

USING THE EXPANDED UVF TO DEMONSTRATE LEARNING

As one assessment of the instructional targets, we wanted students to compose a written piece that would demonstrate their learning of the reading comprehension rubric features and the science standards, but we wanted students to have a more meaningful purpose for writing than to hand it in to their teacher. We also wanted them to experience being able to "show what we know" to someone with whom *they* wanted to share their learning about elephants. Because we hadn't preplanned the unit, and therefore hadn't been able to begin with these types of authentic contexts for learning, we offered students a choice for the end of the unit. This context took us into Phase III of the unit.

Authentic Context

We asked students if they would like to invite guests to the classroom—parents, siblings, and/or friends—to share their learning about elephants.

Figure 5.16. Students compare portable and class UVFs

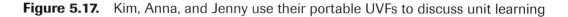

Figure 5.17. Kim, Anna, and Jenny use their portable UVFs to discuss unit learning

This possibility met with enthusiastic response, and the response became more enthusiastic as we unfolded our proposition. Each student would invite a guest to a Guest Day—actually about an hour and a half of an afternoon—that would celebrate the unit's learning. Some students extended invitations to more than one guest, because they had a hard time choosing between inviting a parent or friend.

The guests would play a board game about elephants with their host student. The players had to give information about elephants in order to move on the board. Before playing the game, students would (a) use their UVF portfolio to explain how they had learned about elephants and other unit targets, and (b) read their written piece containing information about elephants to their guests so that everyone would have some common information to play the game. Some Spanish-speaking students were relieved to realize that the game would be available bilingually, because they wanted to invite parents and friends who might be stronger speakers of Spanish than of English.

Elephant Game

As hosts of Guest Day, the students needed to understand the elephant game (Figure 5.18). The text and pictures of this teacher-made game prompted learning from across the reading selections read by the class, as well as knowledge learned from other sources. (Students had been encouraged to continue reading or discussing elephants outside of class, if they wished.) Students threw dice to see how many places they were to move, and then gave any elephant information they could that was related to the word or words on the rectangle where they landed. The object of the game was to traverse the board, and the game did not end until everyone had done so. One of the most important rules was that a person or team member could not repeat information that had been previously shared by someone else who had landed on the same spot.

For students to learn the game and its rules, we divided the class into five teams and put the game on an overhead transparency to play it as a class. When it was a particular team's turn to play, the team spokesperson for that turn was allowed to get help from teammates, if desired (Figure 5.19). Students very early in the game asked if the game rules permitted them to use their UVF portfolios, which they did.

UVF Brings Focus Back to the Whole Unit

Following this introduction to the game, we returned to the expanded UVF to recall the unit focus and where the game and other Guest Day events fit into that. As one student put it in his reflection later, "We had a good review of reading to show what we know, because some of us were forgetting." From our viewpoint, we didn't want students to get so caught up in the game that they

Figure 5.18. Elephant Game

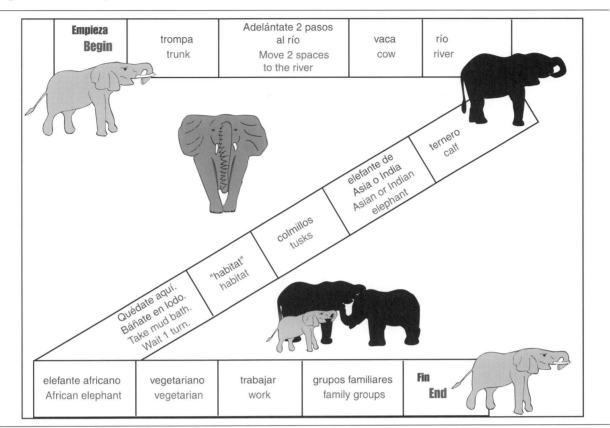

Figure 5.19. Teammates formulate game answer

forgot its purpose or the learning that it served. The game was one way of demonstrating learning after reading. Another way was their expository writing about elephants, which students were ready to begin now that they had knowledge of the game it would help their guests play.

Writing Task

The writing task would require students to integrate their knowledge of writing, the reading comprehension rubric features, and science generalizations using what they understood about elephants, so we used additional support visuals—some co-developed and some provided—consistent with previous visuals students had used. We put up the overhead transparency students had seen at the beginning of the unit showing one version of the writing process (Figure 5.20).

We then co-developed a version that reflected this unit's work and writing task, as well as previously established class writing procedures (Figure 5.21). In this task, consistent with their previous work in the unit, students would not be "selecting" their topic to write about; however, the topic was broad enough to allow student choices of content and varied response. All students were to write to the focus: "Many people think elephants are interesting. Use what you read/learned to tell why." Therefore, we wrote *focus question* by *select* on the writing process visual and discussed the implications of these different ways to begin writing. Similarly, we identified unit-specific tools and references for the rest of the labels on the writing process visual. Though we didn't put illustrations on the co-developed version of the writing process visual, students pointed to images on the UVF and held up their own copies of the various items, such as the planner and little checklist, to show they knew what the visual's text was referencing.

Writing Support: Science Standards GVF

To begin their writing process, students used the planner as they had done when sharing information from each selection read. This time, however, they would be showing their knowledge and interpretation of all the selections they had read, so their "big ideas" had to address the broader generalizations of the science standards. Therefore, students used a GVF for the science standards to help them plan and monitor the science content of their writing (Figure 5.22). Because they had not co-developed the GVF, as a class we read a selection on butterflies and used images from it to help students understand the GVF. We used butterflies because they were another animal-family topic, but not the one they were currently studying, so they all wouldn't end up writing the same thing based on our common work. We also orally elicited a couple of examples from the elephant study for each of the visual's concepts to ensure that students were making the transfer.

Figure 5.20. Global Writing Process Visual

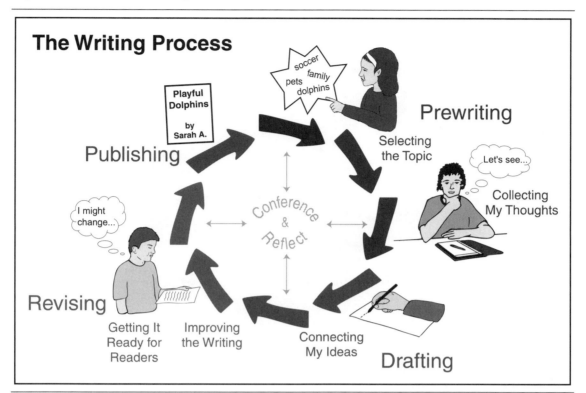

Figure 5.21. Writing Process Visual Co-Developed for the Unit

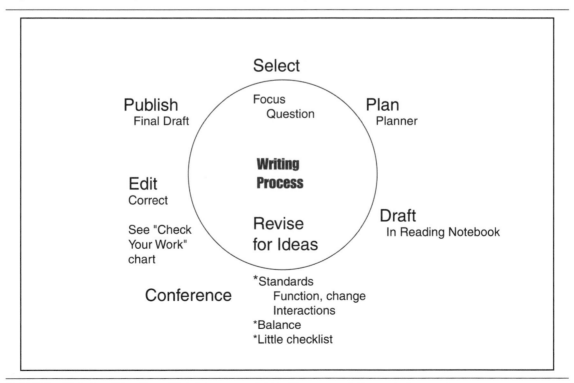

Figure 5.22. Science Standards GVF

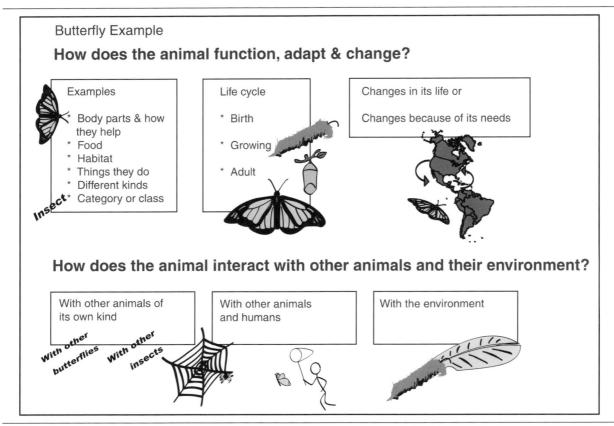

Butterfly Example

How does the animal function, adapt & change?

Examples
* Body parts & how they help
* Food
* Habitat
* Things they do
* Different kinds
* Category or class

Insect

Life cycle
* Birth
* Growing
* Adult

Changes in its life or

Changes because of its needs

How does the animal interact with other animals and their environment?

With other animals of its own kind

With other butterflies   With other insects

With other animals and humans

With the environment

Integrating Content: Adapted Core UVF

To monitor the writing's balance relative to the reading comprehension features, students used an adapted version of their original core UVF (Figure 5.23). This last version of the core UVF brought their unit full circle, and it illustrated the relationships of the disciplines making up the integrated unit.

Students used the writing process visual to follow and report their writing progress each day (Figure 5.24), saying where in the process they were currently working (such as using their planner to finish their first draft) and what their next steps were (revision, for example). In student-teacher conferences during the writing process, students used the supporting visuals to explain, for example, how their piece reflected the science standards and showed balance between knowledge of the articles and their own interpretations. Each of the visuals—the writing process visual, the science standards GVF, the adapted core UVF—was discussed as a part of the unit focus as it was attached to the expanding UVF (Figure 5.25). Here are student and classroom teacher thoughts after writing:

Figure 5.23. Class Core UVF Adapted for Task

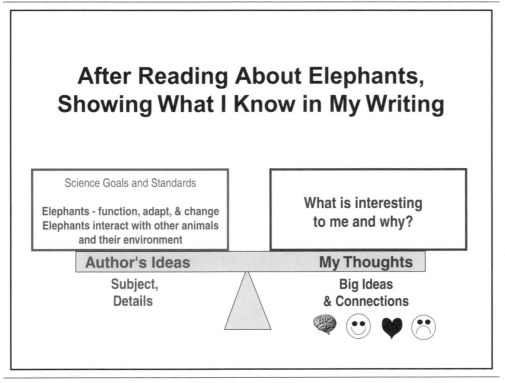

Figure 5.24. Kim tells where she is in the writing process

Figure 5.25. Danny and Olivia discuss and attach visual supports to the class UVF

Student: We had everything we needed: the planner, the UVF. . . .

Student: The science GVF helped me. I liked to check off what I did.

Student: [continuing from the previous one's comment]: Yes, and if I didn't find it, I added and I rechecked it three times.

Teacher: The adapted core UVF helped me know what I was looking for in student papers. I used it in my conferences with students and providing feedback.

Hindsight

Visual Consistency

In Elephant Game

    Images of elephants from Family Groups visual and reading selections

    Vocabulary, concepts, and scenarios on the game board used expressive and academic language from across reading selections and other unit materials

In Writing Process Support Visual

    Consistent process seen in global writing process visual

    Used terms specific to the unit evoking learning experiences, such as focus question, planner, and balance

    Referred to other specific support visuals they would use to complete the task

In the Adapted Core UVF, which made the original class GVF unit-specific

    Used the same images

    Used common text from the class GVF, the class UVF, and the science standards GVF

USING THE UVF PORTFOLIO FOR DEMONSTRATIONS TO GUESTS

When students went over the Guest Day procedure they would follow with guests (Figure 5.26), they had no trouble knowing what to do, because there were illustrations of the very items they had used all along as part of their expanded UVF and UVF portfolios. (Although we used a computer to produce the procedure represented in Figure 5.26, alternatives would have either been (a) to generate the procedure on chart paper for the whole class, putting copies of the actual items as placeholders, or (b) to see if a copier could reduce the items enough to do what was done via computer on this sheet.) Students' portable UVF, the game, their expository writing on elephants, and all the support visuals incorporated into the expanded UVF were in their UVF portfolio.

It was obvious that students and their guests enjoyed the afternoon. Their comments supported that impression:

Figure 5.26. Guest Day Procedure and Photos

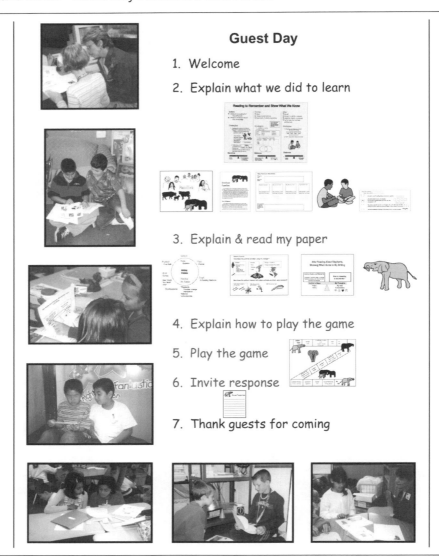

Student: I liked inviting my mom and my friend, and to see the expressions on their faces when they learned something.

Student: It was different; not work like reading and writing.

Student: I'm glad we did this. I would like to do it again.

Guest: Dan had a lot of fun explaining the project. I loved his elephant paper. We played the game twice.

Guest: It was fun to be with my brother and learn about elephants.

We also noticed the evidence we hoped to see: that students understood what they had done and had learned. Parent and student comments supported these observations:

Parent: It was very interesting when Hannah explained about the focus of the paper, big ideas, and strategies. The game then tested out our knowledge. I was used to seeing a web. I talked to Hannah about how different this process was—big ideas went further with details. Hannah mentioned the importance of balance of ideas and facts.

Parent: This was a clever way for children to learn. The best way for someone to learn is to teach it back to someone again, and then it was reinforced and tested with the game.

Student: I learned a lot. I understand it more by playing the game.

VISUAL CONSISTENCIES HELP STUDENT REFLECTION AND EVALUATION

This third-grade class doing the Reading to Remember unit was part of a school and district that measured student enthusiasm and perceptions of their learning. The instrument used was Jeffrey Burgard's (2000) survey, in which students rate the degree to which they liked what they did in a unit of study and how much they felt they learned from the unit.

Evaluating the Unit

Because Reading to Remember and Show What We Know was an integrated unit, we wanted student perceptions about each of the instructional targets, rather than a sweeping opinion of the whole. Figure 5.27 shows how we adapted Burgard's survey and illustrated it to elicit student feedback for each instructional area. The results of the student surveys are also shown.

Evaluating the Impact of the UVF

In addition to evaluating the unit, we wanted student perceptions of if and how their first-time use of UVFs had helped them. We had not used the term *expanded UVF*, so students were asked how the UVF "and other pictures" worked for them. We gave students a visual sampling of the expanded UVF for them to know what the question meant. Because we were running out of time, this was done on the same day as the student surveys. We, therefore, reduced the five-point qualitative scale to two choices because we wanted students to spend their time telling us more specifically how the UVF did or did not help them. It would have been more helpful, had we had additional time, to review once more all that the expanded UVF had entailed or to put it in the visual. Figure 5.28 is the evaluation with the numerical results of the student survey. Here are samples of their specific feedback on use of the UVF:

Figure 5.27. Class Evaluation of the Unit

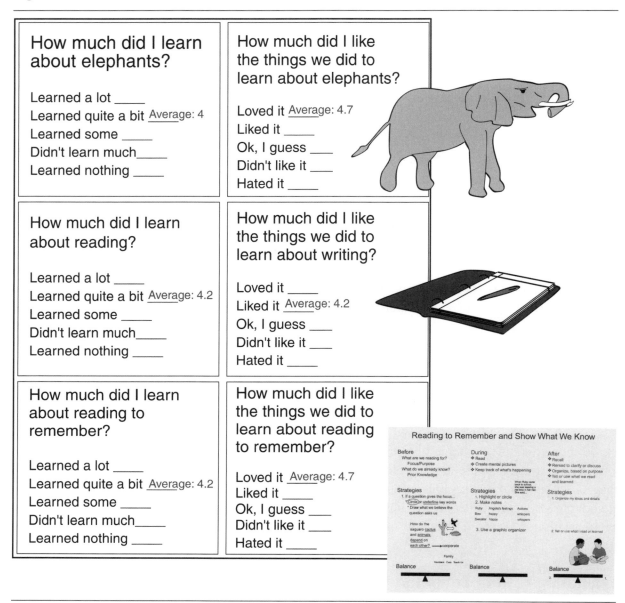

NOTE: Individual responses were averaged to yield the class evaluations.

Focus

I could look at it and see if I am on focus or not. That's what I liked.

Comprehension

It helped us comprehend more. I liked it because I make my connections more.

I would look at the pictures and it would make more sense to me.

I could look back and see what to do if I didn't know.

Thinking

> They would make me think. For example, I couldn't think of something about family groups, so I looked at some pictures.

> They were designed in an understanding way. They tell you useful information.

Communication

> It helped me to explain everything I was trying to tell.

Cumulative Learning

> It said what we learned, and if I forgot something it would tell me again, and when I learn something a second time, it usually sticks in my head and I don't forget it.

MAPPED LEARNING PATHS, RISK-TAKING SAFETY NET

I was delighted to see, both in their end of the day reflections and in their evaluations of the UVF, that students valued cumulative learning. Part of what made it cumulative was the repetition that students mentioned. I believe we often think that repetition will bore students, forgetting that research (Marzano, 2000, pp. 73–76) tells us it takes students approximately 24 practice sessions to have an 80% increase in learning.

The repetition in this unit was not repeating precisely what had been done before, but rather revisiting previous work, carrying it forward, and building on it. For example, students used the balance metaphor in more and more sophisticated ways:

1. For a general understanding of the comprehension features on the first teacher draft and class GVF

2. For more specific interpretation of the comprehension features for before, during, and after reading, as they noted in the three columns of the yellow UVF chart

3. To monitor their understanding and use of comprehension on their checklist in the jigsaw sharing

4. To integrate the reading, writing, and science parts of the unit on the adapted core UVF

Each time material was revisited, it was critical that students recognize previous work so they could use it in a different way. The middle school teacher's statement that opened this chapter—"When I review without a visual framework, students often think it's new material"—tells us that such recognition is not to be taken for granted. So why do UVFs make this

Figure 5.28. Student Evaluation of UVF Use

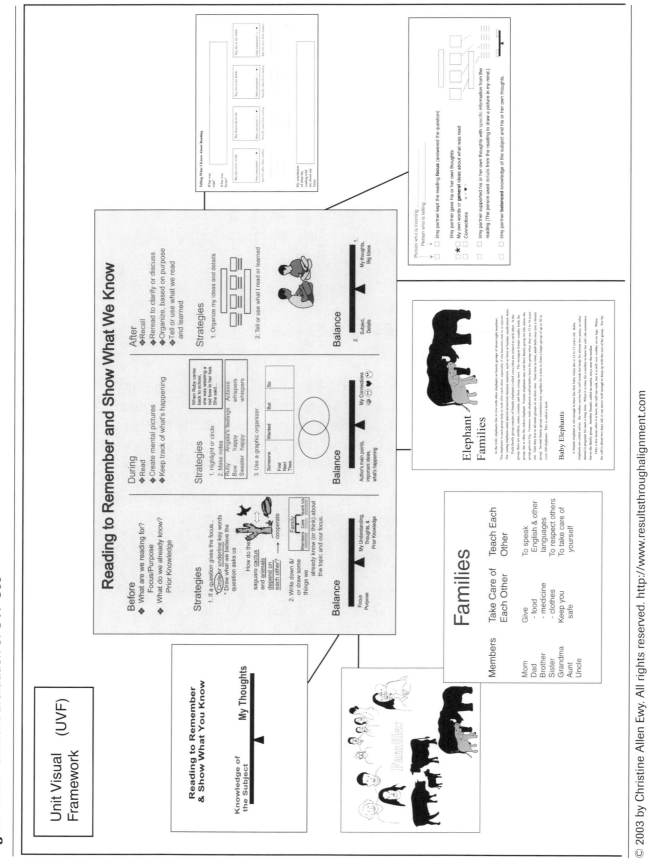

Figure 5.28. (Continued)

My Writing about Elephants

After Reading About Elephants, Showing What I Know in My Writing

Science Goals and Standards

Elephants - function, adapt, & change
Elephants interact with other animals and their environment

Author's Ideas

Subject, Details

What is interesting to me and why?

My Thoughts

Big Ideas & Connections

Butterfly Example

How does the animal function, adapt & change?

Examples
- Body parts & how they help
  - Food
  - Habitat
- Things they do
- Different kinds
- Category or class

Life cycle
- Birth
- Growing
- Adult

Changes in its life or
Changes because of its needs

How does the animal interact with other animals and their environment?

With other animals and humans

With other animals of its own kind

With the environment

Publish
Final Draft

Edit
Correct
See "Check Your Work" chart
Conference

Select
Focus
Question

Writing Process

Revise for Ideas
*Standards
Function, change
Interactions
*Balance
*Little checklist

Plan
Planner

Draft
In Reading Notebook

Please choose and finish the sentence:

I liked __23__ I didn't like __1__

the Unit Visual Framework (UVF) and other pictures ...

because _____

_____

_____

Please choose and finish the sentence:

The Unit Visual Framework (UVF) and other pictures ...

helped me learn __24__ didn't help __0__

because _____

_____

_____

_____

cumulative learning process obvious? We've seen in this chapter how visual consistency and overt linking make learning paths evident, creating both the kind of safety net students described in their evaluation comments and the kind of cohesion that results in cumulative learning.

Mapping Learning Paths

From the opening interactions with students in a unit of study, we begin a bank of experiences that, if visually captured and consistently represented to build on the previous one, optimizes learning. This reading comprehension unit first drew on previous stores of knowledge—the students' previous experience with balances in science. The bank of experiences grew as we elicited and related that prior knowledge to the new context visually, and we maintained and deepened the relationship thereafter through consistent images, color, text, and placement of an item on the page. Consistent images and color have been described elsewhere, so here I'd like to elaborate a little on the latter two, text and placement.

With each new support visual to assist next steps in the unit, we attempted to set up repeated images and text in ways similar to what students had previously seen and/or in the context in which it had been experienced. For instance, the cactus and illustrations anchoring a "Before" strategy on the yellow UVF chart were drawn with the cactus on the left, animals on the right, and arrow in between, just as we had done when we actually analyzed the test focus question with the saguaro selection. These illustrations and the repetition of the actual test prompt about the interdependence of the cactuses and desert animals brought us back to that experience of learning and applying the strategy. When evolution of understanding, or circumstances, required additions and/or adaptations from previous displays, we made overt links and comparisons so students saw the path we had taken and were able to follow.

Student and parent comments included throughout this chapter also attest to the value of consistency in the key text students worked with and recorded in their visual displays. "Focus," "balance," "my thoughts," "big ideas," "author's specific ideas," "details," and "connections" appeared over and over again in the many visuals that made up the expanded UVF, so they became part of students' repertoire.

In like manner, students achieved a command of content-specific terms about elephants (such as those used on the elephant game board) because of their consistent use in the reading selections, on their planners, in their writing, and on the game. Had the unit been preplanned and had the science standards come in earlier in the unit, the same degree of consistency could have occurred with the broader concepts and key text of the science standards.

In summary, when any of the support visuals became part of a new visual or tool, or when whole support visuals themselves were embedded as visual prompts on the Guest Day instruction sheet, student surveys, and UVF evaluation, students easily recognized the previous work first by color, then by illustrations and text. With each recognition, students became more capable of retracing their learning steps on a nonlinear but displayed path, recalling rich experiences and applying prior knowledge to the current situation, with the effect of cumulative learning.

Risk-Taking Safety Net

When I reflect on this unit from a curriculum, instruction, and assessment viewpoint, I am reminded of the coach reflecting on "an ugly win." In the interest of planning for improvement, I acknowledge the weaknesses that occurred. On the other hand, like that coach, I know that some units happen in the same serendipitous way this one did, and I key in on the strengths that made it "a win." The build-as-you-go nature of this sample unit, and the mass of visual supports that helped students work through it, may have lost or overwhelmed students if visual consistencies had not been present all along the way. Instead, the high student satisfaction and enthusiasm, as well as the number of students who felt they learned from and liked the use of the expanded UVF, spoke volumes about the cohesion that occurred. It seems to me, then, that adhering to UVF principles created a safety net that supported the students *and* teachers to take the risks they did in this unit.

CONSISTENCY IN INTEGRATED UNITS

To expand on and illustrate the information provided in Chapter 3 about UVFs in integrated units, there is one last hindsight for this unit.

The driving force of the integrated unit Reading to Remember and Show What We Know was to know *how* to communicate or *demonstrate* their learning across content areas in ways that their audiences or assessors would recognize, specifically by communicating comprehension using the reading rubric features. Opening teaching/learning events made that broad application of the language arts goal the focus by eliciting student experiences when they wanted to "show what they knew" and by the comparison of the reading comprehension features to the way students would demonstrate comprehension in writing and math. Phases II and III of the unit reinforced that focus by employing the comprehension features in science material and expository writing. Therefore, Figure 5.29 would have been a more accurate rendering of the unit's focus and development than the actual expanded UVF that evolved and that is partially shown in Figure 5.28.

As we look at the classroom photos throughout this chapter, or the abbreviated version of the expanded UVF shown in Figure 5.28, it is clear that the central visual ended up being the one showing comprehension within each stage of the reading process—the yellow chart entitled *Reading to Remember and Show What We Know.* This yellow chart became the portable UVF and was

Figure 5.29. Unit Organized for Consistent Focus Across Disciplines

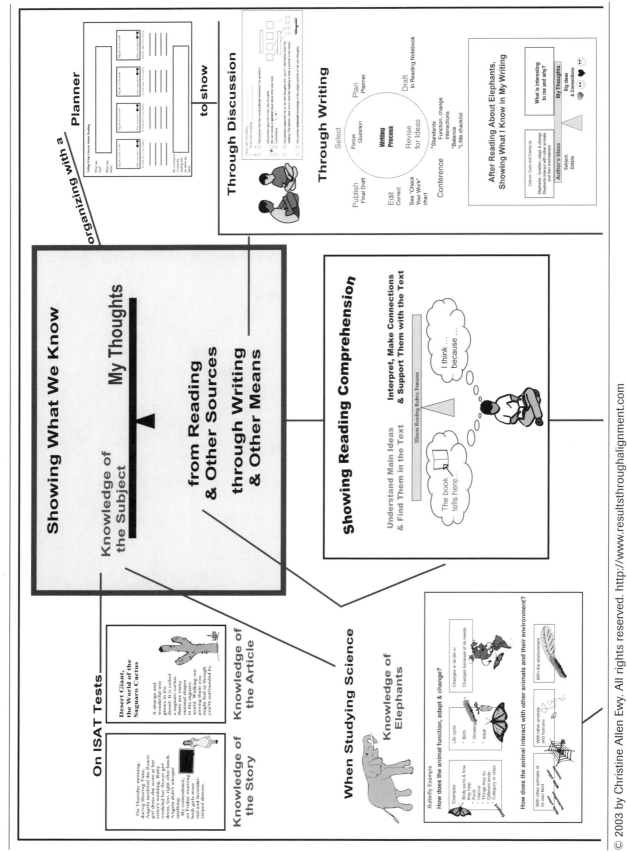

Figure 5.29. (Continued)

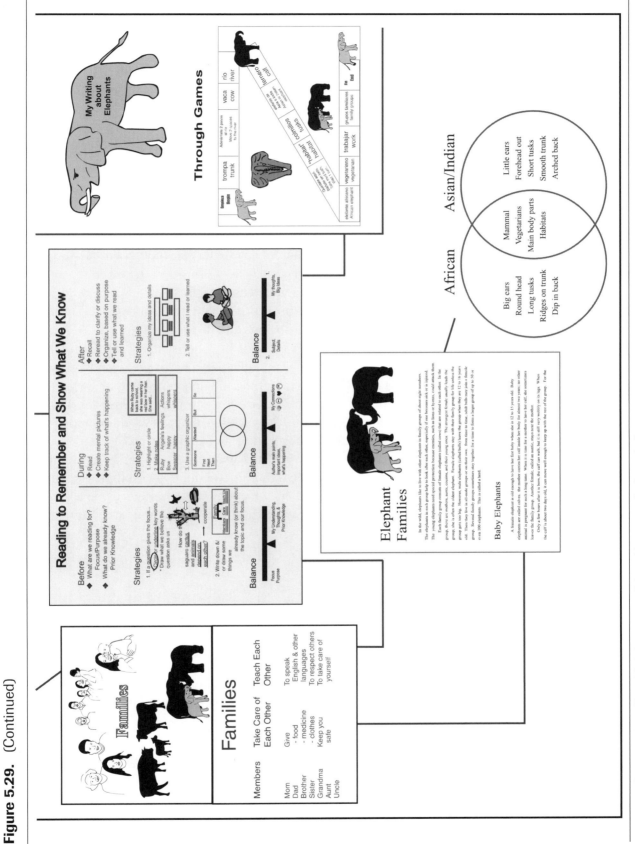

also used to organize all of the support visuals and artifacts to show learning paths and document unit work and learning. So, although the focus was *communicating comprehension* from multiple sources and in several contexts through the reading rubric features, the *reading process* took center stage in the class display and use.

Integration in a Self-Contained Classroom

The organization of the expanded UVF in this case study worked for that class and served similar purposes as Figure 5.29 for two reasons. First, the teacher and student group remained together the whole time (unlike in team teaching, where students form different groups for each content area); second, the class consistently carried the rubric features through their unit.

However, there are two important reasons why Figure 5.29 would have helped this class more readily use the unit's learning in future work. First, the ISAT and science applications are obvious and distinct in Figure 5.29. Hence, when students prepared for other types of ISAT tests, such as their math or writing assessments, or when they studied other content areas, such as social studies or art, they could know where those fit, enabling them to use all they had built in this unit. Second, the organization of Figure 5.29 makes it easier to display broad applications and future learning about how one demonstrates knowledge. Because it sets up categories of application, this UVF encourages the class in the future to expand the list of ways through which they demonstrate their knowledge and their own thoughts about it—a list that is helpful to English language learners and others who might need options when a specific method of demonstration prevents the actual student knowledge from being shared.

Integration in a Departmentalized Situation

Although the way Figure 5.29 is organized might have been an option for the class who did this unit, it is more of a necessity for students in other forms of team teaching with integrated units. If this unit had been co-taught by multiple teachers, the consistency discussed in this chapter would need to be recognizable from class to class. Therefore, the team of teachers would agree on a draft—or the actual—core UVF, such as Figure 5.30.

That last sentence said that teachers "agree on the draft or the actual core UVF." What happened to co-development? The starting point of co-development will be determined by the variables of the teaching and learning situation. One situation might be where a group of students stay together in what we'll call a cohort group, but go to different teachers for each subject area. For this sort of class, co-development occurs from the beginning.

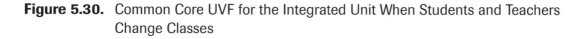

Figure 5.30. Common Core UVF for the Integrated Unit When Students and Teachers Change Classes

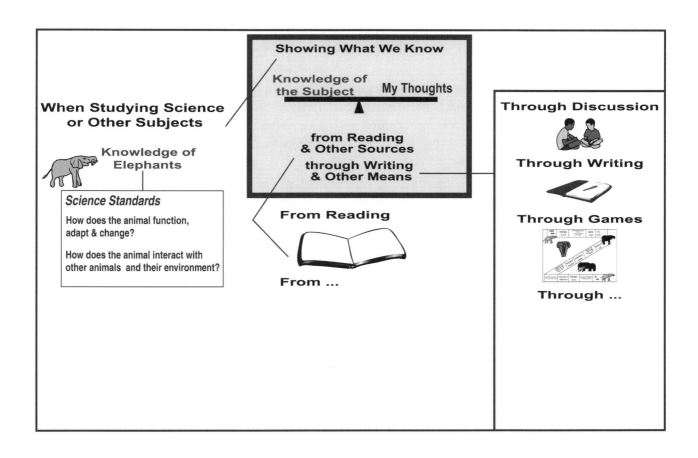

Students could co-develop their core UVF in one class and expand it differently with the respective teacher in each of the content classes they attend.

Another teaching/learning situation is where kids are with different peers in each subject area. In this case, the only constant is that all students study the same content areas, for which their teachers have planned as a team. In such a case, if one core UVF (such as the one in Figure 5. 30) was developed for all classes, either by teachers or by a group of students and teachers, then the common elements of the unit would be more consistently recognizable from one content area class to another. Co-development in this case would begin with the elicitation in each class of student prior knowledge related to the core UVF and/ or with concrete experiences to engage student ownership as they personalized and internalized the core UVF. After that, the expanded UVF would be unique in each class, but organized around consistent, recognizable elements that are taught and assessed in each content area sharing the integrated unit.

CAUTIONS ABOUT GENERALIZATIONS FROM THE CHAPTER'S CASE STUDY

The many support visuals in this unit were included in this chapter to emphasize their consistent characteristics, not their number. Some readers may wonder if it is necessary to have such comprehensive use of visuals if one wants to use UVFs. The answer is an unequivocal "No." Were the unit preplanned or retaught, the number would likely change, as would the unit itself. In addition, had I been the classroom teacher with the students everyday, instead of a visiting teacher with some time in between class visits to generate computer graphics, the visual supports would likely have been fewer and more classroom-generated.

To some readers, the number of visual supports may seem excessive or overwhelming. Personally, when viewing what I perceive to be a lot of information about something that is new to me, I sometimes have a tendency to get overwhelmed. In fact, at times I feel it's more than I can or want to take on, even when I find it interesting, because I think that others have already done it well beyond my own capabilities and maybe I should just put my energies elsewhere. I hope that any reader who is having similar tendencies after reading this or other chapters will pause and remember the middle school student quoted at the beginning of this book. She was amazed at all she, her peers, and her teacher had generated in their unit of study. She wasn't overwhelmed, but rather proud because she had been part of generating it. The number of visual supports in this unit may tend to overwhelm because the reader was not a part of generating the unit, and one is often surprised by the mass of work that occurs in one unit when it is visually documented—which is one function of an expanded UVF.

One reason so many visuals resulted from this unit was that the primary focus of the unit was more on process skills than content material; many of the visuals emerged as an aid to internalizing one or more process. Fortunately, the time spent generating and learning to use these visuals will pay off, because they may be used repeatedly in the future *by these students* who had input into creating them and who can reapply and improve on them if supported in doing so. The core UVF in context (the yellow chart and its portable version) summarizes the use of the reading features in the reading process. The self/peer checklist students used is a precursor for students' using the actual four-point reading response rubric to monitor their communication of comprehension. When students get to that four-point scale, it will have been backed up by experiences, examples, and visuals that will give meaning to the rubric features and descriptors. The writing process and planner graphic organizers integrated previous writing work with the reading rubric features for future application. The science standards GVF can serve more substantive science study where content is the primary focus, just as it served this more limited inclusion of science material. Students may even recycle the elephant game by substituting concepts and illustrations of other content for as long as they find it fun and useful.

Though acknowledging the long-term value of the multiple visuals in this unit, I invoke again the "honest and possible" mantra, suggesting that a draft core UVF is all that is necessary to begin. The rest will occur naturally in ways that serve the particular teacher and students using it, just as each support visual seen in this chapter emerged because of a felt need during the unit's evolution. During this natural evolution, visual consistency across all materials and active co-development will strengthen cohesion.

Chapter Five
Visual Summary

Building Cohesion
Through Visual Consistency

The core UVF organizes the rest

Example: The core UVF — reading comprehension features shown in the context of reading stages — organized and connected everything else.

Images, text, colors, & placement repeat

Example: These symbols and concepts transferred meaning from GVF to UVF, planner, & checklist.

Example: The portable UVF was printed on yellow to be a recognizable copy of the class core UVF.

Visual Consistency

** recalls whole experiences*

Example: Cactus pictures, drawn as previously seen, recalled the saguaro selection & its related strategies.

** allows scaffolding & assists*
cumulative recognition & learning

Example: The repeated "balance" metaphor of comprehension features later united science, writing, and reading in the adapted UVF.

Example: The consistently color-coded graphic organizer/planner connected oral, written, and reading skills.

Example: Miniature pictures of the UVF and support visuals on guest day directions and student surveys helped students use learning for the metacognitive purposes of reflection & evaluation.

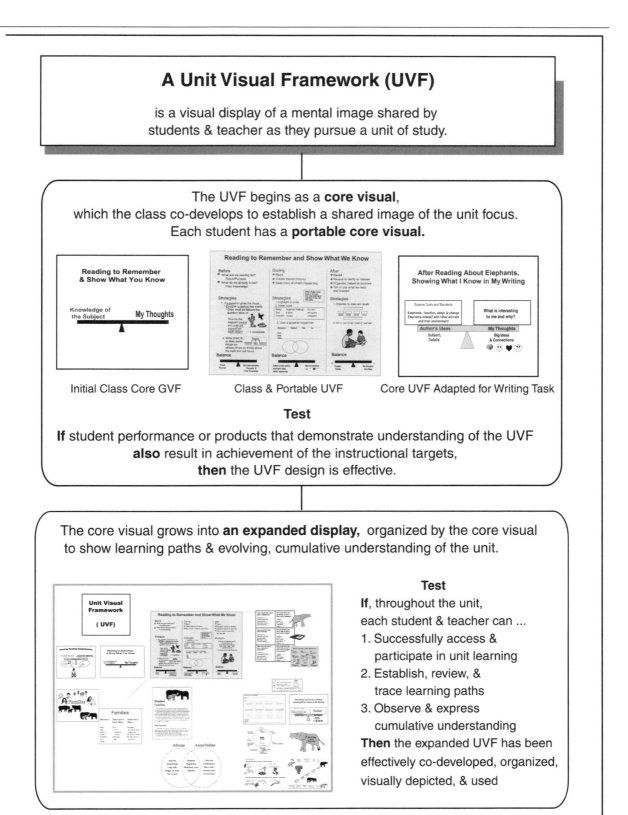

A Unit Visual Framework (UVF)

is a visual display of a mental image shared by
students & teacher as they pursue a unit of study.

The UVF begins as a **core visual**,
which the class co-develops to establish a shared image of the unit focus.
Each student has a **portable core visual.**

Initial Class Core GVF   Class & Portable UVF   Core UVF Adapted for Writing Task

Test

If student performance or products that demonstrate understanding of the UVF
also result in achievement of the instructional targets,
then the UVF design is effective.

The core visual grows into **an expanded display,** organized by the core visual
to show learning paths & evolving, cumulative understanding of the unit.

Test

If, throughout the unit,
each student & teacher can ...
1. Successfully access &
   participate in unit learning
2. Establish, review, &
   trace learning paths
3. Observe & express
   cumulative understanding
Then the expanded UVF has been
effectively co-developed, organized,
visually depicted, & used

A Teacher's Story 6

Moving From Beginning to Experienced Use of UVFs

> *I cannot NOT do this anymore—I've seen immediate results. Making the concepts visual helped me see the big picture. I also saw student learning of the facts and big ideas, and their enthusiasm at being part of the process and empowered to make decisions.*
>
> —Ginger Benning, Sixth-Grade Teacher

Thus far, this book has mostly provided information needed to understand and begin using Unit Visual Frameworks: what they are, how they work, their impact on learning, the teacher's and students' roles, and so on. In fact, Chapter 3 approached getting started from the informational viewpoint of "how to"—"How do I design and prepare to co-develop UVFs with my students?" Chapters 4 and 5 elaborated with details about how teaching with UVFs looked in a couple of different situations and why.

We can now examine the teaching and staff development viewpoints of beginning and integrating UVFs into our practice. A sixth-grade Illinois teacher, Ginger Benning, adds her voice to mine as a primary source of that viewpoint. Ginger compares her experiences of teaching an Earth science unit multiple times—once without and twice with UVFs—to different students over the course of a year. She also mentions insights from co-developing UVFs with her students in a social sciences unit. We will note adjustments she made to her teaching each time and examine her experience of the learning curve that comes with implementing an innovation. Ginger will also connect her understanding of teaching with UVFs to some of her other professional growth interests and experiences. Details about the units will be limited to those needed to understand Ginger's experiences and insights with multiple uses of the innovation.

Though not the primary focus, information about teaching with UVFs will be offered as a by-product of examining this teacher's experiences. Areas that will be introduced or reinforced as we witness co-development with older learners will include

- Teacher guidance in co-development
- Students making their own portable UVFs
- Productive home/school connections through portable UVFs
- Assessment when teaching with UVFs

GETTING STARTED

Ginger Benning has a homeroom in a K–6 school. She also teaches science to the rest of the sixth-grade students on a rotating basis. She meets with one group of sixth graders twice a week for the duration of a unit, and then another group begins the same unit with her.

After an informal conversation and having read drafts of the first five chapters of this book, Ginger decided to implement teaching with UVFs. I asked her to choose a unit that she had already taught so that she could learn about UVFs and how to use them to teach cohesively without the added strain of designing a whole new unit.

Her situation of teaching the same science unit to different students until she had taught all sixth graders seemed an ideal situation in which to learn about teaching with UVFs. When she decided to begin UVF implementation, Ginger had already taught the unit once to her homeroom students, and was about to begin with a new group of students.

To support Ginger, I had approximately three two-hour meetings with her each time she taught the unit to assist her planning, implementation, and reflection of teaching with UVFs. I also typed notes from those sessions for each of us to follow, provided related resources when appropriate, and was in phone contact on an as-needed basis.

Knowledge of the Unit

The majority of our first meeting was spent ensuring that Ginger and I both had a clear conceptualization of the unit. We followed the flow chart familiar to you from Chapter 3 and shown as Figure 6.1.

Ginger described her students and walked me through her Earth science unit to give me a feel for her plans. She had a packet for me with her written objectives, a list of key vocabulary, and other materials. I posed questions like

Figure 6.1.   Getting Started With UVFs

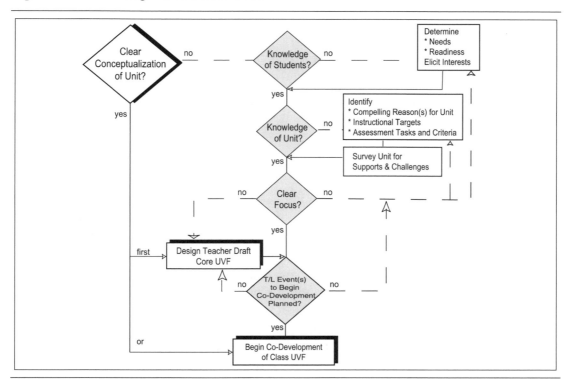

those suggested in Figure 3.2 to identify overtly the state goals and standards, local outcomes, and compelling reason or reasons she had for this study.

I inquired about the way individuals would be assessed and the assessment criteria that would be used. I probed for the clarity Ginger and her students would need to make sure UVF co-development helped them meet their goals. We looked at pre-, post-, and ongoing assessment and alignment among the goals, activities, and assessments to ensure that UVF development would help that flow and give students and teacher the results they wanted.

Last, we generated a few rough sketches of the contents of a UVF, but didn't format them into a teacher draft. Instead we spent the little remaining time brainstorming how UVF co-development might be begun with students.

In order for you to understand Ginger's reflections about this beginning, here is a brief synopsis of the Earth science unit as planned during that session:

Science Goal: Understand the fundamental concepts, principles, and interconnections of the life, physical, and Earth/space sciences.

Standard: Know and apply concepts that describe the features and process of the Earth and its resources.

Key Concept: The Earth is a system.

Guiding Questions:

- What are the layers of the Earth?
- What are the characteristics of each?
- What interactions occur?
- What are results of the interactions?
- What does any of this have to do with you in your life?

Ginger's Initial Thoughts

Before Teaching With UVFs

The first time that I taught this unit, in the fall, it was disjointed. I had ten different activities that the students did at stations. Two or three students worked in a group and worked at one station each day for ten days. At the completion of the ten activities, I gave them a grade based on one hundred points, with each activity being worth ten points. The other assessment was the test.

The students enjoyed working on the activities. They liked the freedom and my ability to work with each group individually. I knew that even though the activities were engaging, the information was not connected. We never once talked about a system. I had no guiding questions. I, as the teacher, knew the facts that I wanted the students to know; however, I did not have in my mind the focus or the enduring concepts that I wanted to convey to the students. Although the students did well on the test, which asked for facts, there was no evidence of a deeper understanding or a connection with their own lives.

Some Ideas That Appealed to Me About UVFs

One of the things that made me know that the UVF was something I wanted to do in my classroom was Christine's statement that "you can see where you are, where you've been, and where you are going in a unit of study at any given time." Indeed, major attractions for me were the UVF's visual aspect, the promise of keeping me focused, the emphasis on co-development with students, and the organic nature of the process.

Planning My First Use of UVFs

After meeting with Christine, I knew that I was missing the unit's deeper understandings and was not connecting the information with each child's own life. Although I had all the facts for Christine to see, it was obvious to me that I was not clear on why I was teaching what I was teaching. In fact, my first meeting with Christine both made me uncomfortable and challenged me. It is very difficult to have someone ask you simple questions that you cannot answer clearly. "Why is this important?" The only answer I could give her at the time was that I have to teach this unit.

Although I felt uncomfortable, I also felt challenged. Maybe Christine would be the person who could push me to begin teaching enduring concepts rather than just facts. I had spent five days at a Differentiated Workshop in Virginia the summer before we met. Christine was asking me the same questions that Carol Tomlinson had asked to a lecture hall full of 150 people. I had understood the questions, but hadn't been sure how to get to the answers. I wanted to make sure I was teaching curriculum that supported the state standards and allowed students to go deeper into a unit of study. So, the journey began.

After two hours of Christine asking questions, looking at our district and state curriculum, and asking more questions, she helped me to develop five guiding questions that would focus me throughout the unit. Although the questions changed somewhat during the months we have worked together, the idea of having questions that repeatedly are asked of students has helped me tremendously. It is very difficult to write the guiding questions, but I found them very valuable throughout the unit. I also thought that teaching with UVFs would make people less afraid of standards: If they are like me, they'll see that standards are not extra work, but are useful aids.

In our first planning meeting, Christine had assisted with a very important piece in my teaching—before I even began to understand the UVF. I realized that Christine's creation of the UVF is actually *a way* of teaching. Before a UVF can be created, a teacher needs to be clear on the focus of the unit. Once the teacher is clear on the focus—not just the facts—the UVF can be co-created with the students. It gives the teacher the freedom to allow the unit to become somewhat "messy" because the focus is the anchor.

The written notes Christine sent after our meeting helped me follow through. They reminded me of what we had discussed, decisions we had made, and planned next steps that I wouldn't have necessarily remembered because I had been concentrating more on Christine's and my questions during our meeting than on taking notes.

THREE UNITS, THREE STUDENT GROUPS, THREE UVFs, AND VARIATIONS ON CO-DEVELOPMENT

First Co-Development of a UVF

Ginger's opening teaching/learning events followed the steps of co-development seen in Figure 4.1, reprinted in this chapter as Figure 6.2.

Figure 6.2.   Co-Development of a Class UVF

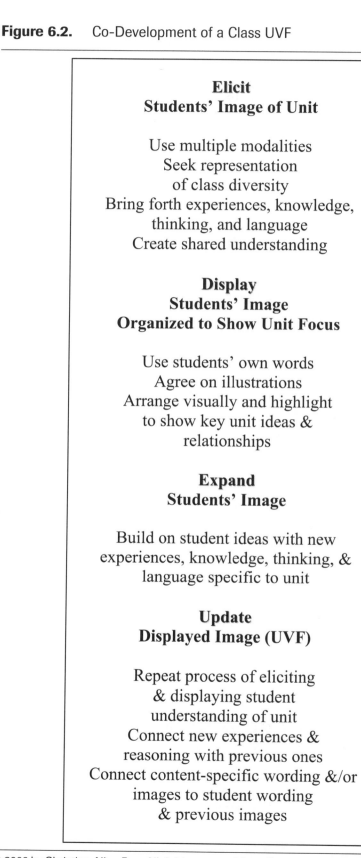

**Elicit
Students' Image of Unit**

Use multiple modalities
Seek representation
of class diversity
Bring forth experiences, knowledge,
thinking, and language
Create shared understanding

**Display
Students' Image
Organized to Show Unit Focus**

Use students' own words
Agree on illustrations
Arrange visually and highlight
to show key unit ideas &
relationships

**Expand
Students' Image**

Build on student ideas with new
experiences, knowledge, thinking, &
language specific to unit

**Update
Displayed Image (UVF)**

Repeat process of eliciting
& displaying student
understanding of unit
Connect new experiences &
reasoning with previous ones
Connect content-specific wording &/or
images to student wording
& previous images

Elicit Students' Image of Unit

Ginger invited student knowledge about systems. They brainstormed several examples, such as a computer, and defined a system as "parts that come together as a whole." Ginger also asked students to do two preassessments:

1. Answer the five guiding questions brainstormed in our first meeting about the layers of the Earth: (a) What are their names? (b) What are their characteristics? (c) How do they interact? (d) What are the results of their interactions? (e) How do they connect with the student's life?

2. Do an individual word sort with unit vocabulary by cutting the words and pasting them on a sheet of construction paper to document their sorts.

Display Student Image Organized to Show Unit Focus

Ginger enlisted her class's help in creating a visual for the unit, comparing the "visual" to a logo to let students know that it was to be more graphic than textual. She asked students each to draw a visual, and they put some drawings on the white board in front of the classroom.

Through discussion and students volunteering to write and draw, the class synthesized individual visuals into a beginning core UVF on chart paper in front of the class. This resulted in a visual model of the Earth and its layers. The students also listed their five assessment questions on the chart as guides for discussion and further learning about the Earth's layers.

Expand Students' Image

With the unit context established and displayed, the topic of plate tectonics was introduced through a cut-and-paste activity and reading from their science text.

Update UVF

The finished product from the cut-and-paste plate tectonics activity was added to the core UVF, with a "plate tectonics" label below it and labels for the ring of fire, mid-ocean ridge, Himalayan Mountains, and Andes Mountains in representative colors, such as brown for mountains and red for ring of fire. Students added the caption, "The Earth is like a puzzle" (later revisited and changed to "The Earth's crust is like a puzzle") and noted "20/7" as a reminder of information about the number of plates on the Earth.

The above teaching and learning experiences occurred in the first three hours of work in the unit. Throughout the rest of the unit, the UVF was revisited each day at least once at the beginning or end of class. Ginger and her students converted the initial chart-paper UVF to a bulletin board in order to make it more manageable and expandable. This new arrangement also

Figure 6.3. Class UVF: First Time Teaching With UVFs

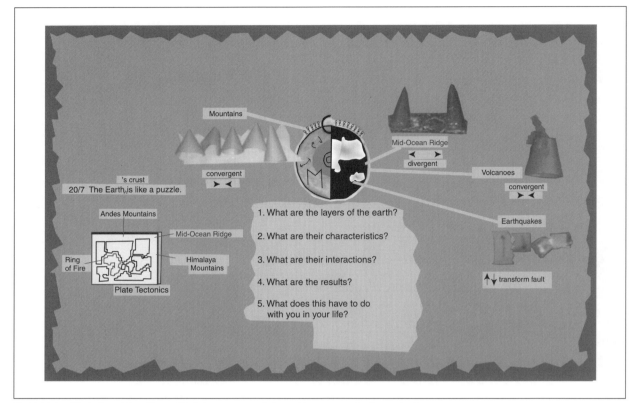

allowed for the centering of concepts for expansion. A third benefit from locating the UVF on the bulletin board was that it gave students the ability to include three-dimensional graphics of such things as the mountains, mid-ocean ridge, and volcano seen in Figure 6.3.

Ginger's Thoughts and Practices After the First Unit

There was an enthusiastic student response to co-developing the UVF. Students in this unit were eager to go up and write and draw on the UVF, including ESL students because they could do it. As students talked with each other about their representations of the content, they helped each other understand. This decreased the need for ESL students to ask basic questions or be left out, because here they had to interact as part of the process. Furthermore, my homeroom students, who had studied the unit without using a UVF, thought the UVF was "cool" when they saw it.

I was also pleased with what occurred. I searched for more connections with students' lives. One student interviewed parents who witnessed the eruption of Mt. Saint Helens in Washington. An ESL student shared experiences about an earthquake in California. Students were allowed to choose related topics they wanted to pursue, because the UVF provided a way to tie those topics back to the core. This confirmed my realization that once I identified my focus and how it would be applied/assessed, I could differentiate instruction for my students' individual needs.

I found what Christine says in Chapter 2 to be true: "A UVF enables divergent thinking and learning experiences to occur without getting lost in activities, life happenings, or the passage of time." Students came to me for science instruction only twice a week. Because there was a five-day passage of time between their Thursday and Tuesday meetings, I felt that the UVF helped the class a lot by making my normal use of review at the beginning of each day's work easier. The UVF also made it visually easier for students to infer, predict, and hypothesize.

I liked the freedom combined with focus: I could go in the directions students went, and the UVF gave a central way to help pull it back together. In fact, it even helped when I had a substitute. When I returned, I just pulled the unit ideas back together with the UVF; we picked up with the unit.

Wanting to pull the unit and the class together forced some rethinking about my planned teaching/learning events. Instead of having ten different activities, like I had the last time I taught the unit, I decided to have only two related activities going on at any given time. That way, within two days, students could debrief and update the class UVF and be on the same topic at the same time.

Second Co-Development of a UVF

Ginger began a social studies unit on Mesopotamia with her homeroom before her UVF-based Earth science unit was complete. Though our work together was mostly centered on the science unit, she decided to teach the social studies unit with UVFs as well. The reason she gave was, "I cannot *not* do this anymore." Teaching with UVFs had become part of her practice. Here are some of her thoughts about this second use of UVFs in her teaching.

My Second Time Using UVFs

I found that every time I read in Christine's book that it is a messy process, I was more comfortable. I felt I was in the middle of a mess that seemed to be working. However, I wasn't always sure I was working with the UVF the "right way." I kept seeing mistakes I'd made. I was glad that in Christine's book she kept reinforcing the idea that it was a process.

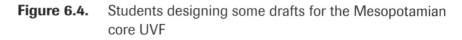

Figure 6.4. Students designing some drafts for the Mesopotamian core UVF

The first time, I was a little nervous about giving the students the power to design the core UVF; the second time, I wasn't (see Figure 6.4 to see students creating drafts in preparation for reaching consensus on a class UVF). With the Mesopotamian UVF, I felt I questioned students better by having them justify the illustrations they wanted to include based on what was important in the core UVF. For example, students were enthusiastic about building and posting a three-dimensional construction of the hanging gardens of Babylon. However, through discussion, they included this representation as part of the expanded UVF, but not in the core because it was interesting and part of their learning, but not essential. When students wanted to include pictures of palm trees in the core UVF, I told them they had to first find

Figure 6.5. Early Class UVF for the Mesopotamian Unit

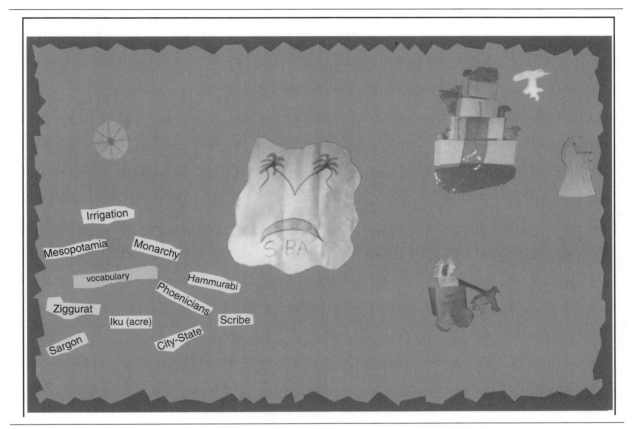

evidence that palm trees belonged there. Students, therefore, went to the three resource books in the classroom and found the evidence that the Mesopotamian area was fertile land, and the illustrations were included. In this second unit, we also put the key vocabulary in a corner of the UVF as a sort of bank ready to be moved and used as labels as the unit concepts developed (see Figure 6.5).

When students made their portable UVFs, they wanted to know the "right way," too, so I asked them, "What does the way you've done it say to you?" If their explanation showed understanding of the unit, I confirmed that their plans or drafts were quite appropriate.

I could tell that students responded positively to the UVF. They liked creating it. They were engaged. They felt it was helpful in remembering information. Therefore, some UVF practices carried into the rest of the day. I had been color coding the UVF, and went on to color code vocabulary word cards they used. I even noticed some of my students using visuals more often on their own outside the unit. We began adding visuals to the vocabulary for our reading and writing bank to help us remember them.

Third Co-Development of a UVF

Ginger made several changes in planning and teaching with UVFs as she led a third group of students through the Earth science unit using UVFs.

Changes During Planning:
Content, Format, and Teacher Draft

Ginger wanted to bring her class to a level of generalization about systems in studying the Earth science unit, because she knew systems to be the basis of other units that were to come. She felt she hadn't done that in her previous uses of UVFs because, as she explained, "I was so busy working on understanding how to create the UVF that I moved away from the original idea of the Earth being a system. I did not even realize I did that." With this new class, Ginger also wanted to consider other types of format for UVF design: "I found myself following the basic graphic organizer of a web for both the Earth science unit and the Mesopotamia unit. I knew I needed to branch out into a more organic UVF that really traced our learning path."

She chose to generate a teacher draft for the first time in order to think through teaching about Earth as an example of a system, as well as to play with different formats. Ginger realized that she was gaining deeper understanding of the unit content herself, along with the students, each time a different class co-developed the UVF.

Changes During Co-Development

Ginger adapted the word sort she had used in previous units as one means of eliciting prior knowledge from students. This time, she asked students not only to sort, but also to give a rationale for the groupings they chose. Some students wrote out a reason, others named each group they made, and others used visuals to show their reasoning by drawing a volcano, for example, and putting all words related to it inside. Ginger talks about the advantages and disadvantages to her adaptation:

> I was beginning to really understand the importance of the preassessment and the postassessment. Although I knew that preassessment was essential, I could honestly say that I didn't always take the time to preassess.
>
> The problem I was having then was that I was trying to teach the unit in sixteen lessons. By spending more time on the preassessments and the sharing of the UVFs, I was not "covering" as much information. However, I was certain that it would help me cover what was essential rather than just the facts.

The "sharing of the UVFs" was another adaptation Ginger made in her way of co-developing the UVF. Students did more individual work before doing a class UVF this time. As they began learning, each student drew an individual

Figure 6.6. Earth Science Class and Portable UVFs

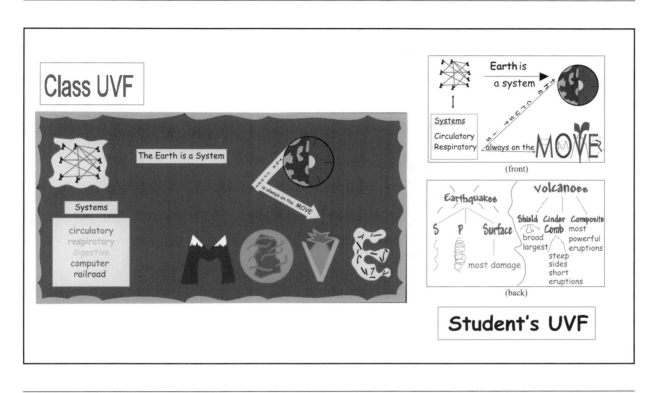

UVF, then viewed each other's, revised their own, and discussed the UVFs. They were, in essence, drafting portable UVFs, and they needed only to reach consensus on accurate representations of the class material. (See Figure 6.6 for comparison of the core class UVF and a student portable UVF.) As a result, Ginger noticed a difference in ownership and flow of co-development:

> The first time I taught with the UVF, I felt the UVF should be somewhat complete before I taught too much information. I am now feeling more freedom in the UVF actually being a visual representation of the students' and my learning path. In addition, because students are forming their own thoughts related to the content and their drawings, I am less apt to lead them in preconceived directions than I had been with previous classes who worked on the class UVF earlier in the unit and more as a whole group.

With greater student ownership and teacher leadership based on clear intent, students got deeper into the content material when they debated the merit of their drawings. For example, Ginger invented an acronym for some of the results of plate tectonics, *MOVE*, which stood for "Mountains, Mid-Ocean

Figure 6.7. Student Draft of Class UVF

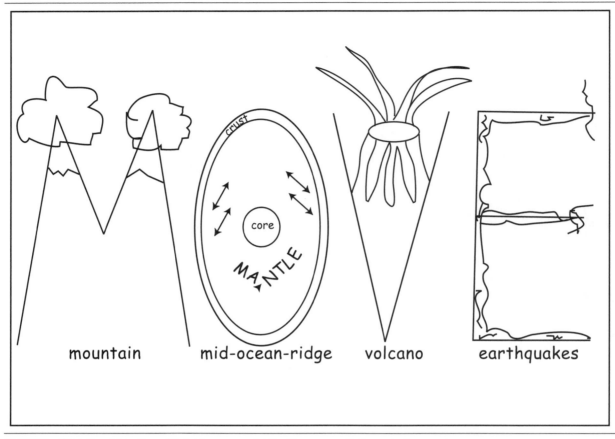

mountain   mid-ocean-ridge   volcano   earthquakes

Ridge, Volcanoes, and Earthquakes." One student objected after observing some of his peers' attempt to use the MOVE acronym to show all of the information they knew at that point (see Figure 6.7). His objection went something like this:

> Why would you put the layers of the Earth in the O? If the other three letters represent "mountain, volcanoes, and earthquakes," the O should be mid-ocean ridge, because those four things are part of the crust. Putting all of the layers into that letter will be confusing.

As this student so clearly demonstrated, these individual drafts held excellent assessment information. They gave Ginger a snapshot of each student's current understanding of the unit concepts and relationships among them, informing her of the next instructional steps needed. In fact, Ginger set up a

procedure: Her signature on students' portable UVFs indicated that the students were able to tell what they knew using their UVF before they took it home to share their learning with their parents.

PRODUCTIVE HOME, SCHOOL, AND RESOURCE PERSONNEL CONNECTIONS VIA PORTABLE UVFS

Beginning with her unit on Mesopotamia, Ginger's students did something similar to what the third graders described in Chapter 5 did: They explained what they had learned to their parents using their portable UVFs. In this case, the exchange occurred at home, giving students and their parents an opportunity to assess student knowledge before the end-of-unit assessment task.

Students took two items home: their portable UVF and a note. The note announced the upcoming test, described the students' task to use the text and visuals to tell their parents what they knew about the subject, and a request for a parent's signature. There were also two places on the note for parent and student comments. Comments seemed to say that students and parents found this a useful means of recalling and discussing classroom learning:

> Parent: My son seems to have grasped most of the information, but needs to study a few missing points. I believe, with a few more details, he will do well on the test.
>
> Student: I think I did well when I explained this, so I think I'll do well on the test.
>
> Parent: This is a great way to learn and retain. I like the visual.
>
> Student: I enjoyed working on this study guide [portable UVF] and I think it will help me out a lot.
>
> Parent: My daughter has gained much knowledge on this subject. The way it was taught appears to be *very* helpful, because she has taken a genuine interest. Thank you.
>
> Student: I enjoyed explaining Mesopotamia to my mother, because it made me feel like I knew everything about it.

One parent made a suggestion: "Bring it home every day to study."

Author's Notes: Portable UVF Use in Coordination and Communication

With guidance to parents that their children should be discussing both individual parts of the UVF and relationships among the parts, UVFs can be a concrete means for parents to understand and assist their child's learning—in any language. Parents who speak the language of instruction will not have difficulty, because that will be documented on the UVFs and supplemented by the student's knowledge of it. Even when parents speak a different language from the text recorded on the UVFs, there are enough visual clues for students and parents conversationally to negotiate the two languages, and if parents have any background in the subject, they can add conceptual depth and terms through the common native language with their children. In some cases, students will teach their parents new information about the topic. In the case of a parent who is dominant in the first language of the child, a student may also incidentally help that parent increase his or her English skills within the respectful context of parent helping child.

Similar exchanges may occur between students and resource personnel or volunteers. Special education students, who see specialists as well as their general education teacher, may use portable UVFs to bridge the two settings. Bilingual or ESL students who receive support services outside their general education classes may do the same.

Miramontes, Nadeau, and Commins (1997) are very specific about the kind of support that will assist students' cognitive and affective lives when there is no opportunity for bilingual students to use their primary language to learn in school. The authors propose that students meet with a speaker of their language (maybe a volunteer) three times per week for 15–30 minutes. The meetings have the explicit purpose of linking new to previous knowledge and extending students' thinking about academics.

Portable UVFs can help guide such support. Because they are prepared as part of class work, the UVFs do not require extra teacher preparation to give to the support person. A copy of the unit targets and the UVF would provide the support person with a clear idea of what students are to learn, even if the teacher was not able to give the adult additional guidance on a particular occasion. This bilingual discussion of students' portable UVFs strengthens class development of it in English. Such support, according to Miramontes, Nadeau, and Commins will give students "a chance to access their underlying conceptual knowledge about the content, and to develop a sound understanding of the material" (p. 75).

EVOLUTION AND RESULTS OF ASSESSMENT

Earlier in this chapter, Ginger explained the assessment she had used when she first taught the Earth science unit: ten points for each of ten activities, plus a chapter test consisting of matching and multiple-choice questions that was administered at the end of the unit. She had also asked the students to do a word sort early in the unit, but did not score it.

When she used UVFs the first time to teach the unit, she no longer did the ten activities the way she had done them before, so she eliminated the 100 points from the activities. She used the newly incorporated guiding questions as a preassessment and gave the chapter test at the end of the unit. Upon reflection, Ginger realized that, though students had demonstrated enthusiasm for the UVFs, she had been too caught up in learning to implement UVFs herself to do the degree of individual monitoring or ongoing assessment that she needed to do all along. As noted above, she remedied that the next time she taught the unit, instituting the practice of signing the students' portable UVFs when they showed her they could use it to demonstrate their unit learning. Let's look at the results of these changes and other assessment modifications she made in the third unit she taught using UVFs.

Alignment

In her third use of teaching with UVFs, Ginger used the guiding questions and word sort with rationale for groups as a preassessment. In addition to the incidental observations she did during class interactions, she initiated the two instances of the portable UVF use for interim assessments: (a) her own signature on each student's portable UVF after the student demonstrated the ability to use it to communicate unit learning orally, and (b) student's self-assessment and parent assessment when students did the same with their parents at home. For post-assessment, she modified the word sort one more time.

As before, students pasted words from the same word list onto an 11 x 14 sheet of construction paper, forming groups that made sense to them. This time, the students had multiple copies of the list, in case they wanted to include a word in more than one group. They attached loose-leaf pages to provide two types of information for each group they made: (a) their reasoning for the grouping, and (b) a definition or explanation of what they knew about each word within the group. (Special education students took the same test giving their rationale and explanations orally.) There were two reasons for the modifications of the word sort assessment.

First, from about the middle of the unit to its end, Ginger expressed the disappointment that she and her colleagues had felt with the schedule during the time allotted for their respective units, noting how meetings with students had been irregular because of so many other schedule conflicts. She was concerned about continuity of the unit for the students and about having enough time to complete the instruction and assessment.

Second, in the postassessment, both continuity/alignment with the content and the learning process were important. The matching and multiple-choice test did assess the factual content, but it no longer fit the way students had been learning. They had been making decisions throughout the unit on how to communicate about unit essentials. These proactive ways of demonstrating knowledge differed from the testing situation of choosing right answers from a list that includes erroneous or distracting information. Furthermore, with the adaptations made to the word sort, instead of showing their knowledge of isolated facts, students now had the opportunity to demonstrate factual knowledge, reasoning, and communication skills with content material. Consider the differences in the following examples.

Ginger's students would probably have had no problem answering the following question because of their unit slogan, "The crust is always on the MOVE":

Earth's crust moves . . .

A. All the time

B. Once each year

C. Only during earthquakes

D. Only in S waves

Compare the above item with the following excerpt of student José Beltrán's explanation for his grouping of the words *crust, core, mantle, magma, volcano,* and *lava*:

The crust is where all of our studies of Earth processes take place. It is the Earth's outermost layer. The mantle is the Earth's inner layer and it is filled with liquid rock, which is called magma. The magma has a lot of pressure, so it tries to escape and that's what causes the crust to move. The core . . . .

Performance Results

Of 19 students in this third unit, 90% received an A or B or its numerical equivalent. This percentage matched the district's achievement goals. Additionally, comparisons of the pre- and postassessment word sorts showed thoughtful regrouping, including students' insertion of a concept in several categories to show relationships among the facts they had learned. Furthermore, as the above excerpt demonstrates, students competently communicated in writing, aptly using content-specific terms. This achievement is a credit to the teacher and students, especially given the disjointed scheduling concerns voiced by Ginger and her colleagues.

Satisfaction/Enthusiasm

Ginger also assessed the students' satisfaction with and enthusiasm for learning with UVFs, and found her impressions to be accurate. Ninety-two percent of students found the UVF helped *quite a bit* or *a lot*, and the remaining 8% found that it helped *some*. With *a lot* given a score of 5 and *not at all* a score of 1, the average class score was 4.6. Some reasons students gave for its usefulness are as follows:

- It had all the information—all in a small visual.

- It helped me visualize everything and actually see it in a different way than just words.

A student who thought it helped *some* gave this reason: "I kind of liked it because it helped me learn, but it also was a little too basic."

Eighty-eight percent of students liked using the class and student UVFs *quite a bit* or *a lot*, and the remaining 12% liked it *some*. Again, with *a lot* given a score of 5 and *not at all* a score of 1, the average class score was 4.5. Examples of why they liked it are as follows:

- We made it so we know the information well.

- It reminded me of everything, and it wasn't boring, standard black and white. It was fun and interesting.

- I enjoyed drawing pictures and it was kind of an easy way to study.

Here are some differing viewpoints:

- Well, it was getting extra homework, so that was a disadvantage.

- It was educational, but I didn't like making it.

The three final comments, for me, verify the emphasis I've had throughout this book about the need to focus on both the visuals and the process of co-creating and using them throughout the unit. These comments speak to either student interest or disinterest in drawing/making the visual, or the "disadvantage" of "getting extra homework." Yet all of the students expressed some degree of enthusiasm, even though sixth graders are apt to "tell it like it is" and choose *not much* or *not at all* when they feel that way. It would seem that Ginger's words at the opening of the chapter were accurate: The UVF's usefulness in helping students learn, combined with the students' role in co-creating the UVF, apparently made up for one student's perceiving it as "too basic," for others' dislike for drawing, and even for the "disadvantage of getting more homework."

OBSERVATION TOOL

Toward the end of her third time teaching with UVFs, I observed Ginger and her class and interviewed some of the students using the structured interview in Appendix A. My intention was to get more firsthand student impressions of learning with UVFs. However, I incidentally again witnessed the ease an observer has in following instruction and knowing priorities when a UVF is integral to the work.

Ginger opened with a whole-class review. The class UVF was on the bulletin board, and students had their portable UVFs in front of them. In a very short time, Ginger asked questions that had students work forward from their initial concept of a system to the concept of Earth as a system, and then to the most recent concepts they had studied about earthquakes. She led students to update their portable UVFs with this information.

Still as a whole class, Ginger led a brief survey of specific text pages, explicitly noting this expository text strategy. After student reading and discussion of the pages' content, the class again updated their portable UVFs.

When the class broke into individual inquiry work, I interviewed six students using the structured interview questions. I did, however, omit the question about what students would do next and added in its place a question about how UVFs served them. Every student with whom I spoke, including a special education student and two bilingual students, clearly knew the main concepts on their UVFs. The variation among students was in the degree to which they were able to explain relationships among the concepts and their ease and flow of communication. Each student was also able to explain the task in which they were individually engaged and how it related to what they were studying. All but one of the bilingual students offered logical reasons for the importance of why they were studying this content. (Whether the student had difficulty with the question or the answer was not ascertained in this brief situation.)

The question I added to the structured interview was, "If I took away this UVF and you didn't use it or the class UVF in this unit, would it have been easier or harder? Why?" (I broke the long sentence up for students.) Here are a couple of answers that were slightly different from the ones quoted in the written UVF evaluation earlier:

Student A: It would be harder if you took it away. We'd have to go all through our science book and find the information.

Observer: But you talk about it in class, don't you?

Student A: Yes, but we'd forget. That's why we have this—to help us remember.

Student B: It helped me understand what's what. Like this [pointing to the drawing of the system they had experienced using string], we did it with string, and it shows . . . [the student told about a system]. It's [the UVF] like a visual, so it says words, but it's a picture.

Students in this class gave us another example of how UVFs can give teachers, students, and observers—be they supervisors, parents, or interested bystanders—a common tool for visually following and assessing classroom work. In addition, the UVF facilitates the articulation of ideas about content and learning. This articulation, in turn, gives each stakeholder the kind of confidence evident in student and parent comments after the homework sharing and in student interviews with me.

GINGER'S REFLECTIONS AFTER MULTIPLE TIMES TEACHING WITH UVFS

I found that creating a UVF helped me create a cohesive unit. As I experimented with the UVFs for the same science unit with different classes, I found I was continually creating a clearer focus on the whole unit of study. The clearer I became, the more freedom I had to move in different directions with each class while continuing the focus of the unit. I was able to use the UVF both as a warm-up for and closure to each lesson. The continuous repetition of the unit goals both orally and visually made things clear for each student.

Creating a clear focus on the big ideas took the longest time, and was the most challenging for me. The UVF had immediate application and results—when I helped students depict the facts visually, they got them easier and were able to hold on to them, even with a basic web to organize them. Although I am pleased with that result, I want to teach more than facts.

I didn't make a teacher draft the first times I taught with a UVF, and I now realize that the draft helps me move into the higher-order thinking, giving me ideas of how to make that visual, and it also helps me envision the backward and forward movement of the unit. Once I have that understanding as a teacher, I can work with the students.

The first time I tried to create a UVF, I was focused more on the actual mechanics of creating it. I kept reminding myself to do what was "honest and possible," as suggested by Christine. In addition, I kept reminding myself that it is a messy process. These two reminders helped me feel more comfortable taking risks and making mistakes along the way.

As I experimented with the process of co-creating the UVF with students, I realized that the process was as important as the product. The product was a given from the very beginning; Pat Wolfe's work on brain research seemed to predict that for me. The process is a way of teaching.

Following Through on Appealing Characteristics

It seems fitting to reflect on Ginger's story in terms of the reasons teaching with UVFs appealed to her in the first place:

- The UVF's promise of keeping her focused
- The organic nature of the process
- The UVF's visual aspect
- The ability to see where the class is, has been, and is going at any given time
- The emphasis on co-development with students

Note that the first item didn't say "*getting* her focused," which is a common prerequisite to all teaching, including teaching with UVFs. Ginger found this prerequisite one of the hardest parts of implementing UVFs, as have some other teachers quoted in this book. Ginger, nonetheless, found the challenge worthwhile and described the benefits she gained from clarifying her focus. One major benefit she named was having an anchor to which to return after related ideas or experiences were explored.

The fact that Ginger needed to return speaks to the organic nature of the process and to the freedom she saw as a benefit of being focused. She mentioned her ability to follow student interests and life connections with any given class, always returning to the focus. She also mentioned, and we observed, the variations she had from class to class with the same unit.

The ability to have that freedom to develop the unit organically while having the confidence of returning to the focus can be partially attributed to the visual aspect of the UVF. The visual did let Ginger and her class see where they were, had been, and were going—whether after the one- to four-day interval between science classes, or after a substitute had been in during Ginger's absence. However, in reality, all of the characteristics that appealed to Ginger merged in her co-development process with students.

Co-ownership was a major factor in keeping the UVF comprehensible to everyone in the class. Students knew the unit priorities because, as one said, "We made it, so we know the information well." The repetitive, cumulative, oral, and visual expansion kept the unit's big ideas clear for students, as teacher, student, and parent comments asserted. Teacher and student clarity enabled each person to relate particular teaching/learning events to the unit priorities, as was evident when I randomly interviewed students. If the five aspects that Ginger listed as appealing to her were interpreted as informal goals for her implementation, Ginger's story and thoughtful reflections have clearly shown how she incorporated them into her practice.

OTHER AREAS OF IMPACT

Some of the items on Ginger's list of reasons described characteristics of teaching with UVFs—the organic nature of the process, the UVF's visual aspect, and the emphasis on co-development. Others were results she anticipated—staying focused and visually recognizing the progress of a unit. Her words at the beginning of this chapter perhaps highlight some unanticipated results—her own and her students' greater understanding of content from being engaged in a collaborative process where they were "empowered to make decisions."

Ginger's content understanding began to deepen when she engaged in the first planning session as she answered those "uncomfortable" questions to identify her focus. It continued with her students as they made decisions about what images and text to put on their UVFs and how to show the relationships among the ideas they represented.

Ginger noted that "making it visual helped [her] see the big picture." Indeed, in at least one case, the decision to "make it visual"—that is, to represent the concept visually—made the picture or ideas to be understood bigger. With her first use of UVFs, Ginger had opened her Earth science unit by eliciting prior knowledge about systems. She explained how she and the class had forgotten to include that in the UVF because of the nervousness and concentration of learning to use UVFs. In the later unit, when Ginger and students included the concept of a system in their UVF, they nested the whole unit in a wider perspective for future recall and application in new contexts.

Decisions often forced movement from isolated information to broader concepts. Forming the slogans "The Earth is always on the MOVE" and "The crust is always on the MOVE," related many pieces of information. To explain those generalizations, students needed to know the smaller details that might otherwise have been separate facts—what causes the Earth or its crust to move, how they move, and the four resulting earth forms contained in the acronym MOVE. Similarly, when the social studies students looked for evidence to decide if they could include palm trees in their core UVF on Mesopotamia, they focused on a broader concept of whether the land was fertile; the results of their inquiry produced more broadly applicable understanding of the content.

Unlike learning activities that simply pass on information, each decision in constructing a UVF requires a critical look at the content. When a student wanted to know if his portable UVF was accurately represented and Ginger asked the student to explain the drawings, she and the student were examining the content from unanticipated viewpoints. The debate about what belonged in the illustrated O of MOVE informed, challenged, and/or confirmed each student's and Ginger's understanding of the content. These and other interactions brought about Ginger's realization that "the process was as important as the product" and that "the process is a way of teaching."

I am fully confident that Ginger's success with these aspects of teaching with UVFs will continue to climb and become consistent. Even as she finished the Earth science unit with the last group described in this chapter, she was developing new ideas about how she and the next group of students could increase the amount of higher-order thinking and application to their lives. In addition to the respect I've gained from working with Ginger, I have confidence in her success, which comes from two sources. First, she didn't approach teaching with UVFs as an add-on or isolated innovation. She integrated it with her continuous improvement process with students, as well as with other growth experiences she had sought out—such as works by Lynn Erickson (2001) on curriculum and instruction, William Glasser (1986) on choice theory and quality in the schools, Carol Tomlinson (1999) on differentiated classrooms, and Pat Wolfe (2001) on brain research. Second, Ginger engaged in all of the components of teaching with UVFs, working on implementing the innovation to its fullest potential. The relationship of the results to the kind of implementation is the subject of the concluding chapter of this book.

Chapter Six
Visual Summary

A Teacher's Story:
Moving from Beginning to Experienced Use of UVFs

First challenge: Conceptualizing Unit
Questions about compelling need, goals, and
standards are uncomfortable, but yield focus.

First Time Teaching With UVFs: Earth Science Unit
* Concentration on learning to co-develop the UVF
* Nervous about giving students power to design core UVF
* UVF captures unit-specific key concepts
* UVF uses a web format
* Immediate results: making concepts visual helps teacher see
  big ideas, students learn facts and big ides, show enthusiasm
  at being part of process and empowered to make decisions
* Guiding questions pre-assessment, end-of-chapter post test

Second Time Teaching With UVFs: Mesopotamia Unit
* Use of questioning to empower students to make more
   decisions about core and portable UVFs
* UVF captures unit-specific key concepts
* UVF uses a web format
* Home/school connection using portable UVFs
* UVF practices move into rest of day, other subjects

Third Time Teaching With UVFs:
Earth Science Unit to New Student Group
* Uses teacher draft for first time
* UVF includes unit-specific key concepts as well as state
   goal's wider perspective for future application of unit learning
* Develops class and portable UVFs simultaneously, with
   more individual student input & critical thinking about content
* UVF format uses cause-effect pattern and slogan
* Home/school connection using portable UVFs
* Pre-, ongoing, & post-assessment, aligned with teaching & learning

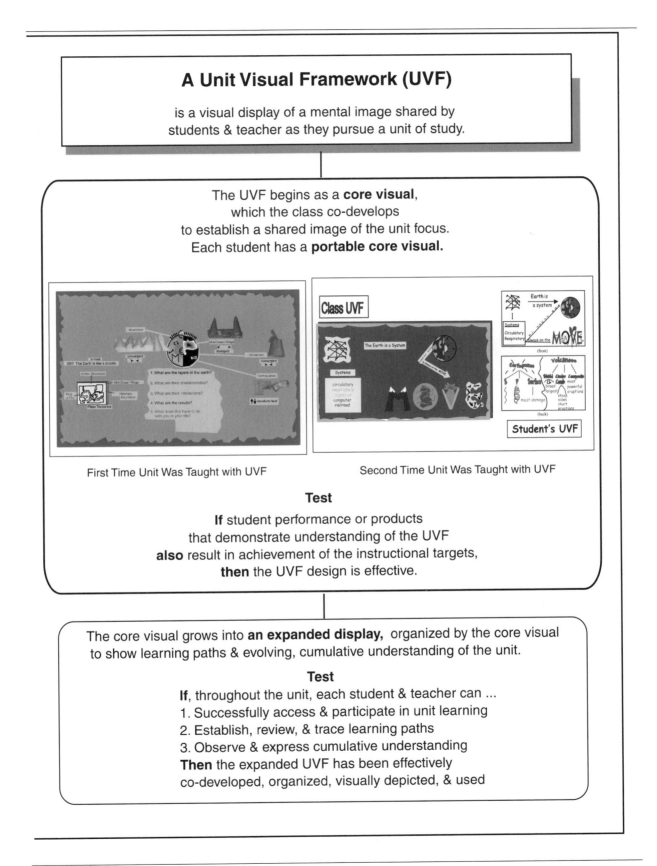

A Unit Visual Framework (UVF)

is a visual display of a mental image shared by
students & teacher as they pursue a unit of study.

The UVF begins as a **core visual**,
which the class co-develops
to establish a shared image of the unit focus.
Each student has a **portable core visual.**

First Time Unit Was Taught with UVF

Second Time Unit Was Taught with UVF

Test

If student performance or products
that demonstrate understanding of the UVF
also result in achievement of the instructional targets,
then the UVF design is effective.

The core visual grows into **an expanded display,** organized by the core visual
to show learning paths & evolving, cumulative understanding of the unit.

Test
If, throughout the unit, each student & teacher can ...
1. Successfully access & participate in unit learning
2. Establish, review, & trace learning paths
3. Observe & express cumulative understanding
Then the expanded UVF has been effectively
co-developed, organized, visually depicted, & used

Getting the Results You Want 7

Today, even guidelines for national policy, such as the No Child Left Behind Act of 2001 (NCLB Act), require that "programs [be] based on scientifically based research" (Title III, Section 3102, [9]). The first chapters of this book provided the theory and research upon which teaching with Unit Visual Frameworks is based. The Office of Civil Rights strengthens the requirements of the NCLB Act through their role of ensuring equal access to education: District programs must show that practices are actually implemented in such a way as to yield what the theory and/or research promised. In fact, theorists and researchers echo that warning with what might be perceived as common sense: Best practices only guarantee results if their original conditions are implemented (Ellis, 2001).

I, therefore, urge anyone who teaches with UVFs to evaluate results by the degree to which all components are actually being implemented, and to use that information to plan improvements. This chapter introduces the Teaching With UVFs Implementation Rubric (Appendix B), which can assist proactive reflection on what was and was not implemented.

Some readers may be wondering about the mantra "honest and possible" that I've used throughout the book and about the previous attention to quelling the seemingly innate fears that accompany our need to do something "the right way." Are those consistent with the recommended rubric? Yes. The use of the rubric to determine what did and didn't happen can prevent fears that thrive on a feeling of "something" not working right, and thus informed, teachers can continue to redefine what is "honest and possible."

Thus, there is a need both to be patient with the process of learning to teach with UVFs and to ensure that you—or others you train—get the desired results through a complete and informed use of the innovation. We saw Ginger Benning practice this patience with the successive units she taught, while improving each new unit through reflection on how she had taught the previous one with UVFs.

Chapters 1 through 6 explained and gave examples of the topics used as features for the Teaching With UVFs Implementation Rubric. This concluding chapter confirms the meaning of each rubric feature and elaborates on the alignment aspect of focus, showing what can occur when instruction departs from planning and how other aspects of teaching with UVFs can help a class recognize that departure and recover. This chapter's case studies, which are very different from those seen thus far, help us recall the fact that the U of UVF means "unit" in its broadest sense, as described in Chapter 1. One of this chapter's examples is of student-directed learning in a primary multiage classroom. The other is of a graduate-level course for teachers, which revisits some considerations of teachers who cannot keep wall displays posted from one class meeting to the next and discusses one concern that some adult and high school students have with UVFs.

TEACHING WITH UVFs: THE IMPLEMENTATION RUBRIC SCALE

My overall priorities are evident in the snapshot of teaching with UVFs in Figure 7.1, which you may recognize as the figure from Chapter 1. The result that I want from teaching is a successful learning community that shares power, leadership, and achievement. That result corresponds to the score or level 3 in the Teaching with UVFs Implementation Rubric (Appendix B). Student and teacher learning are most profound and transferable with this level of implementation.

A score of 2 on the rubric represents basic, competent use of teaching with UVFs, in which some of the components have not been implemented to their fullest potential. Although active co-development of the UVF gives students shared voice and support, level-two implementation does not specifically structure teacher and student use of the UVF to share leadership, support, and accountability for class work. It is probable that, in any given year, some units might be implemented at the third level and others, for various reasons or circumstances, might achieve only the second level.

A score of 1 on the rubric is incomplete implementation of teaching with UVFs. It can improve teaching that is done without visual frameworks. However, the teaching/learning processes may be more difficult, the learning less enduring and/or transferable, and the shared power, leadership, and achievement less likely to occur.

AN EXAMPLE FROM STUDENT-DIRECTED LEARNING

The first case study to illustrate the rubric comes from Darlene Solano's first- and second-grade multiage classroom. The class explored Learning From the

Figure 7.1. Teaching With UVFs: A Snapshot of Its Process and Results

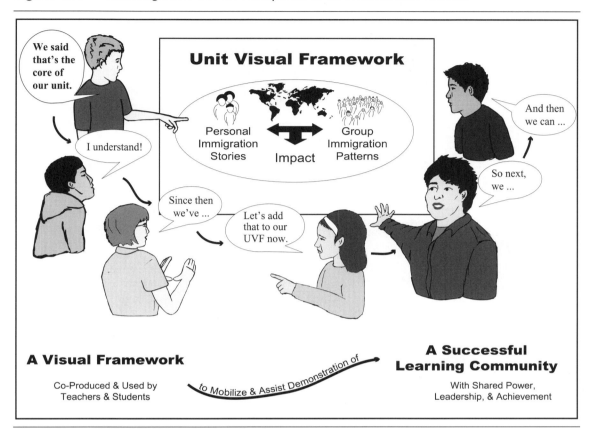

Inside one hour at a time, three times a week for seven weeks. "Learning from the Inside" was defined as

> Learning that comes from a need within the learner and connects with other learners, teachers, and ever-expanding resources. It contrasts with learning that originates with ideas and activities someone else introduces. (Ewy, 1995, p. 1)

Darlene and I team taught Learning From the Inside much the way Paula Bullis and I worked on the Reading to Remember unit described in Chapter 5.

Unit and UVF Focus

The first rubric feature addresses the kind of unit targets reflected in the UVF, their clarity to students and teacher, and the degree to which teaching, learning, and assessment enables and monitors them throughout the unit (see Figure 7.2). Even with student-directed work, clear targets are the only means by which all will achieve their desired results. A variation of the questions in Figure 3.2—"How will we meet curricular targets as part of pursuing our own

Figure 7.2. Focus Feature of the Teaching With UVFs Implementation Rubric

	Partial Implementation	**Complete Implementation for Academic Success**	**Complete Implementation for Academic Success & Shared Leadership**
	1	2	3
Unit & UVF Focus	Part of focus clear to students	All of focus clear	All of focus **clear**
	Unit specific, facts only	Unit & wider perspectives, facts & reasoning evident	Unit & wider **perspectives**, facts & reasoning well integrated
	Student goals/pursuit of interests not addressed	Student goals/pursuit of interests supported	**Student goals**/pursuit of interests supported & assessed
	The content of instruction & assessment aligns with targets & UVF	The content & methods of instruction & assessment align with targets & UVF	The content & methods of instruction & assessment **align** with targets & UVF

goals and interest?"—becomes important. Additionally, for student-directed learning to benefit from teaching with UVFs, there needs to be at least one common goal that the whole class pursues. Thus, students and teacher will need to be clear on both the individual and class goals.

Whole-Class Focus

Learning From the Inside priorities for this class are listed in Figure 7.3. The class would support each other as a learning community to achieve three goals, assessed in the following ways:

1. Acquire a process for meeting their needs as independent learners (needs-satisfying/goal-achievement process), assessed by students' increasing ability to self-direct, articulate, monitor, and complete the process

2. Use a workshop structure to predict and lead the work, demonstrated by the ability of students to know what to do themselves and to be able to lead the class through workshop procedures on any given day, even if a substitute teacher were in the room

Figure 7.3. Goals of Learning From the Inside with a First- and Second-Grade Multiage Class

Teacher Goals for All Students

Shared ownership, power, leadership, and achievement through individual interests pursued as a learning community

- Goal-achievement process: Adapt with students, and help them to internalize, a process they can follow to achieve their interest-based goals
- Shared leadership of class procedures: Adapt a workshop approach with students, which they can manage, so that everyone leads the class, teaches, and learns.
- Curricular achievement within student interest-based goal achievement

Student Goals	**Curricular Goals**
Individually determined	Learning standards and specific curriculum pertinent to student's pursuit
Examples:	Examples:
▪ Not to be afraid flying on an airplane	▪ Oral interviewing, narrative writing
▪ Draw	▪ Expressing ideas through art
▪ Subtracting	▪ Numeration and operations
▪ Read hard books	▪ Read with understanding & fluency
▪ Spell	▪ Spelling strategies for writing
▪ Learn about cats	▪ Use language arts to acquire information

3. Achieve curricular goals pertinent to their interests, assessed with each student based on individual goals and tasks

Although this is not the only type of instruction that specifically targets a level-three UVF implementation, it is a clear example of one.

Alignment

The alignment descriptor in Unit and UVF Focus (see Figure 7.2) is probably readily recognizable by writing teachers, who understand that a written piece must hold its focus from beginning through closure if the writing is to be effective. For similar reasons, the focus of a unit must be carried through in the content and methods of teaching and assessment from the beginning to closure of the unit or course of study. In this pilot of Learning From the Inside, initial misalignment caused some false starts.

Seeking Clarity

The whole-class goals listed in Figure 7.3 were not clear to students in the beginning, because we didn't make them overt. After setting the context of

Figure 7.4.   Student Goals Move From Vague to Clear

Vague	Clear Target & Assessment Criteria
▪ I want to read harder books.	▪ *I want to* read harder books. ▪ *Because* I like reading books and some that look good are hared [hard]. ▪ *Now I already can* read the beginners biybull [Bible]. ▪ *So I want to* read hard insect books. ▪ *I will know my need is met when* I read five hard books. ▪ *I will know that I have done my best quality when* I learn hard wereds [words].

what Learning From the Inside was and why we would spend part of the day using that type of learning, we jumped into content—teaching the needs-satisfying process. We wanted to build on two prior experiences the students had had: (a) discussing things they wondered about and (b) studying five basic needs that William Glasser (1986) identifies.

This brief introduction did not give students the tools they would actually need to meet whole-class goals. They only had a partial awareness of the class goals, the needs-satisfying process was still fuzzy, and they were unaware that the way the class proceeded was based on a structure that would assist their achievement. Therefore, during those first three days, many students' listed very broad areas of interest, which could not truly be pursued satisfactorily or assessed by student and teacher without further definition.

Clarity and Alignment

We developed concrete tools for students to use for the needs-satisfying process they would follow during the doing portion of the workshop. The first tool was a "needs" sheet to clarify individual goals, including self-assessment, planned improvement, and assessment task and criteria. Figure 7.4 shows the difference between one student's initially vague goal and her resulting clear and attainable one after completing the sentence stems on the needs sheet. The teacher's job was to see what academic standard or standards the students' goals and tasks lent themselves to achieving. After students were clear on the relevant standard or standards, the teacher facilitated student pursuit and monitoring of all goals.

Realizing that we had set goals for independent learning but were teaching in ways that kept students dependent on us, we also made other adjustments. On the fourth day, we began building the UVF by revealing the workshop

Figure 7.5.   Beginning to Build the UVF: The Workshop Structure

Parts of Our Workshop	Examples From Our First 3 Days
Planning &/or Mini Lesson	*Day 1: Learning from the inside vs. outside*
Doing	*I wonder...?* *Something we want to do/do better*
Sharing & Celebrating	*How did it go?*

approach we were following (Figure 7.5). Each day thereafter, we had the basic class structure visible for us all to know where we were and what was next.

Everyone in the class was considered both a teacher and a learner. Students generally asked for specific types of expertise during the planning part of the class workshop. For example, working on conquering a fear of flying and moving to California, one student formed a peer and teacher support group to research three areas: flying, moving to a new place and school, and California. Once she asked for resources about these areas, she found that her peers had either experienced one of these things themselves or had parents or friends whom they could consult in order to help the student. The student pursuing her goal scheduled conferences with each of her support group members individually or in groups for the doing portion of the workshop.

For general assistance, we established a simple procedure on the chalkboard: Students would list their names under one of two columns—seeking help from a teacher or from their peers. When students or teachers had reached a point in their work where they were available to act as a resource, they consulted the list and helped the next student.

Thus, through simple procedures co-developed with students and displayed in the room, everyone was able to pursue both individual and class goals. Figure 7.6 shows the unit's content and methods alignment.

UVF Format, Ownership, and Use

The next two features of the Teaching With UVFs Implementation Rubric specifically pertain to the UVF (Figure 7.7). We continue to use the case study to illustrate them.

Figure 7.6. Alignment of the Targets and UVF With Content and Methods

Goals/Targets	Alignment of Content With Targets	Alignment of Instruction & Assessment With Targets
Shared ownership, power, & leadership as a learning community	Shared input into: - Goals - Planning and monitoring of work - Procedures to help get the work done individually and as a community, and - Resources available	- Student & teacher shared roles as learners and teacher/resource for others - Explicit procedures and shared responsibility for individual and class processes & procedures - Class monitoring of progress through UVF displayed process, and participation in "Sharing" part of workshop & "Celebrate" step of goals-achievement process
Goal-achievement/needs-satisfying process	UVF and support forms clearly identified and facilitated each step of the process.	UVF, support forms, & workshop structure provided guidance & sustained time to - Carry out - Internalize - Reflect on - Assess success of the process through demonstration
Curricular achievement within student interest-based goals achievement	- Student choice of individual goals and their assessment - Teacher identification of relevant curricular goals and standards	Teacher facilitation & monitoring of goals-achievement process to help student clarity of all goals, & ensure that the student's learning process & chosen assessment demonstrated achievement of them

Over time, an expanded UVF was constructed on a wall-sized bulletin board (Figure 7.8). Its major task was to clarify the doing part of the workshop structure shown in Figure 7.5, which remained posted as well. This doing consisted of the students following the steps of the needs-satisfying process. Using examples from their own work, students illustrated each step to make sure they knew what it meant and how to complete the process.

This large UVF allowed students to see and physically utilize the needs-satisfying process. They could even stand in front of the displayed step of the process to show where they were working in order for the class visually to see the status of work occurring on any given day. For example, all students

Figure 7.7. UVF Format, Ownership, and Use Features From the Teaching With UVFs Implementation Rubric

	1. Partial Implementation	2. Complete Implementation for Academic Success	3. Complete Implementation for Shared Leadership
UVF Format	Single visual Collection of separate ideas	Evolving display Ideas and main relationships evident	Evolving display Ideas & relationships clearly integrated
UVF Ownership & Use	Teacher-made & teacher-directed use for academic achievement	Co-developed, teacher directed & student unprompted use for academic achievement	Co-developed, shared use for class leadership, support, & academic achievement

currently taking action on a need they had already identified could gather in front of the "Planning and Doing" sign. The folders hanging below that step held their paper, on which they would record their day's work. These forms were color coded, consistent with the color of the sign for that step. Students at the "Planning and Doing" sign would know that their next step would be "Thinking Back" or reflecting on what they had learned and how they had met their need.

The "Celebrate" step had no paper for the students to complete, but was rather a place to post the student's completed forms. In fact, a completed set of the color-coded forms was posted to indicate that students were to put their own set there. Any learning artifacts students desired to post, such as the poetry, letter, and student-made book shown in Figure 7.8, accompanied their forms. This part of the expanded UVF also signaled an occasion to share with and be acknowledged by the class. The teacher gave students a bookmark that illustrated what they had accomplished, listed the steps of the needs-satisfying process, and congratulated them for meeting their need/goal. Some of the bookmarks were added to the UVF for a while as additional learning artifacts.

Participation

Participation when teaching with UVFs means active engagement of students with the priorities of the unit of study (Figure 7.9). A caring teacher once said that she liked UVFs because there's always something on it that English language learners can say something about. Had the teacher elaborated, she might have meant something else, but it triggered a warning for me. It is tempting to feel good that students seem to be participating anytime they can

Figure 7.8. Learning From the Inside Expanded UVF

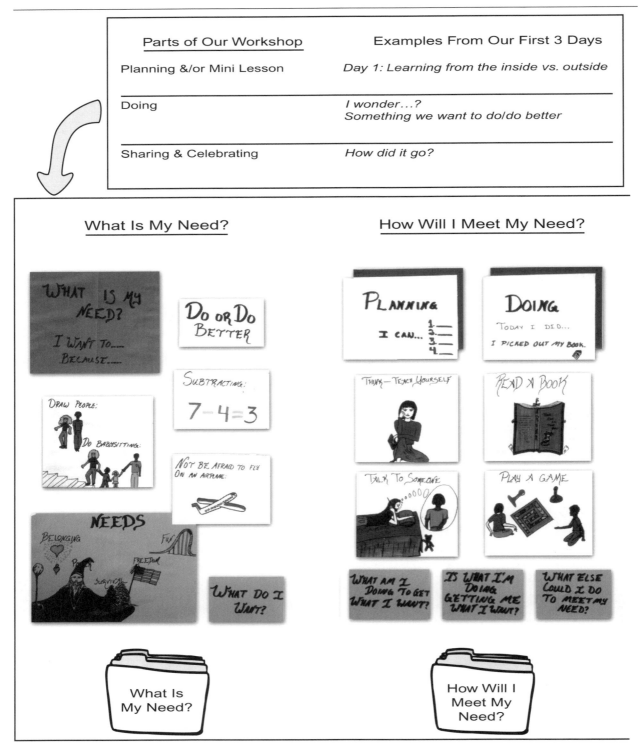

Parts of Our Workshop	Examples From Our First 3 Days
Planning &/or Mini Lesson	*Day 1: Learning from the inside vs. outside*
Doing	*I wonder...?* *Something we want to do/do better*
Sharing & Celebrating	*How did it go?*

Figure 7.8. (Continued)

Figure 7.9. Participation and Achievement Feature of the Teaching With UVFs Implementation Rubric

	1. Partial Implementation	2. Complete Implementation for Academic Success	3. Complete Implementation for Academic Success & Shared Leadership
Participation & Achievement	Many students actively participate throughout unit, varied achievement levels	All students actively participate throughout unit for at least 90% goal achievement	All students monitor their own & class participation and performance throughout unit for at least 90% goal achievement

contribute to or talk about the UVF. However, effective use of UVFs ensures that surface-level contributions move *every* student to the meaningful learning of priorities. We saw examples of this in Chapter 4 when a student said that "pizza" came to mind when thinking about community, and the teacher helped students use that association to understand the unit's focus. The following student-centered case study offers another example.

This multiage class was very diverse in many respects: It had first- and second-grade students, students from varied socioeconomic backgrounds, both learning disabled and behavior-related special education students, students of varied ethnic makeup, and English language learners from several different countries and language groups. Because the nature of Learning From the Inside required active student participation by the whole class, each of these students had to understand the structures, processes, and content of both the class goals and their own; each child was supported and held responsible for achieving both.

One example of how the class ensured equitable success of all its members was the support they gave a beginning speaker of English from Russia. Helping any student identify a need or want they have can be a challenging process. This introspection is even more challenging when what we are asking the child to think through is abstract and not easily communicated in English to a speaker of another language.

We could have used an ESL technique for beginning students: offering picture choices to help both comprehension and the student's limited English production. The student could point to a choice, or answer "yes" or "no." In Learning From the Inside, that technique would not have sufficed, because anyone else's choice may not have gotten to what was most important to the student at the time. Therefore, teachers and peers took the needed time to show the Russian boy their own examples and to rephrase in different ways the same questions they had to answer until he was able to respond verbally and nonverbally. He then identified his desire to learn English, and went on to distinguish his current ability, what he specifically wanted to do during the planned time frame, and how he would know he had met his goal.

Achievement

Students met class and individual goals, satisfying the level-three criteria of teaching with UVF implementation (see Figure 7.9). They had understood the structure enough to have the freedom and power the project intended. This unit was done in the spring. When school ended, all students had been through the cycle from "Needs" through "Celebrate" at least one time. As one would guess, those students who had time to go through it a second time reflected more deeply, were more focused, and understood the process better. Class goals had been met in accordance with the time available for the unit.

Individual achievements were also high. Because teachers no longer had to lead students through the class, there was more opportunity for teaching—such as coaching a student as he wrote his poem, helping another with her book of art, and working with a third to write a letter to an author of a book he had read.

Sixty percent of the students had chosen reading, writing, spelling, or math goals. One student chose an art goal. Others met curricular goals in less obvious ways, such as the student who researched flying, moving, and California. She worked on using the language arts to acquire, assess, and communicate information by interviewing, reading, and later writing about her topic and experiences.

Theresa, a young, shy first grader gives us an example of how she demonstrated her achievement through her own assessment and then through a real-world application. Theresa wanted to "read hard books." She read each day with peers during the doing part of the workshop. Her "celebrate" was to read a book out loud to the class in a voice that they could hear. Later, when the principal visited with the class as a whole group, she asked Theresa to read the personalized bookmark the teacher had given her. Though not a "hard book," the vocabulary on the bookmark was comparable to what she might find in one. We held our breath during the student's long pause, but Theresa refused help from anyone. She read the bookmark on her own with obvious satisfaction and deserved the supportive applause from her peers and learning community.

EXAMPLES FROM TEACHER-
OR CURRICULAR-DIRECTED LEARNING

All of the full-unit examples in Chapters 4 through 6 were teacher- or curricular-directed learning. To round out the kind of examples in this book, we'll look at a university course now that offers examples and nonexamples of the features of the Teaching With UVFs Rubric, particularly of the alignment of content and methods of instruction with the unit targets and UVF.

Unit and UVF Focus

I have taught a graduate course called Foundations of Language Minority Education for many years. The course priorities are shown in Figure 7.10. With the factual information listed under "Major Knowledge" and the reasoning evident in the course description and case study/critical incident analyses, the course design would score a 2 for focus on the Teaching With UVFs Implementation Rubric (see Figure 7.2 and Appendix B). However, the first times I taught the course, methods of instruction actually earned the course a score of 3. Methods included a cohesive approach to the bits of information, beginning with a historical perspective and integrating reasoning through application as we moved forward. Class work modeled work required in projects, the vehicle for students to pursue their own goals or interests and to demonstrate application of course content.

Out of Sight, Out of Mind, Out of Alignment

In its original design, I had not written out the course priorities in a way that showed the cohesion or modeling I built in through teaching. Because as much as two years might pass in between the times that I taught the course, that omission took its toll. Though I continually updated the content to incorporate recent policies and so on, the course goals and types of major knowledge and assessment remained the same.

After teaching the course for many years, I fell into a common error we make when all major priorities are not explicit. I shifted from contextualized, cohesive instruction to isolated coverage of facts for the first half of the course. We went over each piece of information in the "Major Knowledge" list as if it were equally important and in an equally shallow manner.

I "covered" material because of a subconscious separation of policies, practices, and issues. I was trying to "get through" issues and polices because, though important, they had become mere backdrops for the important stuff—the educational implications and practices, where I anticipated the real reasoning and deeper learning.

In my previous teaching of the course, students had interpreted the course description and list of major knowledge as they experienced it, aligned with the course assessment's emphasis on application. With the shift in teaching methods, neither the students nor I were happy that first half of the semester. Students were overwhelmed and resistant, thinking my intent was for them to memorize this mass of information. Furthermore, anxiety on their and my part was high because the assessment emphasis was on application, and time to "get to application" was dwindling.

Figure 7.10. Goals for Foundations of Language Minority Education Course

"Goals" & Assessment	Major Knowledge

Course Description
 	
1. Understand
  • political issues
  • social issues
  • educational issues
that contribute to the formulation of
  • local policies
  • state policies
  • federal policies
and practices for educating language-minority populations.
 	
2. Understand instructional models and programs, their related theory, issues and research, and analyze their degree of local, state, and federal compliance.
 	
Note: Although some classroom, teacher, and individual student variables are considered, course emphasis is on decisions for whole school and district educational services and use of personnel, not the details of instruction, assessment, and culture that are addressed in classes specific to those areas.
 	
Compelling Reasons
To acquire a basis for more detailed study in specific areas and/or a basis for informed decisions, practices, and evaluations of the education of language minority (LM) students
 	
Assessment Tasks & Weights
■ Pre/post — knowledge survey, models matrix, case study: pre-assessment scored, but not graded, postassessment weight 2x
■ Interim case studies/critical incident analyses & midterm quiz: Scored, but not graded
■ Portfolio
  o Philosophy analysis
    Weight 1x
  o 2 reading journals
    Weight 1x
  o Project
    Weight 2x
 	
Rubrics
■ Content-Area Rubric
■ ISAT Literary/Informational Short Answer Reading Rubric
	Federal Policies
	General directive for services, relationship to state guidelines, Castañeda vs. Pickard criteria
	
	State Policies for TBE and TPI programs
	  ■ Criteria for programs and placement
	  ■ Assessment: criteria for services, ongoing, entry/exit requirements/choices
	  ■ Instruction for each type of program
	  ■ Required student interactions
	  ■ Staffing/personnel requirements/restrictions
	
	Local Policies: rights and restrictions
	
	Historical perspective
	  ■ Demographic trends, causes, & misperceptions
	  ■ Notable court cases affecting policies
	
	Research on language acquisition & models' effectiveness
	  ■ Collier, Cummins, Thomas, Ramirez …
	  ■ Controversy and reasoned responses
	
	Issues that impact policies and practices
	  ■ Social: stereotyping, we/they, socioeconomics…
	  ■ Political: immigration, English only, misinformation …
	  ■ Educational: at-risk factors; language, literacy, and cognitive development; job demands/staffing …
	
	Models: content of matrix of each type of model and its level of compliance
	
	Major concepts/terms: BICS, CALP, ESL, OCR, TBE, TPI, acculturation, additive/subtractive bilingualism, compliance, demographics, model types, stages of language acquisition

If I rated the course at midsemester for focus under the Teaching With UVFs Rubric, it would have been about a 1.5 (see Figure 7.2 and Appendix B). The targets and assessment criteria were clear, but facts dominated reasoning, with attempts at wider perspective not making sense because of the methodology. The projects were a vehicle for students' goals and interests, but had lost the stronger connections and support present in earlier teaching of the course. The alignment among targets, instruction, and assessment was of content only, not of the methods of teaching. When we realized the source of the problem, we realigned methods with priorities and assessment.

UVF Format

For this course, the base of the UVF was the course description seen in Figure 7.10. From experienced use of UVFs, I had prepared a teacher draft that took the concepts out of an outline format and showed relationships in a nonlinear fashion. However, we actually worked with the outline the first half of the course. I believe this occurred for three reasons: (a) the comfort level of current adults with outline formats, (b) logistics, and (c) the transmission method of instruction that was occurring.

Many current adults learned in a linear fashion, often using an outline to organize information, just as some high school students have. Therefore, the familiar format made it easy for any of us to lead our routine use of the UVF to review, document what we did, and project what was next. That may not be the case for upcoming high school and adult learners who are seeing nonlinear formats in graphic organizers and in a technology-impacted world in and out of school.

When I taught the course previously, I had used the outline format on overhead transparencies for the UVF and its development. However, its limitations were not as obvious because of the integrative methods I've described earlier. Though students had found the overheads useful and though they were easy for me to transport from session to session, we couldn't see the expansion and interconnections as well as we could with a UVF that is posted on a wall.

With the new class, I wanted to see what else might work. What could I use in this situation, where I was in the classroom only once a week and had nowhere—whether on a wall or in a closet or storage area—to store the UVF between classes? With the ease of today's copiers, I thought we could begin with a much enlarged copy of the outline that I could post and take down each session. From this, we could build a more student-generated UVF and expand in ways similar to what we had done in the past with support visuals on overheads or paper. Unfortunately, for the first half of the course, we stuck with the outline in keeping with the way we marched through the course content.

Limited Ownership and Use

Some Teaching With UVFs practices were used. During the first session, we brainstormed distinctions among the areas we would be studying and decided on illustrations to signal each, as seen in Figure 7.11. We also drew some arrows to show initial understanding of the relationships among those areas. Had we stopped there and gone on to co-developing a UVF, these first steps would have had more impact.

Instead, we did a hybrid of what I had led students to do in past courses and what I was hoping to do with this new wall chart format. As with previous teaching of the course, we further developed on the board and on overheads each of the ideas from the outline. However, how we documented this elaboration departed from the past and backfired.

Concepts Must Be Anchored on UVFs as Complete Thoughts

Because of the limited and fixed space on the outline, we ended up with two kinds of documentation of learning. They are distinguished in Figure 7.12. Consistent with all that has been said since the opening of this book, the results differed for each.

The "Incongruence" drawing in Figure 7.12 is how we began to expand the outline as if it were a core UVF. However, we continued with a predominance of note taking in this limited space, thinking there was enough real anchoring of the related concepts in the support visuals or board elaborations. Wrong! Instead of using images and text to capture concepts, we used short phrases or labels only. These incomplete notes resulted in incomplete ideas for students, especially because teaching methods treated each concept in an abbreviated or shallow fashion, too. Students knew that James Crawford (1999) had written about "misinformation" and "English only," but while they recognized the meaning of the words, they didn't understand the impact of them in relation to the course priorities.

Connecting Visual Supports Is More Than Physically Attaching Them to the UVF

We expanded in ways similar to the Reading to Remember unit in Chapter 5 to overcome space limitations on the actual enlarged outline that was being used as a core UVF. We attached support visuals, such as the one in Figure 7.13. These support visuals had the symbols that students had chosen to represent each area of the course content, so the ideas could readily be connected in this pragmatic way of creating an expanded UVF (note, for example, the apple for "practices" in the upper right hand corner of Figure 7.13).

As with the Reading to Remember unit, this means of expansion could have worked, except for the fact that the teaching methods were not integrating the material. Therefore, these support visuals became one more piece of information, almost defeating the actual purpose of a UVF—to help people focus on what's important in a large amount of material. Because the methods were treating ideas separately, we were in effect making a visual manifestation of the bombardment of ideas students were being exposed to instead of learning. Rather than anchoring secured experiences, we were categorizing surface-level facts.

Figure 7.11. Foundations Class Beginning UVF

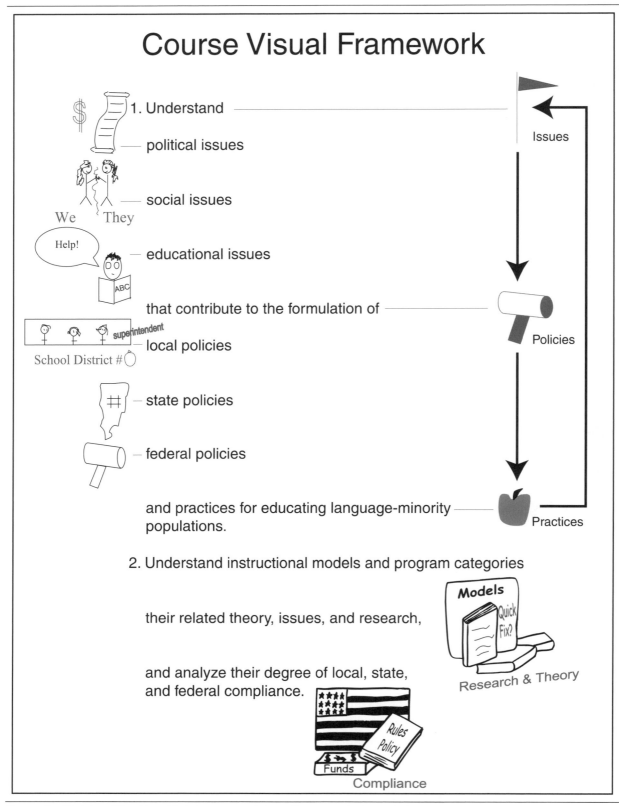

Course Visual Framework

1. Understand
— political issues
— social issues
We   They
Help!
— educational issues
ABC
superintendent
School District #
— local policies
— state policies
— federal policies

and practices for educating language-minority populations.

2. Understand instructional models and program categories

their related theory, issues, and research,

and analyze their degree of local, state, and federal compliance.

Issues

Policies

Practices

Models
Quick Fix?

Research & Theory

Rules Policy
Funds
Compliance

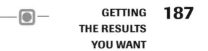

Figure 7.12. Anchored Concepts Versus Note Taking

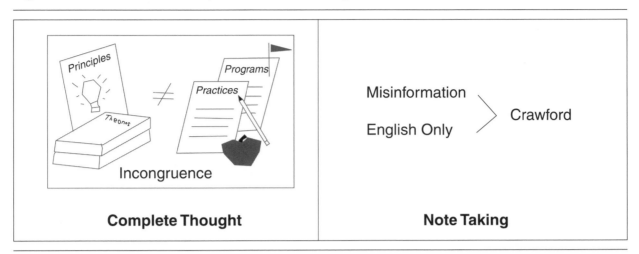

Portable UVF

Work with the "portable UVFs" was similar to previous course teaching. (The quotation marks here acknowledge the facts mentioned earlier that the students actually had little ownership with the outline to this point, so the term "portable UVF" is a misnomer.) Students did a combination of things with their own copy of the posted outline. Some replicated the UVF and made copies of the support visuals. They also used their notebooks to expand the ideas without the space limitations of the outline format, as we did either on the board or on overheads as a class.

Results of Implementation Level

Some of these attempts at teaching with a UVF did assist comprehension, as noted by students in their journals. However, we were working very hard and still not synthesizing information the way we should have. Furthermore, rather than increasing student confidence, we were undermining it. These results were due to a combination of three things: (a) limited ownership, (b) a default rather than designed format, and (c) methods of teaching that were not aligned with targets or assessment. In other words, teaching with UVFs was only partially being implemented.

More Authentic Ownership and Use

In keeping with the midcourse realization of methods misalignment, we made some changes with the UVF and created a real one through co-development. In order to do more thorough reasoning and connecting of ideas, we kept the outline formatted "UVF" posted, but sort of cut up a copy

Figure 7.13. Support Visual as Part of the Expanded UVF

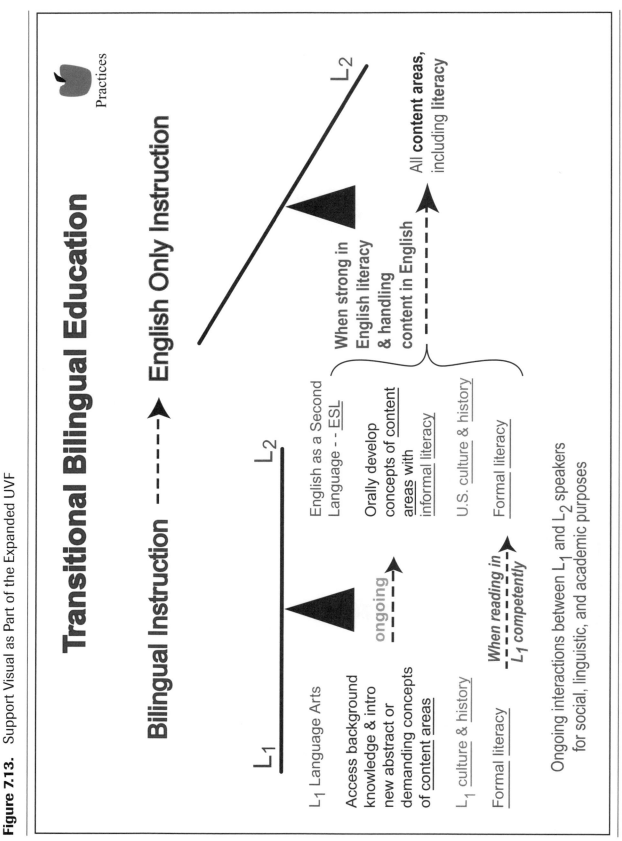

Transitional Bilingual Education

Bilingual Instruction ----→ **English Only Instruction**

Practices

L₂

L₁

L₁ Language Arts

Access background knowledge & intro new abstract or demanding concepts of content areas

ongoing

When reading in L₁ competently

L₁ culture & history

Formal literacy

English as a Second Language -- ESL

Orally develop concepts of content areas with informal literacy

U.S. culture & history

Formal literacy

When strong in English literacy & handling content in English

All **content areas,** including **literacy**

L₂

Ongoing interactions between L₁ and L₂ speakers for social, linguistic, and academic purposes

Figure 7.14. Revising the UVF

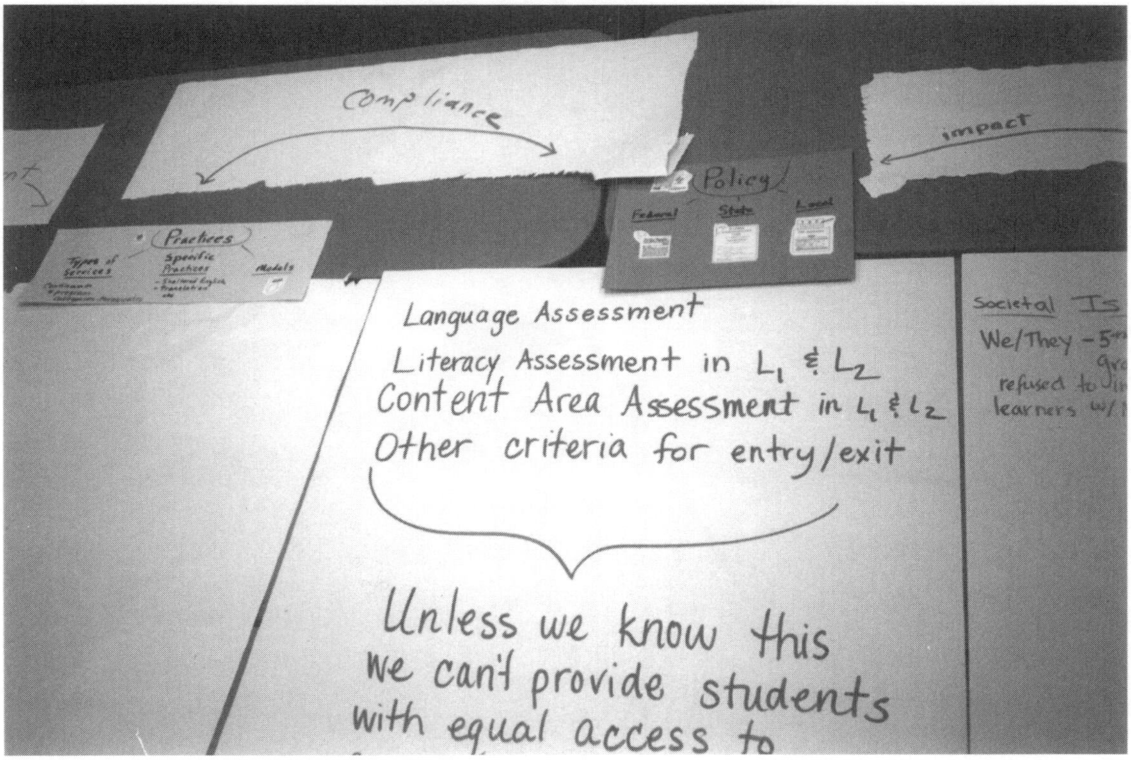

and manipulated the ideas to better show our understanding of the relationships among ideas. We added large chart paper to better display and expand ideas. We carried over the text and student-generated images from the outline-formatted framework to transfer established understanding of the text. See Figure 7.14 for a glimpse of this work in its actual form. Figure 7.15 shows a portable version of the resulting UVF.

Although the new format was still rather linear across the page, it reflected relationships that had been reasoned through by students rather than an outline they had walked into and worked to make their own. This manifestation of student reasoning set the norm for continuing the rest of the course in like manner. When we worked in one area of the course, such as research and theory, we worked the other areas, such as the reasons why the research made sense with our charge as educators, right away as well. We asked if practices and policies were in congruence with that research, and if not, explored the issues that might explain the incongruence or the need that surfaced because of it. Now, rather than simply receiving information, students were constructing and applying it. Active participation was more demanding, but relationships among ideas were stronger, connections more natural, and understanding deeper—even for me. I was pleased to experience the same

Figure 7.15. Portable Revised UVF

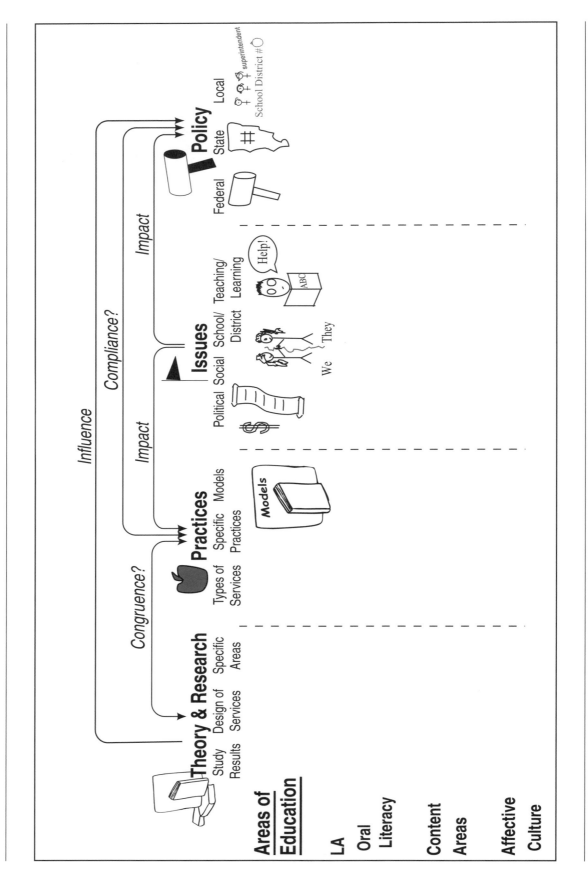

type of learning that Ginger Benning described in Chapter 6. Even after teaching this course for years, when we worked with the ideas organically, together, making sense of the course material, I saw nuances of both content and teaching/learning that would improve my future facilitation of the course.

Participation and Achievement

Students used the UVF and its support visuals each class session individually, with their buddy partner, and as a class. Like the elementary school students quoted in earlier chapters, my graduate students often commented on how the repetition of coming at course material many ways was useful to them. It was the class's routine use of the UVF that helped them recognize and expand previous learning about the targeted areas.

Routine UVF use also served its purpose for informal teacher and self-assessment. This, along with preassessment, ongoing feedback, and postassessment informed and allowed me to adjust my facilitation to be more useful to students and to achieve course goals. It was fun to see students' gain confidence and satisfaction as they realized the knowledge and expertise they gained. At least 90% of each group of students who has gone through the Foundations of Language Minority Education course has achieved course and personal goals. In most cases, all members of the group have. Even in the class where I spent the first half of the semester in what might be called "transmission teaching," students also achieved these goals, but at the high cost of sustained frustration.

Conclusions I Could and
Could Not Make in This Case Study

Student achievement of their own and course goals, relative to the beginning of course, provided evidence of performance growth. Reflection, class dynamics, and student feedback showed me misalignment and helped me to make later adjustments to evaluate my teaching methods and course design. To conclude that teaching with UVFs was or was not effective would have been erroneous, because it had not been completely implemented throughout the course. Overall, the score on the implementation rubric was a level one. Had we not adjusted at midterm, performance results would not have reached the levels they did.

SAFEGUARDS

As both examples in this chapter have shown, if other aspects of teaching with UVFs are present, the problems that lead to low implementation scores on focus will often surface in time to make needed modifications. The kind of modifications will depend on when the problems and their causes are discovered. In the Learning From the Inside example, the incongruence between priorities and what was occurring in the class was evident in the first days. In the university course example, the problems were evident early in the course, but it took until midsemester to discover the causes, because the class met only once a week (albeit three hours per session).

One safeguard that helps realize problems in time to turn them around is ongoing teacher reflection, such as that modeled by the hindsights listed in Chapter 5 and by Ginger Benning in Chapter 6. Another safeguard is for *all* members of the class continually to monitor success—a characteristic that is strongest at level three of the implementation rubric. When students are active learners with ownership and responsibility for the class in a safe environment, they are more willing and more often requested to voice their perceptions of how the class is going, in addition to what and how well they are learning.

Even as I contradicted some of my own values and UVF principles in the first half of the Foundations of Language Minority Education course, I fortunately persisted in efforts to build community and share leadership. Each session, I set up the class in a collegial formation instead of in rows of tables. Besides stated course content, assessment, and evaluation, I made my class routines overt and then asked students to anticipate and lead them using the UVF. I continued to invite students to decide how they wanted to display their knowledge and experiences visually, in spite of the limits established by the outline. Though with less effective support than in past classes, I still kept the degree of choice high and emphasized the purpose of the project as a means for students to meet the goals they had and to demonstrate course priorities. I asked for written feedback on how the course was going several times, reinforcing what students and I thought was working and addressing what was not. Implementation did not reach the third level of shared leadership, but because I aimed for that level, the trust and intent to share ownership with students was sufficient for them to help me realize the misalignment that was occurring in time to rectify it.

DON'T PANIC NOW!

After reading this chapter, one teacher asked, "How will I know if I'm making all these mistakes?" I turned the question back to her, and she had no difficulty generating the following list: "I'll know I am making mistakes by . . ."

- The kind of questions students ask
- Seeing that students are missing the point
- The way students get tangled up in and/or are frustrated with the details
- Seeing that the unit is flat and without depth

May any lurking qualms that surfaced as you read this chapter be quelled by recognition of your own ability to generate a similar list by now.

An unspoken corollary to the posed question might be, "What will I do if I realize I'm making these mistakes?" Perhaps you've already mentally answered that question, too: Return to the rubric, determine what is and is not being implemented, and adjust accordingly.

CONCLUSION

It is my hope that you now have enough information to decide if teaching with UVFs can serve you and your students. This book has offered multiple and varied examples to show what UVFs are. Reasons for why they make a difference have come from students, teachers, parents, theory and research, and my own experiences. The difference they make has been demonstrated both through examples of very successful teaching with UVFs and examples of less-than-optimal implementation accompanied by revealed consequences, hindsight suggestions, and safeguards. Moreover, case studies have demonstrated that one teacher in one classroom with his or her students can make this difference, without waiting for a whole school or district. When effectively implemented, students, teachers, and parents will spread the word to encourage wider use.

I have, throughout, proposed questions to guide planning and examples of the pursuit of academic learning standards. I also voiced cautions about how the term *standards* is applied differently from state to state and in national and international documents, urging pursuit of the broader level of generalizations, which may actually be called *goals* or something else. There was an emphasis throughout and in the Teaching with UVFs Implementation Rubric that teaching with UVFs is also meant to support student and nonacademic goals, which strengthen academic achievement by all students. Indeed, a value for inclusive participation and the success of all students was manifested by the discussion of different age groups, readiness levels, linguistic and cultural backgrounds, and other distinctions that define our diversity.

Teaching with UVFs is no more a panacea than other innovations. However, if you find teaching with UVFs of possible assistance to you and your students, I hope that this book has served to begin your implementation of it and that this chapter has made distinctions to help you get the results you want. I welcome questions, concerns, or responses you might have, as well as tales of any journeys you and your students take through teaching with UVFs. May your initial frustrations of implementing something new be tempered by experiences such as those of the teachers quoted throughout this book who "saw immediate results" and acquired "a wonderful mix of comfort and risk" by making their teaching "more substantial, visible, and accessible" through teaching with UVFs.

Chapter Seven Visual Summary

Getting the Results You Want

Partial implementation yields unreliable results. The rubric in Appendix B helps evaluate the level and purpose(s) of implementation.

For Academic Success

A key factor is alignment of targets and UVF with both content and methods of instruction and assessment.

For Academic Success & Shared Leadership

One safeguard that helps realize problems of mis-alignment in time to turn a unit around is for all members of the class to continually monitor success, a characteristic strongest when implementing to level three on the Teaching With UVFs Implementation Rubric.

A Unit Visual Framework (UVF)

is an organic, collaboratively created, class display (on the wall, if possible) that focuses, supports, & documents a unit of study from its beginning to end.

The UVF begins as

a core visual, with pictures and key text representing the essentials of what is studied and assessed, overtly establishing focus.

Each student has a **portable core visual**.

Test

If student performance or products that demonstrate understanding of the UVF **also** result in achievement of the instructional targets, **then** the UVF design is effective.

Example

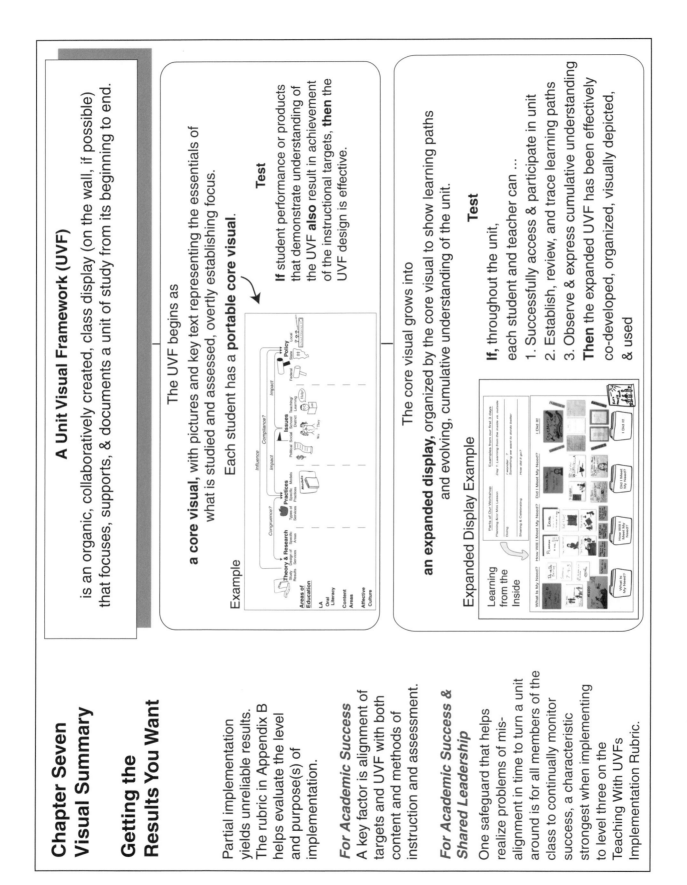

The core visual grows into

an expanded display, organized by the core visual to show learning paths and evolving, cumulative understanding of the unit.

Test

If, throughout the unit, each student and teacher can ...

1. Successfully access & participate in unit
2. Establish, review, and trace learning paths
3. Observe & express cumulative understanding

Then the expanded UVF has been effectively co-developed, organized, visually depicted, & used

Expanded Display Example

Structured Student Interview

Student _____Teacher _____Date_____

Unit Visual Framework for: (list unit name)
Tell me about this (UVF).
What have you learned so far?
What are you doing now? How does it help you learn about . . . ?
What will you do next? Why?
(Ask if student hasn't yet mentioned) What is important about what you're learning? Why?

Teaching With UVFs Implementation Rubric

	Partial Implementation	Complete Implementation for Academic Success	Complete Implementation for Academic Success & Shared Leadership
	1	2	3
Unit & UVF Focus	Part of focus clear to students Unit specific; facts only Student goals/pursuit of interests not addressed The content of instruction & assessment aligns with targets & UVF	All of focus clear Unit & wider perspectives; facts & reasoning evident Student goals/pursuit of interests supported The content & methods of instruction & assessment align with targets & UVF	All of focus **clear** Unit & wider **perspectives**; facts & reasoning well integrated **Student goals**/pursuit of interests supported & assessed The content & methods of instruction & assessment **align** with targets & UVF
UVF Format	Single visual Collection of separate ideas	Evolving display Ideas and main relationships evident	Evolving display Ideas & relationships clearly integrated
UVF Ownership & Use	Teacher-made & teacher-directed use for academic achievement	Co-developed, teacher-directed & student unprompted use for academic achievement	Co-developed, shared use for class leadership, support, & academic achievement
Participation & Achievement	Many students actively participate throughout unit, varied achievement levels	All students actively participate throughout unit for at least 90% goal achievement	All students monitor their own & class participation & performance throughout unit for at least 90% goal achievement
Prerequisites	Identified instructional and assessment targets, based on knowledge of students, curriculum, and materials Core visual, using images and text to show focus Use of Visual Framework from beginning through end of unit		

Appendix C

Software and Hardware Resources

In the classroom, teachers and students will co-develop their own Unit Visual Frameworks using the resources available to them. If technology is a resource, many forms of software and hardware may assist teachers and students in teaching/learning with UVFs, either by helping to create drafts or by allowing what has been created to be used for multiple purposes.

Below is a short sampling of types of resources, rather than a comprehensive list of specific ones. Although I generated or replicated most of the UVFs in this book with these types of resources before my daughter enhanced them, other people are better qualified than I am to speak of technological resources. However, I include this list to indicate how well such resources fit with co-development and teaching with UVFs.

COLOR VERSIONS OF VISUAL FRAMEWORKS FROM THIS BOOK

Full-page, color versions of the UVFs from this book are currently available from my Web site resultsthroughalignment.com in PDF format. As noted, color helps viewers see distinctions, points of emphasis in a core visual, and consistency across items in an expanded UVF. Because printing the book in color would have made it more costly, this avenue provides access to people who still want to see or use the color UVFs.

These color versions may assist anyone wishing to use my examples for work with others: with students as draft examples when exploring or expanding formats, or with colleagues in team planning or staff development. Besides being used as clear examples in handouts, transparencies, or slides, these color versions may be made available for teacher study groups when they read the book to better understand and discuss distinctions I make within the text. Their full-page size also makes them easier to read.

SOFTWARE FOR GRAPHIC-ORGANIZER FORMATTED VISUAL FRAMEWORKS

There are a number of software programs that help generate graphic organizers, including Inspiration Software® (2000) and its primary level counterpart, Kidspiration™ (2000), both by Inspiration Software, Inc.; MindManager® (2002), by Mindjet; and Thinking Maps® (1998) by Innovative Learning Group. These programs are designed to make it easier to generate webs, tree diagrams, flow charts, and other networks of branching concepts. Some programs come with a bank of pictures available to illustrate the graphic organizers, and there are even programs available to generate three-dimensional networks.

All of these programs can help teachers and students generate draft UVFs. However, remember the caution elaborated in Chapter 3 and noted in Chapter 6's case study: The organization of the UVF may have a graphic organizer, metaphor, or other base, depending on (a) the focus and (b) the reasoning of the students and teacher who are making sense of it. Both focus and student reasoning should precede decisions about the format rather than making focus or student reasoning fit a preconceived format. Remember, too, that the pictures or illustrations of a UVF are used specifically to anchor students' own experiences in ways that recall the richness of the learning for scaffolding and recall, not just to make appealing illustrated visuals. Keep that in mind when making choices from a software picture bank, and note that those images may possibly be supplemented by hand or scanned sketches or artifacts.

GENERIC SOFTWARE AND HARDWARE FOR OTHER UVF FORMATS OR VISUAL SUPPORTS

Microsoft's PowerPoint® (1987–1999) is widely used by teachers and students. It is fairly user friendly and can interface with other resources to offer flexibility in formatting and illustrating ideas. A class can incorporate a pattern generated with one of the graphic organizer software programs into a

UVF, and then illustrate it or other aspects of the focus with the searchable clipart, word art, draw, or other PowerPoint® tools or by scanning something into PowerPoint®. In addition, the program will accommodate a number of different graphics embedded into one.

Adobe's Illustrator® (2000) is a sophisticated art production tool that offers the double-edged sword of abundant capabilities and complexity of use. All of the visual frameworks in this book were ultimately created in Illustrator®, but most classroom-generated UVFs would not require the sophistication offered by this program. It can, however, be particularly useful for capturing expanded UVFs, if desired, because the program allows the use of a mass of images and text, offers precise scaling of text and images, and can make isolated or broad changes.

A camera—conventional or digital—can be handy for at least two purposes: (a) capturing student experiences in photos, instead of in drawings, and (b) keeping UVFs of previous units in view throughout the year so that they may serve as scaffolding for new learning. The same cautions hold in the use of photos as for other types of pictures. First, their purpose is to illustrate the focus or its related learning, so the choice of what to photograph or what photographs to display should be made with that criterion. Second, photographs need to be large enough and clear enough to be seen from afar if the UVF is always at a distance and the photos are not transferred to the portable UVF.

A scanner can also be of great help, whether by contributing to draft UVFs generated by computer or in scanning class-generated work as part of a core or expanded UVF.

With the exception of classrooms where technology has been integrated and used by all members of the class, these types of resources will be used at limited times. Graphic design is very time-consuming and involves a lot of decisions. Trying to generate a UVF on the computer at the same time that one is learning unit content would be very challenging.

There are several situations, described in the case studies, in which teachers will want to use these tools to reproduce what was generated in class. The teacher who does not have the ability to keep a UVF on display from one class session to the next, for example, may want to photograph a class-generated UVF, and then transfer the photograph to an overhead transparency or portable UVF using some of the above resources. The Reading to Remember case study in Chapter 5 used these resources to generate a visual set of procedures for students and their guests to use to share all of their learning and its process. There were also examples of putting part or all of an expanded UVF at the top of a survey to remind students of the learning and methods they were being asked to evaluate.

Teachers and students who are using technology extensively are bound to create additional ways of combining that and teaching with UVFs. I hope to hear about those, too.

References

Adobe Systems Incorporated. (Producer). (2000). Illustrator® [Software]. San Jose, CA: Adobe Systems Incorporated.

Bayer, A. S. (1990). *Collaborative apprenticeship learning: Language and thinking across the curriculum, K-12.* Mountain View, CA: Mayfield.

Beane, J. A. (1995). What Is a Coherent Curriculum? *Toward a coherent curriculum, the 1995 ASCD Yearbook.* Alexandria, VA: ASCD.

Belenky, M., Glinchy, B., Goldberger, N., & Tarule, J. (1986). *Women's ways of knowing.* New York: Basic Books.

Burgard, J. J. (2000). *Continuous improvement in the science classroom.* Milwaukee, WI: ASQ Quality Press.

Cawelti, G. (Ed.). (1995). *Handbook of research on improving student achievement.* Arlington, VA: Educational Research Service.

Clarke, J. H. (1990). *Patterns of thinking, integrating learning skills in content teaching.* Needham Heights, MA: Allyn and Bacon.

Clarke, J. H. (1991, April). Using visual organizers to focus on thinking. *Journal of Reading, 34*(7), 526-527.

Crawford, James. (1999). *Bilingual education: History, politics, theory, and practice.* Los Angeles, CA: Bilingual Educational Services, Inc.

Ellis, A.K. (2001). *Research on educational innovations.* Larchmont, NY: Eye on Education.

Erickson, Lynn H. (2001). *Stirring the head, heart, and soul.* Thousand Oaks, CA: Corwin.

Ewy, C. (1995). Learning from the inside. *Journal of the Illinois Association for Multilingual Multicultural Education, 1,* 1, Fall.

Ewy, C., et al. (1998a). *Conflict and resolution: Interpersonal & political, an Illinois content-based assessment exemplar for sixth grade–twelfth grade.* Springfield, IL: Illinois State Board of Education, Division of Standards and Assessment.

Ewy, C., et al. (1998b). *Immigration stories, an Illinois content-based exemplar for third grade–fifth grade.* Springfield, IL: Illinois State Board of Education, Division of Standards and Assessment.

Ewy, C., et al. (1998c). *People and places in community.* Springfield, IL: Illinois State Board of Education, Division of Standards and Assessment.

Gardner, Howard. (1992). *Multiple intelligences: The theory in practice.* New York: Basic Books.

Gardner, Howard. (1993). *Frames of mind: The theory of multiple intelligences* (10th Anniversary Edition). New York: Basic Books.

Glasser, W. (1986). *Choice theory in the classroom.* New York: Harper Perennial.

Hyerle, D. (1996). *Visual tools for constructing knowledge.* Alexandria, VA: ASCD.

Hyerle, D. (2000). *A field guide to using visual tools.* Alexandria, VA: ASCD.

Illinois State Board of Education. (1997). *Illinois Learning Standards* (adopted July 1997).

Innovative Learning Group. (1998). Thinking Maps®: Technology for learning [Software]. Raleigh, NC: Innovative learning Group.

Inspiration Software, Inc. (Producer). (2000). Inspiration Software®. Portland, OR: Inspiration Software, Inc.

Inspiration Software, Inc. (Producer). (2000). Kidspiration™ [Software]. Portland, OR: Inspiration Software, Inc.

Institute for Research on Learning. (1993). *A new learning agenda, Putting people first.* Palo Alto, CA: Institute for Research on Learning.

Joyce, B., & Weil, M. (1996) *Models of teaching.* Needham Heights, MA: Simon & Schuster.

Lenz, B. K., Bulgren, J. A., Schumaker, J.B., Deshler, D. D., & Doudah, D. A. (1994). *The unit organizer routine.* Lawrence, KS: Edge Enterprises.

Lenz, B. K., Marrs, R.W., Schumaker, J.B., & Deshler, D. D. (1993). *The lesson organizer routine.* Lawrence, KS: Edge Enterprises.

Madison, W. (1971). *Maria Luisa.* New York: J.B. Lippincott Company.

Marzano, R. (2000). *Transforming classroom grading.* Alexandria, VA: ASCD.

Marzano R., Pickering, D., & Pollock, J. (2001). *Classroom instruction that works.* Alexandria, VA: ASCD.

McClanahan, E., & Wicks, C. (1993). *Future force.* Chino Hills, CA: PACT.

Mehan, H. (1991). *Sociological foundations supporting the study of cultural diversity.* Washington, D.C.: National Center of Research on Cultural Diversity and Second Language Learning.

Microsoft Corporation. (Producer). (1987-1999). PowerPoint® [Software]. Redmond, WA: Microsoft Corporation.

Mindjet. (Producer). (2002). MindManager® [Software]. Larkspur, CA: Mindjet

Miramontes, O., Nadeau, A., & Commins, N. (1997). *Restructuring schools for linguistic diversity.* New York, NY: Teachers College Press.

National Academy of Sciences. (1995). *National Science Education Standards (NSES).* Washington, D.C.: National Academy of Sciences.

National Council of Teachers of Mathematics. (2001). *Principles and standards for school mathematics.* Reston, VA: NCTM.

Novak, J.D., & Gowin, R.B. (1984). *Learning how to learn.* Cambridge, England: Cambridge University Press.

Tomlinson, C.A. (1999). *The differentiated classroom.* Alexandria, VA: ASCD.

Wolfe, Patricia. (2001). *Brain matters: Translating research into classroom practice.* Alexandria, VA: ASCD.

Wycoff, J. (1991). *Mindmapping, your personal guide to exploring creativity and problem-solving.* New York: Berkley Books.

Index